SELF-DIRECTED LEARNING:

APPLICATION AND RESEARCH

Huey B. Long & Associates

ii

TABLE OF CONTENTS

TABLES AND FIGURES

<u>Tables</u>

Figures

PREFACE

Self-Directed Learning: Application and Research is a product of the Fifth International Symposium on Adult Self-Directed Learning. It, as the four previous volumes released following the 1987, 1988, 1989 and 1990 symposia, is not a proceedings of the conference. Approximately forty papers and posters were presented at the symposium. The twenty-three chapters that follow, with the exception of chapter one, were selected for inclusion after the authors reworked their papers. Revisions and modifications of the present papers were based, in part, on the helpful criticism provided by symposium participants. Finally, the chapters included here were submitted to additional scrutiny and review. Thus, they have experienced two screening stages: first for acceptance as a paper and second as revised versions of the papers in chapter format. The chapters were selected from all submissions to provide as complete a picture as possible of the current efforts in self-directed learning application and research.

In preparing this volume, we experienced several constraints. First, it was desirable to select the best manuscripts. Second, it was important to stratify the chapters according to content in order to provide the gestalt for which we were searching. Third, it was desirable to keep the price at an appropriate level. Each of these goals interact with production issues. If we used smaller type we could reduce the bulk and cost of the volume, but we would also reduce the substantive value of the book by making it more difficult to read. As a result, the decision was made to do several things.

First, we strongly encouraged the authors to limit the length of their manuscripts even though they believed that in doing so they may have to leave out important information. Second, we used smaller fonts for references, quotes, and other composition elements. The use of smaller fonts for quotations does not denigrate those elements. Rather, it may draw attention to them. Finally, I have abdicated the normal practice of providing descriptive introductory material to each of the chapters. With twenty-three chapters to describe, I felt that I could not do justice to all of the authors within the production constraints. All in all, these compromises should not reduce the value and usefulness of the book.

Huey B. Long
Norman, Oklahoma

CHAPTER ONE

LEARNING ABOUT SELF-DIRECTED LEARNING

Huey B. Long

Self-direction in learning is becoming an increasingly popular topic. The idea that learners are expected to assume and manifest responsibility for learning somehow appears to have been a radical concept when Malcolm Knowles made it a cornerstone of his philosophy of andragogy in 1970. Even if Malcolm had kept still about the idea, the work of Allen Tough (1967) and others (Long and Ashford 1976) may have encouraged further thought. Certainly, Tough contributed to a cerebral frenzy with his work on learning projects as numerous replications of his dissertation were conducted around the globe. Hence, the time seems to have been right for the study of self-direction in learning.

The papers contained in Self-Directed Learning: Application and Research constitute one small part of the expanding literature on self-directed learning. Approximately one hundred papers were presented at the first five symposia on adult learning between 1986 and 1991. These papers addressed a range of topics on self-directed learning from theoretical/conceptual treatises to empirical research reports to papers on practical application. Many of these papers were selected for publication in books such as this one. The first in the series by Long and Associates (1988) was entitled Self-Directed Learning: Application & Theory. The second was Self-Directed Learning: Emerging Theory and Practice (Long and Associates, 1989). Advances in Research and Practice in Self-Directed Learning (Long and Associate, 1990) was the fourth. Finally, Self-Directed Learning: Consensus and Conflict (Long and Associates 1991) is the latest volume preceding this one.

1

As indicated in the Preface the International Symposium on Self-Directed Learning, formerly the North American Symposium on Adult Self-Directed Learning began, in 1986, as a means to stimulate and encourage researchers and practitioners interested in self-directed learning. Even though the volume of research on the topic continues to expand annually the need for a forum continues to exist. The symposium is a source of stimulation that provides an opportunity for many to continue to learn about self-direction in learning. This chapter provides a brief, but hopefully, informative overview of some things that we are learning about self-directed learning and the literature on the topic. Some of these new insights as discussed in the following paragraphs include the nature of the published and unpublished work on self-directed learning, the questionable accuracy of some of the criticism, and some revised concepts of self-direction in learning.

LITERATURE

After reading some of the published items on self-directed learning research, several years ago, I became concerned about the propensity of some writers to ignore the larger body of literature on self-directed learning as they described the area through some inspirational stimulant. The problem was compounded when the pronouncements were attributed to reputational scholars whose enthusiasm for comment exceeded their devotion to scholarship. Consequently, in 1989 I began to work on a idea of abstracts of self-directed dissertations. The idea finally matured in 1991 with the publication of <u>Self-Directed Learning Dissertation Abstracts</u> (Long & Redding, 1991). The publication identified 173 doctoral dissertations concerning self-directed learning listed in <u>Dissertation Abstracts International</u> between 1966 and January of 1991. The majority of the dissertations were completed after 1980.

As this chapter is being written Gary Confessore and I are working on two additional volumes of abstracts. These volumes contain abstracts of works other than dissertations published from 1966 to 1991. Even though the books are not completed at the time this manuscript is being written we have identified approximately 400 articles, books and chapters that focus on self-directed learning. The abstracts of this body of work coupled with the dissertation abstracts indicate that the breadth and depth of the self-directed learning literature exceed that which is normally suggested by the citations listed at the end of published works.

Furthermore, the above literature suggests that researchers may be embarrassingly ill-informed by and about the literature. For example, even though the Guglielmino Self-Directed Learning Readiness Scale (SDLRS) and the Oddi Continuing Learning Inventory (OCLI) are clearly the better known instruments designed to measure aspects of self-direction in learning several additional scales are reported in dissertations. Smith (1968) developed one of the first instruments reported in contemporary literature designed to measure self-direction in learning. She labeled her scale Teacher Facilitation of Self-Direction Inventory. Skaggs (1981) reports the use of a scale identified as the Self-directed Learning Activity Survey. Kratz (1978) describes an instrument he calls the Self-Directed Learning Situation-Reaction Instrument (SDLRI). Finally, Six (1987) reports the use of an instrument referred to as the Classroom Learning Scale (CLS) that is designed to measure a teacher's perception of a a student's behavior in a classroom learning situation. I cannot recall any reference to any of the last group of instruments, except for articles citing Skagg's general work and Six's articles based on his dissertation. It is obvious from the work reviewed by Long and Redding (1991), Confessore and Long (in press) and Long and Confessore (in press) that Guglielmino's SDLRS is the instrument most frequently mentioned in the literature, but why have the others been so conspicuously neglected?

Scholars and practitioners currently interested in self-directed learning are in an enviable position. the literature base including philosophical, conceptual, theoretical and empirical information is increasingly available. It is rewarding to believe that the International Symposium on

3

Self-Directed Learning has contributed in some small way to the expansion of literature. Three of the publications resulting from symposia (1987, 1988, and 1989) have been identified as among the most important sources on the topic of self-directed learning.

Another illustration of failure to learn from earlier literature concerns the nature of self-directed learning activity. Despite some rather clear evidence to the contrary, students of self-direction in learning have demonstrated an amazing, persistence in equating self-directed learning with a Lone Ranger approach. Even a casual reading of Knowles (1970, 1975) would have revealed that he was concerned with self-direction in group learning situations. Guglielmino's dissertation (1977/78) was equally instructive on this point. Finally Skager (1984) said it very well when he noted that learning need not be independent or individualistic in order to be self-directed. His position is comparable to that of mine as expressed in chapter two of this volume. Motivation to choose to learn and act on that choice, e.g. maintaining psychological control (Long, 1990) is more important than the social environment in which the learning activity occurs. With the increasing interest in distance education, however, we should be careful that we do not fall into the error of simply equating distance learning with self-directed learning. A review of various proposals submitted for the different symposia on self-directed learning suggests that such a development is possible.

Yet, we have a long way to go in synthesizing the vast array of research findings and conclusions currently available. We are also challenged to move more directly into application of what we have learned.

CRITICISM

Other critical observations reported in the literature, when considered against the background of the voluminous work available now seem to have been over stated. For example, Brookfield (1984) severely criticized the self-directed learning research for being "methodolotrous." According to Brookfield the research was based on one research method, quantitative analysis; one instrument, the SDLRS; and one kind of sample, White middle-class people. Candy (1991) and, to a lesser degree, Caffarella (1988) share Brookfield's assertion concerning the need for more qualitative research. Unfortunately, these three respected scholars convey an inaccurate picture of the characteristics of the self-directed learning research. Reviews of the research by Long and Redding, and Confessore and Long indicate that the criticism that is most nearly accurate concerns sample characteristics. Even though an examination of the literature indicates that non-White samples and individuals other than middle-class persons have been included in the research more often than implied.

CONCEPTS

We are also learning other things about self-directed learning. For example, Tough approached the related area of learning projects or self-teaching from a more independent perspective. According to this view self-directed learning in groups, particularly classroom learning, was at best a peripheral concern. It was easy for self-directed learning quickly to be identified with the exotic electronic media based instruction and the more traditional correspondence study programs. Surprisingly, we seem to have ignored the difference between Tough and Knowles. Knowles' andragogical ideas were directly associated with classroom learning. Hence, self-direction in learning in the classroom was central to his work. It now appears that a rapprochement between these two views has taken place with either perspective acceptable.

Yet another significant development seems to be taking place. Some of the criticism of the construct upon which Guglielmino's SDLRS has focused on the nature of self-direction (SD) in learning. For example, is SD a constant attribute? or is it variable according to situations and other conditions? Recently, I made another suggestion concerning the way we might think about SD (Long, 1991). I proposed that SD be viewed as a variable attribute that may be manifested in non-pathological or pathological ways. Assuming that SD is a normal human trait we should be concerned when conditions interact with the trait in such a way that SD is pathologically manifested. According to this view unhealthy SD may occur at either extreme. When it is so great that it interferes with a learner's consideration and optimal use of instruction SD is as debilitating as it is when it is almost non-existent and the learner is overly dependent upon instruction. This view mutes the criticism that says that SD cannot be measured because it is not a constant thing. Instruments such as the SDLRS may at least provide us with an index to an individual's SD in learning in the same way that an IQ test is an index to the individual's intelligence. As all bright people do not always act intelligently, all individuals who score high on the SDLRS may not always manifest exemplary SD.

Two recently completed reviews of selected bodies of self-directed learning research illustrates the kind of information that is available to us, if we choose to search for it. Long (in press) reports that studies of self-directed learning with elderly subjects has produced some useful information. For example, the research indicates that self-direction in learning is positively associated with life satisfaction. Additional findings that should be of interest to individuals in the helping professions who serve older adult clients are also available. These findings suggest that self-directed learning may be a productive way for older adults to addresss health and financial learning needs.

A second area of inquiry focused upon the study of self-directed learning in community/junior colleges. This review of the literature yielded some exciting findings and conclusions concerning the relationship between self-directed learning and college achievement and retention, among other things.

CONCLUSIONS

Through the International Symposium on Self-Directed Learning and related activities we are expanding our knowledge of self-direction in learning. As discussed above we are learning that the literature is much richer, broader and deeper than perhaps most realize. We are learning that much of the literature is overlooked by writers. For example, seldom are other instruments designed to measure self-direction in learning mentioned in the literature despite their presence.

We are learning that some of the conspicuous criticism is undeserved.

We are also learning that SD is not a direct function of the social setting in which learning occurs. SD in learning can occur equally in individual socially isolated persons or in students interacting in a classroom. Interaction with other learners does not negate or prevent self directed learning.

Finally, I think that we are learning more about the construct of self-direction in learning. By conceptualizing the idea as a normal human trait that is subject to a variety of insults and encouragers we can explain the ebb and flow of SD as well as unhealthy or self-defeating learning activity.

REFERENCES

Brookfield, S. (1984). Self- directed learning : A critical paradigm. Adult Education Quarterly, 35,59-71.

Caffarella, R. & O'Donnell, J. (1988). Research in self-directed learning Past, present and future trends. In H. Long & Associates, Self-directed learning: Application and Theory, Athens, Georgia: Adult Education Department, University of Georgia, 65 98.

Candy, P. (1991). Self-direction for lifelong learning. San Francisco, California: Jossey-Bass.

Confessore, G. and Long, H.(in press). Abstracts of literature self-directed learning 1983-1991. Norman, Oklahoma: Oklahoma Research Center for Continuing Professional and Higher Education, University of Oklahoma.

Guglielmino, L. (1977). Development of the self-directed learning readiness scale. Dissertation Abstracts International, (1978), 38, 6467A.

Knowles, M. (1975). Self-directed learning: A guide for learners and teachers. Chicago: Follett Publishing Co.

Knowles, M. (1970). The modern practice of adult education: Andragogy versus pedagogy, Chicago: Association Press.

Long, H. (1990). Psychological control in self-directed learning. International Journal of Lifelong Education, 9, 4, 331-338.

Long, H. (in press) Self-directed learning by the elderly: A review of dissertation abstracts, 1966-1991. Journal of Educational Gerontology.

Long, H. and Ashford M. (1976) Self-directed inquiry as a method of continuing education in colonial America. Journal of General Education, 28,3, 245-255.

Long, H. and Confessore, G. (in press). Abstracts of literature in self-directed literature 1966-1982. Norman, Oklahoma: Oklahoma Research Center for Continuing Professional and Higher Education, University of Oklahoma.

Long, H. and Redding, T. (1991). Self-directed learning dissertation abstracts 1966-1991. Norman, Oklahoma: Oklahoma Research Center for Continuing Professional and Higher Education, University of Oklahoma.

Skager, R. (1984). Organizing schools to encourage self-direction in learners. Hamburg: UNESCO Institute for Education.

Tough, A.(1967) Learning without a teacher. (Educational Research Series No. 3, Ontario, Canada: The Ontario Institute for Studies in Education.

CHAPTER TWO

PHILOSOPHICAL, PSYCHOLOGICAL AND PRACTICAL JUSTIFICATIONS FOR STUDYING SELF-DIRECTION IN LEARNING*

Huey B. Long

This chapter addresses the question of why self-directed learning should be studied. It contains six topical subsections: first, the problem is described; second, a definition of self-directed learning is provided and discussed along with seven assumptions about learning; third, philosophical justifications are noted; fourth, psychological reasons for studying self-directed learning are provided; fifth, practical justifications are identified; and sixth, a summary and conclusions complete the chapter.

PROBLEM

Self-directed learning is one of the most frequently researched topics in contemporary adult education (Garrison 1989; Long and Agyekum 1988). Scholars have examined numerous aspects of self-direction in learning including such diverse concerns as the nature of self-directed learning, the relationship of self-directed learning readiness with other variables, and measurement of self-directed learning attitudes and propensities (Guglielmino, 1989). Despite the volume and diversity of the research writers have not always clearly explicated the justification for the inquiry. Even though a number of reasons for studying self-directed learning are

* This research was supported by the Oklahoma Research Center for Continuing Professional and Higher Education, University of Oklahoma, Norman, Oklahoma.

found in the literature, the issue of why great expenditures of energy should be made on behalf of research into self-directed learning has not been confronted in depth.

A few examples of the justifications for studying self-directed learning reveal that writers on the topic have a range of opinions. A review of ten different works on the topic produced ten different kinds of reasons for asserting that it is important to study self-directed learning (SDL). Suggestions range from the simple notation that it is a human characteristic and more specifically, on occasion, it is perceived to be an adult attribute (Bonham, 1989; Mezirow, 1981). Others identify self-direction as a desirable goal or philosophical ideal (Bonham, 1989; Brookfield, 1988; Candy, 1990;). Some identify it with general desirable human development (Candy, 1990; McCune and Garcia, 1989), with specific practical needs of adult workers (Candy, 1990; DeJoy and Mills, 1989; McCoy and Langenbach 1989) and problem-solving (Peters, 1989). West and Bentley (1990) indicate that understanding self-directed learning may be helpful in understanding the natural learning processes. Finally, the study of self-directed learning is justified on the basis that it is something that is being done by large numbers of people (Eisenman, 1990; Penland, 1979; West and Bentley, 1989). In addition to the above valued attributes of SDL, others have asserted that it has significant implications for the field of adult education.

Mezirow (1985) identified it as the central concept in adult education. Brookfield (1985), at one time, described it as the aim of adult education. Knowles (1980) hailed SDL as a unifying concept for the field of adult education. Later Brookfield (1988: 13-14) suggested that self-directed learning reflects the "democratic humanism of our traditions." Candy (1990:9) says that it has been promoted

> because it contributes to the development of the whole person, and on the instrumental grounds that it allows people to be more responsive to the market-oriented workplace.

DeJoy and Mills (1989) also cite the importance of SDL in a rapidly changing information society where remaining competent is an increasing challenge.

Given the above positive comments on the value of self-directed learning that generally encourage study of the topic, it could be asserted that SDL research requires no defense. Yet, a few authors have challenged the importance and value of SDL. Brookfield, who early spoke of the value of SDL, as noted above, changed his position in 1988 and called the high level of interest in the topic " a danger to our field" (p. 12). Brookfield's recanting of the importance of SDL seems to have arisen out of his concern over what he identified as the ambiguities and possible contradictions that exist among the various research reports and hortatory essays on the topic. According to Confessore and Confessore, who were conducting a delphi study concerning self-directed learning at the time (personal communication), others who have studied the topic have recently suggested that self-directed learning is a hoax. The reasons behind such recent negative opinions are unclear. Nevertheless, it is obvious that there are two contrasting opinions on the topic.

Part of the problem seems to reside in the failure to adequately address the topic previously. Despite the number of comments on the importance of SDL, no comprehensive discussion of why the topic may be important has been identified. Most authors that provide comments justifying inquiry into the topic seem to be satisfied with brief "throw-away" comments. That is, a statement is made to the effect that it is important, but the author assumes that the reason for the observation is self-evident. As a result no further effort is made to persuade the reader of its significance.

This chapter is designed to address the problem by identifying and discussing some of the reasons for studying self-direction in learning. The intent is to present rational arguments to the effect that the study of self-directed learning is not a danger to the field, and that failure to study the phenomena may pose a greater danger. The justifications fall into three broad categories : philosophical, psychological and practical. Each of the broad categories contain one or more specific reasons for conducting research into the topic. The following pages are devoted to the above topics plus a definition of the term and some assumptions.

DEFINITION

The literature contains various definitions, descriptions, and conceptualizations of self-directed learning. Increasingly, the definitions and conceptualizations have moved away from equating SDL with sociologically independent learning to an interactive concept that places emphasis upon learner mental behavior and corollary efforts to secure informational resources (Long, 1989). Elsewhere (1987) this writer has defined self-directed learning as "a purposive mental activity." This purposive mental activity may be described as being designed to answer a question (inquiry), solve a problem, retain information, develop a new understanding or awareness, perform a new motor-skill activity, etc. Self-directed learning is, thus, a cognitive process that is dependent on meta-cognitive behaviors such as attending, focusing, questioning, comparing, contrasting, etc. that are personally controlled or managed by the learner with little or no external supervision by a powerful other. Self-directed learning involves freedom of choice in evaluating and using informational resources in the purposive mental activity (Straka & Will, in progress; Weinert, 1982).

SDL may occur in group learning situations (Long, 1989; Weinert, 1982) or individual and solitary activities. Regardless of the setting for learning, the necessary and sufficient criterion is psychological control by the learner. Incidental or serendipitous learning may occur as a corollary to self-directed learning, but until it changes the learner's mental purpose, or conscious awareness, such learning is not self-directed.

SDL is more than making a choice. For example, some have suggested that if a learner chooses to submit himself or herself to the instruction of another the choice changes the learning setting into a self-directed one. It is difficult to agree completely with this proposal. Deciding to learn through a class or group method coupled with other self-managed/controlled behaviors, may be identified as self-directing. But, in some instances, the decision may lead to the abdication of personal responsibility. The determining criterion of retaining and exhibiting optimal psychological control has not been met merely by choosing to enroll in a class or to hire a tutor or coach. What happens at the mental level, rather than at the social level, between the learner and the coach, tutor or teacher is critical. The critical locus of action is at the intersection of information or content and the mental processes. The main question is, does the learner surrender SDL activities such as aggressively attending, focusing, comparing, contrasting, questioning and reorganizing mental constructs to become merely a reflecting, reciting, repeating, acquiescing drone? See Sgroi's (1990) work on self-directed learning of dancers. The dancing environment is rigidly controlled, the dance master may be very authoritarian in demeanor. But the mental constructs required to execute the motor skills require strong self-discipline.

Numerous studies (Long, 1966) have revealed that some individuals deny their own perceptions and passively accept obviously erroneous judgments of others, while other individuals maintain independence of judgment. This kind of independence is critical in self-directed learning. Self-directed learners are aware of the discrepancies between their perceptions and judgments and those of others, but they maintain their cognitive independence despite the authority or numbers of others who differ with them.

Justifications for studying self-directed learning flow from the above definition and the following seven assumptions:

1. Learning is a natural adaptive act.
2. The quality of learning is variable.
3. The quality of learning is associated with learning skills and controlling processes (Gagne and Briggs 1974).
4. The learning process is more complex than the mere receipt of information.

5. Learning can proceed in the absence of instruction.
6. Educators have an interest in understanding learning that proceeds from instruction or otherwise.
7. Complex social-technical environments require increased learner responsibility for learning.

Given the above definition of SDL and assumptions, the importance of studying the phenomenon can be explored. To organize the justifications, into some kind of workable framework, I have identified three categories of reasons for studying SDL. They are philosophical, psychological and practical. I have chosen to begin with the more abstract, but fundamental philosophical justifications and to conclude with the more concrete practical reasons for being interested in the topic. Therefore, the rest of my comments treat, in order, philosophical, psychological and practical justifications before ending with a brief summary statement and conclusions. First, attention is directed to the philosophical justifications for understanding SDL.

PHILOSOPHICAL

There are important philosophical reasons for investigating SDL. There is an equally logical reason for discussing philosophical reasons prior to the cognitive and practical. While each of the three sub-areas of philosophy may be instructive. I am more interested at this time in the axiological and epistemological concerns, specifically, ideas concerning the nature of the human being and knowledge. Some of these reasons grow directly in the soil of human definition. Our concept of the human may very well justify or interfere with any justification for studying SDL. If one takes a highly mechanistic view of the human it may be easy to deny the importance of SDL. This perspective of humanity represents men and women and girls and boys as "instructed" responding or reacting beings. The most simple version of this perspective represents human learning as a kind of photographic or recording process. Accordingly, information is arranged and displayed by a teacher so that the learner faithfully reproduces it for later recall and repetition. James (1983) eloquently demolished the mechanistic view in his concerns with the "will."

A contrasting view translates into a perception of the human as an active, inquiring, searching organism. According to this concept, information processing is more complicated than presented in the mechanistic school. Information is not a static thing that is dumbly received by the brain. Data are selected from an information rich environment according to the interaction of many complex variables, some of which are under the conscious control of the learner. The receiving system is also active in the process of receiving and encoding the information which is subsequently given meaning. As a result, some learners attend to different information within the same environment, learners may interpret what is reasonably identified as the same information in different ways, thus arriving at different meanings. For others who ignore the information, it has no meaning. For example, cloud formations may be perceived quite differently by a poet and a meteorologist, while others are oblivious to the sky. Thus, in addressing the issue of why self-directed learning should be studied we must confront our beliefs about the nature of human determinism as found in the works of Descartes, James, Kant and Nietzsche, to name a few, and its relationship to our view of the human as a learner.

Beliefs about humans are not only limited to ideas about us as learners. We must also address other opinions that we hold concerning human behavior in general. One useful model is provided by McGregor's X and Y concepts. According to the X view, the human is indolent, lacking in initiative and in need of close supervision. The Y concept is in contrast and is best reflected in the work of Carl Rogers and Malcolm Knowles.

Philosophically we are challenged to relate our concepts of human nature with our concepts of human learning. If human learning proceeds effectively in a self-directed manner then how do we justify a rigid authoritarian instructional environment and failure to study SDL? Conversely, if the type X view of humankind is accurate, there can be little justification for self-directed learning.

A second philosophical justification emerges from the nature and purposes of education. The preferred concept of education is normally related closely to one's view about human nature. If the mechanistic view is subscribed to, education is conceptualized as a banking type of activity designed to fill the heads of learners with information; thus, SDL is not a very attractive option. Yet, if educators perceive of the human being as an active free agent, education is likely to be seen as a liberating power. As a result, SDL frees the individual from the conforming pressures of the mob. Please note that the concept of the mob as used here is quite broad so that I am also including the mob rule of intellectual orthodoxy, dogma, or political correctness. Educators of adults have long identified empowerment as a goal of education and learning. Self-directed learning appears to be much more congruent with empowerment ideals than a teaching-learning construct that retains an emphasis on other directed authoritarianism. Can educators rationally subscribe to a philosophy in which learner empowerment is central while either adhering to a pedagogical concept that is contrary to the position, or by denying the need to have a better understanding of the potential of self-directed learning?

It is possible to justify the study of self-directed learning on grounds other than the philosophical. The hard-headed pragmatist challenges us to support our values by knowledge - therefore, let us turn our attention to the psychological justifications.

PSYCHOLOGICAL

One psychological justification is of a cognitive nature, it is concerned with knowledge about, and of, a phenomenon. Therefore, a fundamental cognitive consideration in the effort to justify the study of SDL is involved in the following three questions: (a) what do we need to know to better understand the learning process? (b) why will the study of self-direction in learning be helpful in understanding learning? and (c) how will the study of self-directed learning affect the knowledge base of human learning? If we are certain that the study of SDL will not produce results that contribute to our understanding of the learning process, one justification is removed. Furthermore, if there is no potential positive impact on the human learning knowledge base it is difficult to justify SDL in terms of cognitive reasons, other than to know the negative. Stated in other terms, there may be some benefit in discounting the idea of SDL, and thereby obviate the continued expenditure of energy on the topic. On the other hand, if the study of self-directed learning has the potential to improve awareness of human learning processes and to result in better explanations of learning no further cognitive justification is required.

Most would agree that educators need to understand how the learning process proceeds. One of the great recent changes in educational literature has been the shift from teaching to learning. Educational psychologists and others recognize that learning is a private activity that often proceeds in public places. Teaching does not necessarily lead to learning. Learning may exist independent of teaching. It is obvious that children and adults often learn many things without the benefit of being instructed in those things. Thus, teaching and learning appear to be two different behaviors with the optimum consequence coming about when the two are most compatible. In order to make teaching more compatible with learning it is desirable, if not necessary, to learn more about how learning occurs. Those who deny the value of studying SDL today are similar to the behaviorists of an earlier period who rejected the need to study the so-called black box of mental processes. Thankfully, cognitive and humanistic psychologists resisted those opinions. It is strongly asserted that we may have a better understanding of how learning occurs in instructional settings by increased knowledge of self-directed learning.

Unfortunately, the early identification of self-directed learning with Robinson Crusoe-like activity has done much to distract from other aspects of self-directed learning. This distraction resulted in an over-emphasis on individual pedagogical procedures at a cost to interest in the psychological aspects of SDL. For example, long term memory is often associated with deep processing skills. Deep-processing skills, in turn, are often associated with certain control processes such as interest and attention. Theoretically, these are the same control processes that are important in SDL. Thus, the study of self-directed learning may be improved by knowledge of meta-cognitive control processes. A better understanding of the consequences of improved meta-cognitive control processes, in turn, may be improved by greater knowledge of SDL (Straka and Will, in progress).

If learning is a natural behavior, it is plausible to assume that SDL is the first kind of learning in which the human being engages. Study of self-directed learning may help us to understand how to better merge the positive attributes of the natural learning process with instructional procedures used in educational institutions.

Given the possibility that SDL may help educators to have a better understanding of the learning process and how to better organize the teaching-learning interaction it is important to study it. A better understanding of SDL also may have implications for knowledge of meta-cognition and intrinsic motivation. When one considers the range and stature of scholars, such as Dewey, Piaget, and Rogers whose work is some how associated with self-directed learning concepts as defined above it is obviously an area too important to be ignored.

PRACTICAL

Despite the rather convincing philosophical and cognitive reasons that can be given for studying self-directed learning, the justifications appear to be more often couched in pragmatic or practical terms. For example, the idea that individuals must continuously renew their competence because of rapidly changing knowledge, is a frequently given reason for encouraging SDL. A related incentive is found in the observation that traditional educational resources are too expensive and are inadequate in a rapidly changing world where almost everyone is engaged in systematic learning. Yet a third justification is found in the increasing acceptance that schools can't teach everything that is important. As a consequence, it is asserted that some things must be learned through the personal responsibility of the learner. As a result of the above observations, SDL is recommended as a means by which systematic continuous learning can proceed.

Failure to study self-directed learning leaves a host of significant assertions unanswered. For example, Knowles (1975, p. 14-15) lists the following three important consequences of self-directed learning:

> (a)...there is convincing evidence that people who take the initiative in learning (proactive learners) learn more things, learn better, than do people who sit at the feet of teachers passively waiting to be taught (reactive learners).

> (b)...self-directed learning is more in tune with our natural processes of psychological development.

> (c)...many of the new developments in education--the new curriculums, open classrooms, ...--put a heavy responsibility on the learners to take a good deal of initiative in their own learning.

> The above advantages of self-directed learning, if true, commends the practice to all levels of education. Research is needed to confirm or reject these, and similar, beliefs.

Another practical way of looking at the question of why study SDL is to raise the question of the consequences of a decision to study it or not to study it. A number of contrasting outcomes seem to be related to the way the question is answered.

If we fail to study SDL at least five important consequences can be identified. They are as follows:

1. It suggests we have accepted the notion of the "instructed" learner.
2. We deny that SDL is a worthy goal.
3. We cannot provide any guidance for developing SDL among learners.
4. We cannot provide any assistance to practitioners who wish to encourage SDL.
5. We continue to emphasize instruction devoid of a complete understanding of the relationship between learning and instruction.

If we continue to study SDL, the six following positive benefits are suggested:

1. We subscribe to a view of the human as an active, learner, adapting being.
2. We reveal a belief in the value of the human as a self-directing being.
3. Our findings may be helpful in developing curricula and practitioners skillful in developing self-directed learners.
4. We may contribute to empowered learners who are not dependent upon the universal guidance of teachers.
5. Learning may be enhanced through the development and mastery of control processes that are required in all kinds of learning, but which are especially critical in SDL.
6. We may free up human resources that might otherwise be consumed by travel to educational meetings, instructional time and so forth.

CONCLUSIONS AND SUMMARY

This chapter was designed to provide a more comprehensive discussion of the justifications for studying self-directed learning than is currently available. It was noted that numerous authors briefly have stated reasons for studying the topic, but these reasons have usually been pronounced ex cathedera with little explanation or justification. In addition they have been reported without defining self-directed learning or identification of basic assumptions.

Justifications for studying self-directed learning as gleaned from the literature were presented. The chapter also provides a definition of SDL that emphasizes mental characteristics of the phenomenon. Seven basic assumptions about learning were provided. Finally, three classes of reasons for studying the topic were discussed. They are philosophical, psychological and pragmatic reasons.

SDL is identified with the organismic view of the human thus, the greatest philosophical justification is to be found among those who conceive of the human as an active, self-initiating, inquiring being.

Psychological justifications primarily are associated with questions of what kind of knowledge is important to understanding how learning occurs and what kind of knowledge is generated by SDL research.

Practical justifications relate to the increasing need for continuing learning in a complex, rapidly changing civilization and the consequences of failing to study SDL.

Given the justifications identified in the chapter, it is difficult to explain why educators should ignore self-directed learning as a topic of inquiry or practice. Suggestions that the area should be forgotten simply because there are problems with nomenclature and conceptual confusion begs the question. The history of human development is filled with examples of important questions that were pursued despite greater difficulties.

REFERENCES

Bonham, L. A. (1989) Self-directed orientation toward learning: A learning style. In H. B. Long and Associates, <u>Self-directed learning: Emerging theory and practice</u>. Norman, Oklahoma: Oklahoma Research Center for Continuing Professional and Higher Education, University of Oklahoma, 13-42.

Brookfield, S. (1985) Self-directed learning: A critical review of research. In S. Brookfield (Ed.), <u>Self-directed learning: From theory to practice</u>. San Francisco: Jossey-Bass, 5-16.

Brookfield, S. (1988) Conceptual, methodological and practical ambiguities in self-directed learning. In H. B. Long and Associates, Self-directed learning: Application and theory. Athens, Georgia: Adult Education Department, University of Georgia, 11-38.

Candy, P. (1990). The transition from learner-control to autodidaxy: More than meets the eye. In H. B. Long and Associates, Advances in research and practice in self-directed learning. Norman, Oklahoma: Oklahoma Research Center for Continuing Professional and Higher Education, University of Oklahoma, 9-46.

Confessore, G and Confessore, S. (Personal communication, January 31, 1991).

DeJoy, J. and Mills, H. (1989). Bridging theory and practice: Applications in the development of services for self-directed learners. In H. B. Long and Associates Self-directed learning: Emerging theory and practice. Norman, Oklahoma: Oklahoma Research Center for Continuing Professional and Higher Education, University of Oklahoma, 99-112.

Eisenman, G. (1990). Self-directed learning: A growth process? In H.B. Long and Associates, Advances in research and practice in self-directed learning. Norman, Oklahoma: Oklahoma Research Center for Continuing Professional and Higher Education, University of Oklahoma, 93-122.

Gagne, R. and Briggs, L., (1974) Principles of instructional design. New York: Holt, Rinehart and Winston, Inc.

Garrison, D. R. (1989). Facilitating self-directed learning: Not a contradiction in terms. In H. B. Long and Associates Self-directed learning: Emerging theory and practice. Norman, Oklahoma: Oklahoma Research Center for Continuing Professional and Higher Education, University of Oklahoma, 53-62.

Guglielmino, L. M. (1989). Development of an adult basic eduction form of the self-directed learning readiness scale. In H. B. Long and Associates Self-directed learning: Emerging theory and practice. Norman, Oklahoma: Oklahoma Research Center for Continuing Professional and Higher Education, University of Oklahoma, 63-76.

James, W. (1983). The works of William James: Talks to teachers of psychology, Cambridge, Mass.: Harvard University Press. (Original work published 1910)

Knowles, M., (1980) The modern practice of adult education: From pedagogy to andragogy, (Second Ed.). Chicago: Follett.

Long, H. (1966). Relationships Between Conforming Judgment and Employee Rank and Between Conforming Judgment and Dogmatism in an Employment Group. (Doctoral dissertation, Florida State University).

Long, H. (1987). Self-directed learning and learning theory. Unpublished paper presented at the Annual Meeting of the Commission of Professors of Adult Education, Washington, D.C.

Long, H. (1989). Self-directed learning: Emerging theory and practice. In H.B. Long and Associates, Self-directed Learning: Emerging theory and practice. Norman, Oklahoma: Oklahoma Research Center for Continuing Professional and Higher Education, University of Oklahoma, 1-12.

Long, H. and Agyekum, S. (1988). Self-directed learning: Assessment and validation. In H. Long and Associates Self-directed learning: Application and theory. Athens, Georgia: Department of Adult Education, University of Georgia, 253-266.

McCoy C. and Langenbach, M, (1989). Self-directed learning among clinical laboratory scientists: A closer look at the OCL1." In H.B. Long and Associates, Self-directed learning: Emerging theory and practice. Norman, Oklahoma: Oklahoma Research Center for Continuing Professional and Higher Education, University of Oklahoma, 77-86.

McCune, S. and Garcia, G., Jr. (1989). A Meta-analytic study of the relationship between adult self-direction in learning and psychological well-being: A review of the research from 1977 to 1987. In H. Long and Associates, Self-directed Learning: Emerging Theory and Practice. Norman, Oklahoma: Oklahoma Research Center for Continuing Professional and Higher Education, University of Oklahoma, 87-98.

Mezirow, J. (1981). A critical theory of adult learning and education, Adult Education, 32, 3-27.

Mezirow, J. (1985). A critical theory of self-directed learning. In S. Brookfield (Ed.), Self-directed learning: From theory to practice. San Francisco: Jossey-Bass, 17-30.

Penland, P., (1977) Self-planned learning in America. Pittsburgh: Book Center, University of Pittsburgh.

Peters, J. (1989). Self-direction and problem-solving: Theory and method. In H.B. Long and Associates <u>Self-directed learning: Emerging theory and practice</u>. Norman, Oklahoma: Oklahoma Research Center for Continuing Professional and Higher Education, University of Oklahoma, 43-52.

Sgroi, A. (1990). The drive to learn: Self-directed learning in a formal institutional setting. In H.B. Long and Associates, <u>Advances in research and practice in self-directed learning</u>. Norman, Oklahoma: Oklahoma Research Center for Continuing Professional and Higher Education, University of Oklahoma, 249-264.

Straka, G. and Will, J. (in progress). Self-directed learning in the Federal Republic of Germany. An unpublished paper.

Weinert, F. (1982). Selbstgesteuertes lernen als voraussetzung, methode und evaluation von studienunterstutz ungen. <u>Unterrichtswissenschaft</u>, (2), 114-127.

West, R. and Bently, E., (1990). Structural analysis of the self-directed learning readiness scale: A confirmatory factor analysis using LISREL modeling. In H.B. Long and Associates <u>Advances in research and practice in self-directed learning</u>. Norman, Oklahoma: Oklahoma Research Center for Continuing Professional and Higher Education, University of Oklahoma, 157-180.

CHAPTER THREE

IN SEARCH OF CONSENSUS IN THE STUDY OF SELF-DIRECTED LEARNING *

Gary J. Confessore & Sharon J. Confessore

During the past decade there has been rapid growth in both the quantity and quality of research into self-directed learning (Long, 1991). Over that same period of time there has been a growing concern that the field has become mired in "semantic chaos" (Brookfield, 1988, p. 11). Candy (1990) suggests "it seems likely that any term that can be used by such a diverse range of authors might also mask a certain conceptual confusion" (p. 9). Long (1991) reports, "the field of self-directed learning is characterized by ad hoc propositions rather than by any broad nomological frameworks" and "Consensus concerning definitional and conceptual properties of self-directed learning is at best in the emerging stage" (pp. 1-2).

As manuscripts to be presented at the Fourth International Symposium on Adult Self-Directed Learning arrived at the Oklahoma Research Center for Continuing Professional and Higher Education, during the months of November and December of 1989, it became apparent that many authors proceeded from an assumption of conflict, or at least an absence of consensus, regarding concepts and issues that would seem to be at the very heart of the field. In response, the symposium organizers instituted think-tank sessions on theory and application. In part, this was done in

* This research was supported by the Oklahoma Research Center for Continuing Professional and Higher Education, University of Oklahoma, Norman, Oklahoma.

an effort to focus the attention of active researchers in the field on the nature and role of these assumptions and on how they may influence our understanding of self-directed learning.

The think-tank sessions held at the symposium were well attended and they generated animated discussions that yielded only limited agreement on critical issues. Thus, Long (1991) was moved to note, "self-directed learning as a theoretical, research, and applied topic may be compared to a gangling adolescent whose physical growth has not been matched by social, emotional, and mental maturity" (p. 2).

The manuscripts selected for inclusion as chapters in the book published subsequent to the Fourth International Symposium on Adult Self-Directed Learning, and the think-tank reports from that symposium, clearly emphasized the extent to which philosophical, methodological, operational, and personality conflicts dominate discourse in the field. Indeed, this pattern was so clear the 1991 book by Long and Associates was titled, "Self-Directed Learning: Consensus and Conflict."

Moreover, where consensus emerged in the think-tank sessions it did so in a diffuse and tentative way. As active participants in both think-tank sessions, we were left with the sense that perceived conflicts grew more out of limitations of time and process that forestalled emergence of consensus than out of actual disagreement. That is to say, it seemed the activity was too brief and the process did not allow for full consideration of a broad range of ideas in a non-confrontational setting. Hence, no individual or group of individuals had sufficient opportunity to stimulate the formation of consensus around critical issues in the field.

At the close of the Fourth International Symposium the authors determined to undertake a comprehensive effort to discover the extent to which consensus regarding the recent accomplishments and near future objectives of the field might be formed. Properly structured such an effort might help researchers distinguish between areas where there is true conflict and areas where existing consensus has not been reported as such.

METHODOLOGY

The Delphi technique was developed by Norman Dalkey and Olaf Helmer for use by the Rand Institute in the early 1950's (Dalkey & Helmer, 1963). Basically, the process is designed to provide a non-confrontational environment in which diverse views on a topic may be elicited and receive thorough consideration as to the extent to which others agree or disagree with those views. This process is often used to arrive at consensus on issues which cannot be settled empirically such as predicting future events. In other cases it has been used to form a consensus as to the relative merit or importance of attitudes, assumptions, or research findings.

In order to use the Delphi technique a panel of "reputational experts" must be selected. These "experts" may share specific experiences, skills, knowledge, or membership in a community of common concern. Once the panel is impounded, the members participate in a paper exercise in which their contributions and responses to the contributions of others are never identified by source to anyone but the research managers. In the first iteration panelists are asked to respond to open-ended questions. Their answers are then compiled, without editing, into a single report using a code system, such as identification numbers. This allows panelists to track their own contributions while masking the source of items contributed by others. In the second iteration, the panelists are asked to indicate the degree to which they agree or disagree with each contribution using a Likert-type scale. These responses are analyzed to discover which, if any, have elicited a response pattern that represents a statistically significant consensus.

In the present study, response patterns were subjected to analysis using the Kolmogorov-Smirnov one sample test (Siegel, 1956) to determine whether the actual cumulative distribution of responses to each item deviated significantly from a theoretical cumulative distribution. The result of this calculation is referred to as the value of "D." In the second iteration items were differentiated according to whether they had attracted a simple majority of the panel indicating agreement or disagreement.

In the third iteration each panelist received individually structured survey forms that asked for responses to only those items for which his or her second iteration response fell outside the emerging consensus. Sufficient information was provided to inform each panelist of the magnitude, direction, and distribution of the emerging consensus, and a record of his or her outlying response. Panelists were asked to review their second iteration response in light of the emerging consensus. If they wished to change their response they were welcomed to do so. In the alternative, if they wished to provide an explanation of their reasons for remaining an outlyer, that information would be of value in understanding the limits of the emerging consensus.

In the third iteration, the Kolmogorov-Smirnov was used again to determine the significance of the response patterns. Additionally, in this final iteration only those items whose volume of agreement was at least one standard deviation above the mean for responses found to have a statistically significant response pattern were retained in the consensus (See Table 3.1).

THE DELPHI PANEL

Because this study was motivated by observations made at the Fourth International Symposium on Adult Self-Directed Learning, it was decided that the Delphi panel should be composed of individuals who had some formal connection with one or more of the four international symposia on adult self-directed learning. An effort was made to balance the panel according to important philosophical and methodological issues by including quantitative and qualitative researchers, some of whom believe the field is on the right track, others who have expressed substantial concern that the field is an important distraction to adult educators, and some of whom have recanted their earlier substantial involvement in the field. Application of these criteria yielded a list of forty-nine possible panelists representing seven countries. For purposes of this study these individuals were designated "reputational experts."

These reputational experts were provided an outline of the present study and of the Delphi process. They were then asked to respond to ten open-ended questions regarding their judgement about issues in self-directed learning. Consensus was sought on the following items:

1. In your judgement, what are the three most important research findings that have been reported to date in the literature on adult self-directed learning?

2. In your judgement, what are the three most important trends in research into adult self-directed learning?

3. Please list the three most important changes in educational <u>theory</u> that, in your judgement, are attributable to research into adult self-directed learning.

4. Please list the three most important changes in educational <u>practice</u> that, in your judgement, are attributable to research into adult self-directed learning.

5. Please provide the citations for the three most important published works that, in your judgement, should be read at the outset of ones introduction to the field of adult self-directed learning.

6. Please list the three most important issues in adult education that, in your judgement, should be researched between now and the year 2000.

7. Please list the three most important changes in educational <u>theory</u> during the 1990's that will, in your judgement, be precipitated by research into adult self-directed learning.

8. Please list the three most important changes in educational <u>practice</u> during the 1990's that will, in your judgement, be precipitated by research into adult self-directed learning.

9.   Please list the three most important sources that, in your judgement, will produce researchers in the field of adult self-directed learning during the 1990's.

10.   Please list the three most important questions not included above that, in your judgement should be asked in future surveys.

QUANTITATIVE FINDINGS

Twenty-seven panelists representing five countries participated in the study and returned completed first iteration response forms. Figure 3.1 reveals the rate at which a general consensus emerged. Note that the number of "possible" responses to this survey was set at 810. This reflects the fact that 27 panelists agreed to provide up to three responses to each of ten questions. In order to avoid missing the potential importance of differences in language that appeared to the researchers to be of no real importance, all items obtained in the first iteration were retained in their original form throughout the entire process. The actual number of items obtained in the first iteration was 634 or 78.27% of the diversity possible, assuming every item differed in content or purpose from every other.

In the second iteration, twenty-three panelists returned completed surveys. Four hundred and fifty-two of the 634 responses (71.29%) attracted a simple majority agreement, the pattern of which was not likely to be a chance distribution.

In the third iteration, twenty-two panelists returned completed surveys. One hundred and one of the original 634 responses (15.93%) had response patterns that were not likely to be a chance distribution and the volume of agreement with these items was at least one standard deviation above the mean volume of agreement for all such items.

Table 3.1 reports the number of statements provided in the first iteration in response to each of the ten survey items. For example, 72 statements were made in response to survey item one and 76 were made in response to survey item two.

Figure 3.1
Emergence of Consensus Over Three Delphi Iterations

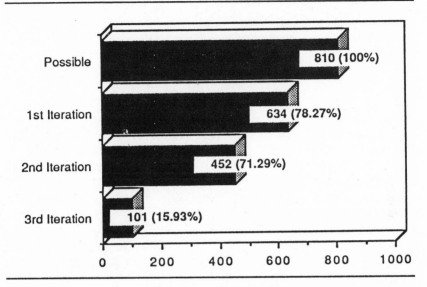

By comparing the volume of responses to survey items in the first iteration one can get a general picture of the relative diversity of opinion on that topic at the beginning of the Delphi process. For example, the greatest diversity was registered in response to items two and six. The respective topics of these items were "important trends in research into adult self-directed learning" and "important issues in adult education that . . . should be researched between now and the year 2000." It is important to note that initial diversity of response does not necessarily equate directly to lack of agreement. Indeed, in the case of survey item six initial diversity carried through to the third iteration in the form of the greatest number (17), greatest portion (22.37%), and the

Table 3.1
Formation of Consensus by Item Over Three Delphi
Iterations

Item	1st Iteration Responses	2nd Iteration Majority .05	3rd Iteration Mean	SD	+1SD	Consensus Responses
1	72	55	16.45	3.30	19.75	13
2	76	53	15.30	2.37	17.67	11
3	64	45	14.67	2.43	17.10	10
4	70	51	16.18	2.48	18.66	10
5	34	24	15.92	2.59	18.51	4
6	76	61	15.44	1.89	17.33	17
7	62	39	14.72	2.29	17.01	8
8	65	48	15.98	2.37	18.35	9
9	63	42	16.21	3.38	19.59	10
10	52	34	14.74	2.08	16.82	9
	634	452				101

most homogeneous reaction (SD = 1.89) of statements on which a significant consensus was eventually reached (See Table 3.1). Conversely, survey item five, which sought citations for "important published works that . . . should be read at the outset of ones introduction to the field of adult self-directed learning," yielded the least initial diversity and the narrowest final consensus. This should not be mistaken for evidence of the greatest initial strength of consensus. Note in Table 3.1 that by the completion of iteration three, four other survey items achieved higher mean scores and seven others achieved narrower standard deviations than did item five. Thus, when established through the Delphi process, relative strength of consensus is an expression of deviation from the norm calculated for the survey item.

QUALITATIVE FINDINGS

The objective of this study was to discover the extent to which consensus might be formed regarding the recent accomplishments and near future objectives of the field. In order not to inject our own perceptions into the process, we elected to report only those items for which the third iteration consensus was significantly strong even when compared to those items for which it could be said there was an apparent general agreement. This section includes the full text of each item obtained for which the number of panelists who agreed with the statement was one standard deviation above the mean for all items that attracted 12 or more votes (a simple majority) and for which the value of D was .05 or less. Table 3.1 reports the number, mean and standard deviation of responses that met these criteria for each survey item. Finally, each response is preceded by two numbers, for example 20 .01. The first reports the number of panelists who formed the third iteration consensus and the second reports the value of D. Keep in mind that there were twenty-two third iteration panelists.

The report for each item is followed by a brief summary comment.

Item #1: In the panel's judgement, these are the most important research findings that have been reported to date in the literature on adult self-directed learning.

1. 22 .01 Allen Tough's research and subsequent book provided a springboard for much of what has followed -- that adults do engage in learning projects that are somewhat self-directed and seek resources outside institutional settings.

2. 21 .01 Self-directed learning is not a linear, step-by-step process.

3. 21 .01 The extent of self-learning (Tough).

4. <u>21 .01</u> Pervasiveness of self-directed learning activity over a range of areas; not just those areas pertaining to work/occupation. e.g., intentional changes.

5. <u>21 .01</u> The extent to which self-directed learning occurs among various groups, e.g., all social groups, ethnic groups, etc.

6. <u>21 .01</u> The impact that environment plays in "shaping" the learning effort -- possibly the fact that no learning effort is solely tied to "self."

7. <u>21 .01</u> Recognition that self-directed learning does not take place in isolation, that learners actually draw upon many sources/people in their search for learning.

8. <u>21 .05</u> Adult's aren't equally self-directed in their learning; not all are self-directed.

9. <u>20 .01</u> Tough's research on <u>The Adult's Learning Projects</u>.

10. <u>20 .01</u> That there are things that adult educators do that can be helpful in facilitating self-directed learning.

11. <u>20 .05</u> The environment (e.g., the circumstances in which learners find themselves) is an important aspect of self-directed learning.

12. <u>20 .05</u> Tough's findings regarding the descriptive nature of self-directed learning -- <u>The Adult's Learning Project</u>.

13. <u>20 .05</u> The way planning is done probably is not detailed and linear.

Summary: The work of Tough provided the impetus for study of self-directed learning. Since Tough's work was completed, important areas of research have focused environmental factors and processes which can be used to define and develop self-directed learning.

Item #2: In the panel's judgement, these are the most important trends in research into adult self-directed learning.

1. <u>21 .05</u> How conditions can be organized to enhance self-direction.

2. <u>20 .01</u> Contextual examination of self-directed learning research constructs within other psychological theories and research constructs. In essence, researchers attempting to identify the relationship between characteristics of the learner, the environment, the teaching-learning transactions to self-directed learning.

3. <u>19 .01</u> Conceptual model building of self-directed learning.

4. <u>19 .01</u> Theories to explain self-direction.

5. <u>19 .01</u> Attempts to understand the role instructors/facilitators can play in enhancing self-directed learning.

6. <u>18 .01</u> Search for personal characteristics and factors that correlate with self-directed learning vigor.

7. <u>18 .01</u> Search for environmental effects that account for self-directed learning directions.

8. <u>18 .01</u> Examining individual differences in the way self-directed learning occurs.

9. <u>18 .01</u> How to facilitate or stimulate adult self-directed learning.

10. <u>18 .01</u> Continued use of qualitative methods to gain insight into the nature of self-directed learning.

11. <u>18 .05</u> Research to develop the understanding of the learning processes involved in self-directed learning (i.e., what happens to the individuals, not methodological processes).

<u>Summary:</u> It appears that researchers are primarily focused on (improving) enhancing self-directed learning by manipulating process (learning) and environmental factors.

Item #3: These are the most important changes in educational theory that, in the panel's judgement, are attributable to research into adult self-directed learning.

1. <u>20 .01</u> The importance of understanding learning that goes on outside of formal institutions.

2. <u>20 .01</u> Focus on the learner as important.

3. <u>20 .01</u> A second theoretical aspect i.e that autonomy and self-direction can be considered as important characteristics of learning in adulthood.

4. <u>19 .01</u> Re-definition of <u>effective adult learning</u> as embedded within the learner, as opposed to effectively designed curriculum/instruction or effective teaching/learning environment actions.

5. <u>18 .05</u> Greater understanding of self-directed learning as a process rather than merely as a method.

6. <u>17 .01</u> Very little theory in general educational theory directly attributable to self-directed learning, but some changes such as increasing students' responsibilities for learning as well as student options are reinforced by the self-directed learning research.

7. <u>17 .01</u> Increasing emphasis on the characteristics and learning experience/practice of adult learners.

8. <u>17 .01</u> A first theoretical aspect is that people do not necessarily learn in a linear or sequential way.

9. <u>17 .01</u> A third theoretical aspect is that we must consider both environment and individual as reciprocal determinants in a learning activity.

10.   17 .01 That there is considerable learning activity existing outside formal structures/programs.

Summary: The panel believes that educational theorists are now focusing more on the individual and on individualized learning concepts.   This focus is providing self-directed learning researchers with information directly applicable to self-directed learning in terms of learning situation, environment, and process.

Item #4: These are the most important changes in educational practice that, in the panel's judgement, are attributable to research into adult self-directed learning.

1.   21 .05 Increasing involvement of the learner in the teaching-learning transaction, such as mutual goal setting, alternative activities, etc.

2.   20 .01 Recognition of the notion of facilitation of self-directed learning as a part of a more formal learning process.

3.   20 .01 Increased efforts to solicit and use learner input.

4..   20 .01 An increasing emphasis on program design on setting a climate that is conducive to self-directed learning.

5.   19 .01 Use of learning contracts and other ways of individualizing instruction.

6.   19 .01 Association of learning contracts with self-directed learning in adult education graduate programs.

7.   19 .01 Providing more opportunity for participants/learners to design and carry out independent projects.

8.   19 .01 A shift in teacher training away from emphasis on skills in using techniques of transmission and control to using techniques of learner-involvement and responsibility.

9.   19 .01 The incorporation of self-directed learning in professional continuing education.

10.   19 .05 Legitimation of learning which occurs outside formal institutional setting.

Summary: Focus on the learner and meeting individual needs by way of learning contracts is seen as an important contribution of self-directed learning research.   The legitimization   of   "informal"   individually-focused methodologies in education is also seen as having occurred as a result of self-directed learning research.

Item #5: These are the citations for the most important published works that, in the panel's judgement, should be read at the outset of one's introduction to the field of adult self-directed learning.

1.   22 .01 Tough, A. (1979). The adult's learning projects. 2nd Edition. Toronto: Ontario Institute of Studies in Education.

2.   20 .01 Houle, C.O. (1961). The inquiring mind, 2nd Edition. Madison, WI: The University of Wisconsin Press.

3.   20 .01 Long H.B. and Associates (1988). Self-directed learning: Application and theory. Athens, GA: University of Georgia, Department of Adult Education.

4.   19 .01 Brookfield, S. (1985).   Self-directed learning: From theory to practice. New Directions for Continuing Education, No. 25. San Francisco: Jossey-Bass.

Summary: A statistically significant majority consensus formed around eight other published works which are listed here for those who wish to use a more extensive introductory reading list.   They are listed here in order of the strength of consensus: 1) Knowles, M. (1975). <u>Self-directed learning: A guide for learners and teachers</u>. Chicago, IL: Follett. 2) Long, H.B. & Associates (1989). <u>Self-directed learning: Emerging theory and practice</u>. Norman, OK: Oklahoma Research Center for Continuing Professional and Higher Education. 3) Spear, G.E. & Mocker, D.W. (1984). The organizing circumstance: Environmental determinants in self-directed learning. <u>Adult education quarterly</u>. <u>35</u> 1, 1-10. 4) Tough, A. (1978). Major learning efforts: Recent research and future directions. <u>Adult education</u>. <u>28</u> 4, 250-63. 5) Long, H.B. & Associates (1990). <u>Advances in research and practice in self-directed learning</u>. Norman, OK: Oklahoma Research Center for Continuing Professional and Higher Education. 6) Brookfield, S. (1986). <u>Understanding and facilitating adult learning</u>. San Francisco: Jossey-Bass. 7) Caffarella, R.S. & O'Donnell, J.M. (1987). Self-directed adult learning: A critical paradigm revisited. <u>Adult education quarterly</u>. <u>37</u> 4, 199-211. 8) Tough, A. (1981). <u>Learning without a teacher: A study of tasks and assistance during adult self-teaching projects</u>. Toronto: Ontario Institute for Studies in Education.

<u>Item #6:</u> These are the most important issues in adult education that, in panel's judgement, should be researched between now and the year 2000.

1. <u>20 .01</u> Longitudinal research on individuals in their use and enhancement of self-directed learning knowledge, skills, and attitudes. In particular the consideration of the impact of education, involvement in community or organization experiences, impact of work and family roles.

2. <u>19 .01</u> What are the critical and necessary properties of the self-directed learning construct?

3. <u>19 .01</u> The relationship of self-directed learning to critical thinking and other prominent concepts in adult education.

4.   18 .01 Further conceptualization of the term self-directed learning.

5.   18 .01 Identify the competencies one should develop to become an effective self-directed learner and identify the corresponding methods and techniques that should develop those competencies.

6.   18 .01 How can self-directed learning strategies help the workers increase their competencies on their job?

7.   18 .01 Conduct a longitudinal study of adults to identify successful and unsuccessful self-directed learning activities amongst this group and analyze reasons for each.

8.   18 .05 Agreement on clear definition of what is self-directed learning.

9.   18 .05 Conduct a longitudinal study of adults focusing on how adult self-directed learners develop or hone the necessary skills and techniques for learning in various subject/knowledge domains and various situations/contexts.

10.   17 .01 The role of self-directed learning in personal and social change.

11.   17 .01 Ways of enhancing readiness for self-directed learning.

12.   17 .01 What are the mechanisms by which learners decide whether to proceed more deeply into a learning project, or to abandon it?

13.   17 .01 Conduct a longitudinal study of adults focusing on how they conceive and approach learning in (1) various subject and knowledge domains; and, (2) various situations and contexts.

14.   17 .01 Determination of how self-directed learning is translated into improved professional practice.

15.   17 .01 What role do personal learning networks or personal learning communities have in promoting or facilitating self-directed learning?

16. 17 .01 Promoting self-directed learning/individuals: Origins and ways to develop self-directed learning attitudes among individuals in adult education.

17. 17 .01 Ways/techniques/instruments for measuring various aspects of self-directed learning.

Summary: It appears that more longitudinal research needs to be done in self-directed learning. Emphasis should be placed on decisions made by the learner within the context of self direction. What, why and how do they study within a self-directed learning context? How do we relate to self-directed learning so it can be considered a legitimate method of learning? By answering these questions, researchers may be able to provide insight with regard enhancing self direction in all learners.

Item #7: These are the most important changes in educational theory during the 1990's that will, in the panel's judgement, be precipitated by research into adult self-directed learning.

1. 19 .01 The importance of experience (e.g., being an expert versus being a novice) in how one processes information.

2. 18 .01 Development of a more complex and multidimensional understanding of adult learners. In particular, the re-framing of the concept of self-directed learning into levels or positions of action, practice and reflection premised upon the post-Piagetian concepts of Perry and others. In essence the quality of meaning, knowledge context, and understandings of self-directed learning would greatly differ between a 5 year old, a 20 year old college student, a 40 year old illiterate, and a 40 year old college professor.

3. 18 .01 Extensive theory-building related to the self-learning process and ways to enhance readiness for self-directed learning.

4. <u>18 .01</u> Development of models of facilitation for self-directed learning.

5. <u>18 .01</u> An increasing focus on the learner in contrast to the teacher in theorizing about the dynamics of the teaching-learning process.

6. <u>18 .01</u> Learning theory, grounded in self-directed learning, will explain the need to modify public institutions that provide educational experiences (such as libraries, museums, parks, and zoos) to incorporate notions of self-directed learning in order to improve the opportunity for individuals to learn what they choose to learn.

7. <u>17 .01</u> Development of a variety of models of self-directed learning according to the different aspects and nature of what is self-directed learning.

8. <u>17 .01</u> Hopefully, a clarification of the multiple definitions of self-directed learning.

<u>Summary:</u>   The panel believes a clear definition of self-directed learning will emerge in the 1990's. Some believe increased understanding of individual learning preferences will contribute to methods for enhancing readiness for self directed learning. Others believe increased understanding of individual learner characteristics will improve our ability to enhance self-directed learning in individuals.

Item #8: These are the most important changes in educational <u>practice</u> during the 1990's that will, in panel's judgement, be precipitated by research into adult self-directed learning.

1. <u>22 .01</u> A shift in teacher training away from emphasis on skills in using techniques of transmission and control to using techniques of learner-involvement and responsibility.

2. 21 .01 Greater emphasis on learning how to learn techniques and skills.

3. 21 .05 Teachers, instructors, and others will place greater emphasis on learners' personal responsibility for learning, hence greater choice, options, alternatives will be available to learners.

4. 19 .01 A better delineation of the role of the facilitator.

5. 19 .01 Identification of strategies and methods to develop "learning how to learn" competencies.

6. 18 .01 Acceptance of greater diversity in how and whether people prefer to be self-directed in educational settings.

7. 18 .01 Building self-directedness concepts into education for learning-how-to-learn; helping people know themselves better so they can make the most appropriate choices about kind and degree of self-directedness in specific contexts.

8. 18 .01 Increasing acceptance of learner autonomy and teacher facilitation within formal educational settings.

9. 18 .01 Improved sophistication in the provision of services to adults, especially provision in facilitating self-directed learning.

Summary: Increased emphasis on individual learning, cited previously, will continue to provide focus for educational practitioners. All participants believed teacher training emphasis will shift from focusing on transmission and control to the development and use of techniques of learner involvement and responsibility. This theme of responsibility was interpreted to include teaching "learning how to learn" concepts and methods of facilitating student learning via individualized instructional techniques.

Item #9: These are the most important sources that, in the panel's judgement, will produce researchers in the field of adult self-directed learning during the 1990's.

1.   <u>22 .01</u> Doctoral programs in adult and continuing education.

2.   <u>22 .01</u> The professors who are now concerned with self-directed learning will continue to produce researchers in the field (students of Master and Ph.D. degree programs).

3.   <u>22 .01</u> Adult education (doctoral level) degree programs.

4.   <u>22 .01</u> Adult education graduate programs which emphasize qualitative research.

5.   <u>22 .01</u> Graduate programs in adult and continuing education.

6.   <u>22 .01</u> Graduate programs of adult education in universities.

7.   <u>21 .01</u> Academic field of adult education.

8.   <u>21 .01</u> University research into adult education in general, and mainly into adult learning. Research teams, networks.

9.   <u>20 .01</u> Adult education Ph.D. programs in the U.S.A.

10.   <u>20 .01</u> Graduate programs of adult education in North America.

Summary: There was overwhelming agreement that graduate programs will provide the next researchers in self-directed learning. It is anticipated that nearly all research into self-directed learning will be conducted by persons associated with graduate programs in higher education settings.

Item #10: These are the most important questions not included above that, in the panel's judgement, should be asked in future surveys.

1. <u>19 .01</u> What are the major gaps in self-directed learning research?

2. <u>18 .01</u> What are the necessary and sufficient conditions for self-directed learning?

3. <u>18 .01</u> Should self-directed learning continue to be a major trend of research in adult education?

4. <u>18 .01</u> What were major turning points in theory building that allowed expansion of self-directed learning?

5. <u>18 .01</u> What, in your opinion, are the three greatest blockages to improved research in adult self-directed learning?

6. <u>17 .01</u> How can self-directed learning skills be best developed?

7. <u>17 .01</u> What areas of research are in need of clarification?

8. <u>17 .01</u> What current works seem to show most promise for future directions?

9. <u>17 .05</u> How can we develop an elegantly clear and conceptually distinctive definition of self-directed learning?

Summary: The panelists appeared to be most concerned with areas of research. Areas of suggested investigation research include the need for clarifying areas of research, gaps in the research, and blockages to effective research. A sub-theme of developing self-directed learners, either by providing appropriate conditions by developing effective methodologies also emerges in these statements.

CONCLUSIONS

This study found consensus in rather substantial breadth and depth related to ten central issues among leaders in the field of self-directed learning. Yet, this consensus is limited temporally and in terms of content. The Delphi technique has proven to be effective in allowing this consensus to emerge among these panelists, on these issues, at this time. It is hoped that other Delphi surveys on topics in self-directed learning will be conducted with other panels in the future. Such studies may benefit from the topical guidance provided in the items obtained in response to survey item ten which sought advice as to what questions should be asked in future surveys.

REFERENCES

Brookfield, S.D. (1988). Conceptual, methodological and practical ambiguities in self-directed learning. In H.B. Long & Associates. Self-directed learning: Application and theory. Athens, GA: Department of Education, University of Georgia, 11-37.

Candy, P.C. (1990). The transition from learner-control to autodidaxy: More than meets the eye. In H.B. Long and Associates. Advances in research and practice in self-directed learning. Norman, OK: Oklahoma Research Center for Continuing Professional and Higher Education, 9-46.

Dalkey, N. & Helmer, O. (1963). An experimental application of the Delphi method to the use of experts. Management science. 9 3, 458-77.

Long, H.B. (1991). Self-directed learning: Consensus and conflict. In Huey B. Long & Associates. Self-directed learning: Consensus and conflict. Norman, OK: Oklahoma Research Center for Continuing Professional and Higher Education, 1-9.

Siegel, S. (1956). Nonparametric statistics for the behavioral sciences. New York, NY: McGraw-Hill.

CHAPTER FOUR

A UNIFYING FRAMEWORK FOR DATA-BASED RESEARCH INTO ADULT SELF-DIRECTED LEARNING

Claudia Danis

Data-based research efforts in the field of adult self-directed learning are presently faced with three major difficulties. The first difficulty is related to the fact that many researchers have tended to overemphasize the importance of too few components, often to the detriment of other components or elements. Studies regarding the nature of the self-directed learner, for instance, have mostly focused on the individual learner's psychological characteristics (Guglielmino & Guglielmino, 1988; Caffarella & O'Donnell, 1988a), while paying relatively little attention to other aspects of both individual and collective self-directed learners. The second difficulty is related to the need, in trying to define and explain the self-directed learning phenomenon, to focus on more dynamic aspects of the complex self-directed learning processes (Penland, 1981; Knowles, 1981; Peters, 1981; Kasworm, 1983; Spear & Mocker, 1984; Danis & Tremblay, 1988; Long & Agyekum, 1988). In the last fifteen years or so, a multiplicity of theoretical models have been proposed as hypothesized representations of the self-directed learning processes or of some of their corresponding notions (Danis, 1988b). The main models are Tough's management model (1975), Kasworm's lifespan developmental model (1983), Martin's information-processing model of self-instruction (1984), and Spear & Mocker's "alternative conceptualization" (Caffarella & O'Donnell, 1988a) centered around the notion of "organizing circumstance" (1984). Yet, in a theory-building perspective, researchers are still in need of more comprehensive and inclusive models or frameworks (Long, 1990). The third major difficulty concerns the specificity of self-directed learning as a field of research, as opposed to other closely related fields such as cognitive psychology and adult learning in general. The actual conceptual ambiguity regarding the study of internal change ("learning" as a gerund) as opposed to the study of corresponding self-instructed learning activities or behaviors ("learning" as a verb) (Brookfield, 1988) illustrates the need, for the self-directed learning field of research, to delimit explicitly its own boundaries and its own contribution.

Given this problematic context, the purpose of the present study is to propose a broad, unifying framework that could encompass and guide the various data-based self-directed learning research efforts. This new framework should provide an overview of the main components to be investigated, put forward a dynamic conceptualization of these various components' interrelations, as well as delimit the boundaries of the self-directed learning field of investigation. The purpose of this framework is not to prescribe any one particular way of theorizing or of operationalizing self-directed learning research. What this tentative framework aims to provide is a coherent, general "map of the territory" (de Winter Hebron, 1983) within which researchers can locate self-directed learning's main components and bring into play its essential relationships.

THE PROPOSED FRAMEWORK

The proposed framework is based on the notion of self-regulated learning processes. Self-instructed learning has already been conceptualized as a process (Tough, 1975) and even as a combination of various processes (Penland, 1988; Spear, 1988; Danis & Tremblay, 1988). "Learning processes" are defined, within this framework, as "the various possible interactions of a series of interdependent components which lead to the acquisition and/or application of new knowledge". These processes do not refer to the internal, cognitive aspects of learning. "Self-regulation", which characterizes these processes, is defined here as "the control exerted by the learners themselves with regard to the purpose, agency, and instrumentality of their learnings" (Zimmerman & Martinez Pons, 1986).

The self-regulated learning processes' inherent components along with their mutual interactions constitute the present framework. The components and sub-components (see Table 4.1) were derived from a synthesis of relevant data found in three main research bases: research in self-directed learning as such, research in self-instruction, and research in learning and study strategies. The framework's components are the following: I- the self-regulated learning STRATEGIES, II- the PHASES of the self-regulated learning processes, III- the LEARNING CONTENT, IV- the LEARNER, and V- the CONTEXT.

Strategies (I)

Viewed as the operationalization of the various self-regulated learning processes, self-regulated learning strategies constitute the core of the present framework (Danis, 1988a).

Until now, self-directed learning research has focused very little on the notion of strategies (Danis, 1988a). Research in self-instruction and in learning and study strategies has mainly focused on the teaching of study strategies and on reading, writing, or problem-solving strategies (Dansereau, 1978; Weinstein & Mayer, 1986; Zimmerman & Martinez Pons, 1986; Wilson, 1988). It has mostly been carried out in artificial contexts (Dansereau, 1978; Zimmerman & Martinez Pons, 1986), with children and adolescents rather than with adult learners (Palmer & Goetz, 1988), and has studied relatively isolated elements rather than strategies in relation to more global and interactive theoretical contexts.

Within the present framework, "strategies" are defined as "the learner's explicit behaviors and thoughts (Weinstein & Mayer, 1986) that are intended to influence how he/she acquires or applies new knowledge". They are viewed in terms of approaches (Schmeck, 1988) or ways of proceeding (Danis, 1988a).

A certain relationship between the study of self-regulated learning processes and the theoretical base offered by Bandura's Social Learning Theory (1971, 1977, 1982) has been established (Penland, 1981; Spear, 1988). The same relationship has also been established, more specifically, between this same theoretical base and the study of self-regulated learning strategies (Zimmerman & Martinez Pons, 1986). This "consensus theoretical framework" (Penland, 1981) "suggests an interactive relationship among environmental, behavioral, and personal elements that modify and determine the life process of individuals" (Spear, 1988, p. 220).

Two categories of strategies are considered in the present framework. The first category corresponds to the "strategies" that are used directly in order to acquire or apply new knowledge. The second category corresponds to the "meta-strategies" that are used and refers to the learner's awareness of his/her own use of particular strategies (Meichenbaum, Burland, Gruson, & Cameron, 1979; Jones, Sullivan Palincsar, Sederburg Ogle, & Glynn Carr, 1987).

The related sub-components are the following:

Strategies (A)

1. REPERTOIRE of the strategies used to monitor one's own learning (Dansereau, 1978; Smith, 1982; Weinstein & Mayer, 1986; Zimmerman & Martinez Pons, 1986; Weinstein, 1987; Weinstein, Zimmerman, & Palmer, 1988). This repertoire includes two main categories of strategies: (a) the strategies used to acquire and/or apply new knowledge, and (b) those used to provide affective and motivational support (Dansereau, 1978; Weinstein, 1987; Weinstein, Zimmerman, & Palmer, 1988).

2. ORIGIN of the strategies used by the learner (Hrimech, 1990).

3.   MODIFICATION(S) of the strategies used by the learner (Hrimech, 1990).

4.   TRANSFER of the strategies in use to (a) similar learning tasks (Hrimech, 1990), (b) different learning tasks (Danis & Tremblay, 1985; Hrimech, 1990), and (c) teaching tasks that are related to the newly acquired/applied knowledge (Danis & Tremblay, 1987; Hrimech, 1990).

Meta-Strategies (B)

The same four corresponding sub-components apply to this second category of strategies:

1.   REPERTOIRE of the meta-strategies used to monitor one's own learning. This repertoire includes two main categories of meta-strategies: (a) those that are used to acquire and/or apply new knowledge, and (b) those that are used to provide affective and motivational support (Meichenbaum et al., 1979; Danis & Tremblay, 1984).

2.   ORIGIN of the meta-strategies used by the learner.

3.   MODIFICATION(S) of the meta-strategies used by the learner.

4.   TRANSFER of the meta-strategies in use to (a) similar learning tasks, (b) different learning tasks, and (c) teaching tasks that are related to the newly acquired/applied knowledge.

Further research into this component's constituents could lead to a better understanding of the relative importance of each strategy/meta-strategy or cluster of strategies/meta-strategies used by the learner (Hrimech, 1990) and to a better understanding of the interaction between strategies and meta-strategies.

Within the proposed framework, the Strategies component (I) has a direct impact on the Phases (II), on the Learning Content (III), and on the Context (V) components. The Strategies component (I), in turn, is directly affected by the Learner (IV), the Phases (II), and the Context (V) components (see Figure 4.1. a, b, c). Research into these dynamic interrelations between the first component and the other four components of the self-regulated learning processes could lead to important findings. It would be most interesting, for example, to study the transfer of specific strategies to different self-instructional tasks (I,A,4,b) in relation to the type of learning content that is being acquired (III). It would also be interesting to study, among other things, the impact of a self-instructed learner's previous experience (IV) on his/her use of particular meta-strategies (I,B,1) (see Figure 4.1.a).

Phases (II)

Descriptive self-directed learning research has long focused on the existence of pre-established "steps" or "episodes" (Tough, 1975) that are related to the planning, implementation, and evaluation of self-directed learning projects (Caffarella & O'Donnell, 1988a). From this viewpoint, planning seems to be as crucial as learning itself (de Winter Hebron, 1983), and the setting of goals or objectives, an essential part of the underlying decision-making process (Danis, 1988a). Research in self-instruction (Martin, 1984) and in learning and study strategies (Dansereau, 1978; Weinstein, 1987; Zimmerman & Martinez Pons, 1986) has also focused, although less directly, on the various recursive "phases" (Jones et al., 1987) or "sequences" involved in any learning process. Researchers differ on the extent to which specific phases should be delineated and on the various labels that should be used (Jones et al., 1987). A synthesis of relevant literature, however, always seems to bring out three general phases: (1) preparing for learning, (2) acquiring the new knowledge, and (3) consolidating and extending the new knowledge (Jones et al., 1987).

Within the present framework, "phases" are defined as "the distinct stages in the sequence of learning activities" (Spear, 1988). These stages are interrelated and may be recursive (Jones et al., 1987; Danis, 1988b).

The related sub-components correspond to the various recursive phases involved. They are the following:

1. REACTING TO A TRIGGERING EVENT/SITUATION that becomes the starting point of the self-regulated learning processes (Spear, 1988). GOAL SETTING (Martin, 1984; Zimmerman & Martinez Pons, 1986), if present, is assumed to be less frequent in this particular mode of learning (Danis & Tremblay, 1985; Spear, 1988).

2. SEEKING AND SELECTING (a) the specific knowledge/information to be acquired (Martin, 1984; Zimmerman & Martinez Pons, 1986) and (b) the available sources/resources (Zimmerman & Martinez Pons, 1986).

3. ORGANIZING AND STRUCTURING both (a) the knowledge to be acquired (Zimmerman & Martinez Pons, 1986) and (b) the strategies to be used (Hrimech, 1990). A detailed PRE-PLANNING of the learning processes does not seem to correspond to the self-regulated way of learning (Spear & Mocker, 1984; Danis & Tremblay, 1985), even though the learners do seem to proceed with deliberateness (Spear & Mocker, 1984) and purpose (Penland, 1988).

4. ACQUIRING AND INTEGRATING the new knowledge (Smith, 1982; Zimmerman & Martinez Pons, 1986).

5. ASSESSING THE QUALITY of both (a) the learning outcome (Martin, 1984; Brookfield, 1988; Caffarella & O'Donnell, 1988b) and (b) the learning strategies used (Hrimech, 1990). This assessment may be carried out (a) during the learning processes as well as (b) after (Caffarella & O'Donnell, 1988b), either by the learner himself/herself (Zimmerman & Martinez Pons, 1986; Caffarella & O'Donnell, 1988b) or with the help of others (for example, peers or experts) (Zimmerman & Martinez Pons, 1986).

6. APPLYING the new knowledge (Baskett, 1986; Jones et al., 1987).

Further research into this component's dynamic processes of reciprocation could lead to more accurate descriptions of the self-instructed learning syntax (Danis, 1988b).

Within the proposed framework, the Phases component (II) has a direct impact on the Strategies (I) and on the Learning Content (III) components. The Phases component (II), in turn, is directly affected by the Strategies component (I) (see Figure 4.1. b, c). In order to be specific to the self-directed learning field of research, investigations should explicitly take into account the link between this second component (II) and the self-regulated learning strategies used by the learner (I). Such investigations could therefore focus on the link between the learner's self-regulated ways of proceeding (I) and any one particular phase (II), and, for example, subsequently focus on the link between these two sub-components and specific types of learning contents (III). More specifically, this could bring about studies linking, among other things, the repertoire of self-regulated learning strategies used by the learner (I,A,1) to the phase of integration (II,4) of new attitudes (III,1) (see Figure 4.1.b).

Learning Content (III)

Until now, data-based self-directed learning research has focused very little on the nature, quality (Brookfield, 1988; Caffarella & O'Donnell, 1988b), and role of the learning content itself. Research in learning and study strategies has mostly focused on types of "subject matter knowledge" (Thomas & Rohwer, 1986), from an academic perspective.

In the present framework, "learning content" is defined as "any new knowledge that is acquired by the learner". This new knowledge corresponds to any type of content that the individual or collective learner may acquire: for example, psychomotor skills (Singer, 1978), technical skills or abilities, communicative and problem-solving skills or abilities, attitudes, affective and value orientations (Kasworm, 1983), meaning of abstract notions and constructs, interpretation of personal and social reality (Marton & Saljo, 1979;

Brookfield, 1988). The focus is on the learning outcome which may be inferred from the learner's own perception and/or performance. Cognitive processing as such (Dansereau, 1978) is excluded.

The related sub-components are the following:

1. TYPES OF OUTCOMES as such (Marton & Saljo, 1979; Danis, 1980; Mayer, 1988).

2. LEVELS OF COMPLEXITY of the acquired learning content, mostly regarding the structure of the knowledge to be acquired and/or applied (Baskett, 1986).

3. The LINK between NEWLY ACQUIRED KNOWLEDGE and relevant PRIOR KNOWLEDGE (Jones et al., 1987; Spear, 1988). This integration of new knowledge with pre-existing knowledge has already been related to the notions of meaning and MEANINGFUL LEARNING (Van Rossum & Schenk, 1984; Jarvis, 1987).

Further research into this component's constituents could provide findings that are essential to our understanding of adult learning in general.

Within the proposed framework, the Learning Content component (III) has a direct impact on the Learner component (IV). The Learning Content component (III) is, in turn, directly affected by the Strategies (I) and Phases (II) components (see Figure 4.1. a, b). In order to be specific to the self-directed learning field of research, investigations should, therefore, take into account the link between this component (III) and the self-regulated learning strategies used by the learner (I). For instance, such investigations could first focus on the link between the modification of specific self-regulated learning strategies (I,A,3) and the learning content's structural complexity (III,2) and, subsequently, focus on the link between these two sub-components and the learner's competencies (IV,A,1) (see Figure 4.1.a).

Table 4.1
Components and Sub-Components of the Proposed Framework

I. <u>STRATEGIES</u>

    A) STRATEGIES
        1. REPERTOIRE
        2. ORIGIN
        3. MODIFICATION(S)
        4. TRANSFER to
           a) similar tasks
           b) different tasks
           c) teaching tasks

    B) META-STRATEGIES
        1. REPERTOIRE
        2. ORIGIN
        3. MODIFICATION(S)
        4. TRANSFER to
           a) similar tasks
           b) different tasks
           c) teaching tasks

- -

II <u>PHASES</u>

        1. REACTING TO A TRIGGERING EVENT/SITUATION
        2. SEEKING/SELECTING
           a) knowledge
           b) sources/resources
        3. ORGANIZING/STRUCTURING
           a) knowledge
           b) strategies
        4. ACQUIRING/INTEGRATING
        new knowledge

Table 4.1 Continued

    5. ASSESSING THE QUALITY
       a) of learning outcome
       b) of strategies
    6. APPLYING
       the new knowledge

III LEARNING CONTENT

    1. TYPES OF OUTCOMES
    2. LEVELS OF COMPLEXITY
    3. LINK between NEW and PRIOR KNOWLEDGE

IV LEARNER

A) INDIVIDUAL LEARNER
    1. LEARNING ABILITIES/COMPETENCIES
    2. INDIVIDUAL IDENTITY
       a) self-concept
       b) readiness to learn
       c) individual styles:
          i) cognitive styles
          ii) learning styles
       d) perception of the learning-teaching transaction
       e) motivation
       f) attitudes
       g) interests
       h) emotions
       i) locus of control
    3. DEVELOPMENTAL FACTORS
       a) developmental stage of
          i) the individual
          ii) his/her work/career
       b) previous experience
          i) learning content
          ii) procedural knowledge

Table 4.1 Continued

4. CULTURAL/ETHNIC FACTORS
   a) cultural:
      i) beliefs
      ii) values
      iii) traditions
   b) ethnic:
      i) racial
      ii) religious
      iii) linguistic traits
5. SOCIAL FACTORS
   a) socioeconomic factors
   b) sociopolitical factors

B) COLLECTIVE LEARNER
   1. LEARNING ABILITIES/COMPETENCIES
      a) learning content
      b) procedural knowledge
   2. COLLECTIVE IDENTITY
      a) group structure
         i) executive levels/processes
         ii) membership composition
      b) goals/mandate
         i) as a collective entity
         ii) as a self-regulated learning group
      c) norms/normative control
      d) affective structure
         i) behavioral level
         ii) emotional level
      e) perception of the learning-teaching transaction
   3. DEVELOPMENTAL FACTORS
      a) developmental stage of group
      b) previous experience
         i) learning content
         ii) procedural knowledge
   4. CULTURAL/ETHNIC FACTORS
      a) cultural/multicultural:

Table 4.1 Continued

   i) beliefs
   ii) values
   iii) traditions
  b) ethnic/multiethnic:
   i) racial
   ii) religious
   iii) linguistic traits
 5. SOCIAL FACTORS
  a) socioeconomic factors
  b) sociopolitical factors

- -

V <u>CONTEXT</u>

 1. CONDITIONS/CIRCUMSTANCES
 2. RESOURCES/CHANNELS:
  a) human: i) separate:
     1- peers
     2- family/friends
     3- experts
     4- clients
    ii) combined:
     1- networks
  b) material: i) separate:
     1- print
     2- other media
    ii) combined:
     1- multimedia

Learner (IV)

Until now, adult self-directed learning research -particularly North American research- seems to have overemphasized the importance of the individual learner component. This is probably so because of the strong influence Humanistic Psychotherapy (Maslow, Allport, Rogers) has exerted on this area of investigation (Brookfield, 1988). Data-based self-directed learning research has focused mostly on personality constructs and motivation to learn (Caffarella & O'Donnell, 1988a). Guglielmino's Self-directed Learning Readiness Scale (SDLRS) (1978) and Oddi's Continuing Learning Inventory (OCLI) (1986) are the two prevailing instruments that have been used to measure mostly given personality characteristics of adult learners. Experiential learning styles of self-taught adults (Theil, 1984) have also been studied, along with the corresponding use of general strategies (Danis, 1988a). Study and learning strategy research is stressing the learners' individual differences with regard to their abilities and capacities (both genetic and acquired), developmental factors (related to past learning and training experiences) as well as social and cultural factors (related to the learners' interests, attitudes, and motivation to perform and to persevere) (Singer, 1978). Other studies in this same field of research have directly linked the use of learning and study strategies to specific characteristics of the learners, for example, to their learning styles and personal characteristics (Schmeck, 1988) and to developmental factors (comparing experts/skilled learners with novices/less proficient learners, and young with older students (Jones et al., 1987). Regarding the use of strategies, some researchers point out the fact that adult learners have received until now but scattered and sporadic attention, and the consequent need for research into the adults' background knowledge, abilities, affect, and metacognitive knowledge (Palmer & Goetz, 1988).

In the present study, the "learner" is defined as "any individual or collective entity that acquires new knowledge".

Self-taught groups or associations (Tough, 1975; Danis, 1980; Mvilongo-Tsala, 1990), as well as self-taught adults are thus taken into account.

Within the proposed framework, this component is divided into two sets of sub-components: one set is related to individual learners (A), the other, to collective learners (B). These sub-components are as follows:

Individual Learner (A)

1. LEARNING ABILITIES (Singer, 1978) and COMPETENCIES (Baskett, 1991) that are related to both (a) the learning content and (b) procedural knowledge (Thomas & Rohwer, 1986).
2. INDIVIDUAL IDENTITY which, as a sub-component, is mostly related to the individual learners' distinctive personal features, and often, even to the individuals' personality traits as such (Fox & West, 1983). It may include combinations of factors such as: (a) self-concept as a learner (Palmer & Goetz, 1988), (b) readiness to learn (Guglielmino, 1978), (c) individual styles, mainly (i) cognitive styles (Schmeck, 1988) and (ii) learning styles (Theil, 1984; Schmeck, 1988) (Self-directed learning has been found to be most compatible with Kolb's Experiential Learning Theory (Penland, 1988) and its four modes of "grasping" and "transforming" knowledge (Theil, 1984; Rossing, 1988; Danis, 1988a), and (d) perception of the learning-teaching transaction (Danis, 1980). This sub-component may also include specific factors such as: (e) motivation (i) to learn (Kasworm, 1988), (ii) to perform, or (iii) to persevere (Singer, 1978), (f) attitudes (Singer, 1978), (g) interests (Singer, 1978), (h) emotions (Palmer & Goetz, 1988) that are related to learning, and (i) locus of control that is related to the learners' personal autonomy (Fox & West, 1983; Caffarella & O'Donnell, 1988a).
3. DEVELOPMENTAL FACTORS which, as a sub-component, are mostly related to: (a) the developmental stages of (i) the adult learner as an individual (Kasworm, 1983: Sexton-Hesse, 1984) and of (ii) the individual's work or career. (Any particular developmental stage may be linked to the individual's receptivity to acquire and apply new knowledge (Baskett, 1986; Kasworm, 1988), and (b) previous experience of the learner with regard to (1) past learnings in general, (2) specific training experiences (Singer, 1978), or even (3)

consequent teaching of the newly acquired knowledge (Danis & Tremblay, 1987). This background knowledge may be related to both (i) the learning content and (ii) procedural knowledge. (Both the distinctions between young and older learners and between experts and novices are most relevant within this developmental context (Jones et al., 1987.)

4. CULTURAL FACTORS which include the individual learner's (i) beliefs, (ii) values, and (iii) traditions, and ETHNIC FACTORS which include the individual's shared (i) racial, (ii) religious, and (iii) linguistic traits.

5. SOCIAL FACTORS which are mostly related to (a) socioeconomic factors and (b) sociopolitical factors.

Collective Learner (B)

1. COLLECTIVE LEARNING ABILITIES and COMPETENCIES that are related to both (a) the learning content and (b) procedural knowledge.

2. COLLECTIVE IDENTITY which, as a sub-component, is related to the learning group's distinctive features and may include various factors such as (a) the group structure, with regard to (i) the executive levels and processes and (ii) the membership composition (Danis, 1980; Mvilongo-Tsala, 1990), (b) the group goals or mandate, (i) as a collective entity (Mvilongo-Tsala, 1990), including its activities and clientele (Danis, 1980), and (ii) as a self-instructed learning group (Tough, 1975; Danis, 1980; Mvilongo-Tsala, 1990), including the related task(s) to accomplish, (c) the group norms and normative control (Mvilongo-Tsala, 1990), (d) the affective structure (Mvilongo-Tsala, 1990) with regard to (i) a behavioral level and (ii) an emotional level (Mvilongo-Tsala, 1990), and (e) perception of the learning-teaching transaction (Danis, 1980).

3. DEVELOPMENTAL FACTORS which, as a sub-component, are mostly related to (a) the developmental stages of the group as such. (Any particular stage may be linked to the group's receptivity to acquire and apply new knowledge), (b) previous experience which is related to the group's common past learning experiences. This common background knowledge may be related to both (i) the

learning content and (ii) procedural knowledge. (The distinction between skilled groups and less proficient learning groups could be most relevant within this developmental perspective.)

4. CULTURAL FACTORS (Mvilongo-Tsala, 1990) which include any homogeneous self-instructed learning group's (i) beliefs, (ii) values, and (iii) traditions, and ETHNIC FACTORS which include this same group's shared (i) racial, (ii) religious, and (iii) linguistic traits (Mvilongo-Tsala, 1990), or MULTICULTURAL and MULTIETHNIC FACTORS which correspond to heterogeneous self-directed learning groups.

5. SOCIAL FACTORS which are mostly related to (a) socioeconomic factors (Danis, 1980; Mvilongo-Tsala, 1990) and (b) sociopolitical factors (Danis, 1980; Mvilongo-Tsala, 1990).

Further investigations into this component's collective (B) as well as individual (A) characteristics could prove to be crucial to extend the scope of self-directed learning research objects. Given the fact that the last two sub-components (4 and 5) may exert a strong, direct or indirect influence on all other sub-components (1, 2, 3), these cultural/ethnic or multicultural/multiethnic factors and social factors should be more explicitly taken into account.

Within the proposed framework, the Learner component (IV) has a direct impact on the Strategies component (I). The Learner component (IV), in turn, is directly affected by the Learning Content component (III) (see Figure 4.1.a). Findings regarding the Learner component (IV) alone, do not characterize the self-instructed mode of learning. The individuals' or the groups' abilities (1), identity (2), or development (3), for example, may probably describe many types of proactive, efficient learners; these characteristics may not be uniquely correlated with self-instructed learning. In order to describe, and eventually explain, the self-regulated learning phenomenon, studies should therefore link explicitly the Learner component (IV) to "the behaviors and thoughts that are intended to influence how (the learner) acquires and applies new knowledge" (I). For example, self-directed learning research could focus on the interrelation between an individual's developmental stage (IV,A,3,a,i) and the modifications of his/her repertoire of self-regulated learning meta-strategies (I,B,3), and, subsequently, focus on the link between these two sub-components and the corresponding types of learning outcomes (III,1). Self-directed learning research could equally focus, among other things, on the impact of heterogeneous collective learners' beliefs or values (IV,B,4,a) on their repertoire of self-regulated learning strategies (I,A,1) and, subsequently, study the impact of these two sub-components on these learning groups' integration of new knowledge with their pre-existing knowledge (III,3) (see Figure 4.1.a).

Context (V)

Until now, self-directed learning research has focused mainly on the identification and description of one contextual variable: the human and non-human resources that are related to the individual learners' self-directed learning projects (Tough, 1975; Spear, 1988; Caffarella & O'Donnell, 1988a). Research in self-directed continuing professional education has related these resources more specifically to different kinds of newly acquired knowledge and to some phases of the self-instructed learning processes (Baskett, 1986). Recently, some self-directed learning researchers have also emphasized the importance of studying the effects of the natural environment on the self-regulated learning processes (Spear, 1988; Danis, Tremblay, Brouillet, Theil, & Mvilongo-Tsala, 1989; Tremblay & Theil, 1991). Learning and study strategy research has given very little attention to the context component, mostly limiting itself to the study of the individual learners' formally structured environment and to the study of these learners' use of very few corresponding strategies (Zimmerman & Martinez Pons, 1986).

Within the present framework, the "context" is defined as "the external factors that, within the self-regulated individual or collective learners' environment, facilitate, inhibit, or modify the acquisition and/or application of new knowledge" (Baskett, 1986; Danis et al., 1989). Such factors may be consistent or fortuitous (Spear, 1988; Tremblay & Theil, 1991).

The related sub-components are the following:

1. The CONDITIONS OR CIRCUMSTANCES that influence the self-regulated learning processes, with regard to time or place (Spear, 1988).
2. The RESOURCES AND CHANNELS that are used by the learners with regard to the access, handling, and exchange that are related to their new knowledge (Penland, 1988). These resources and channels may be (a) human and refer either to (i) separate resources such as (1) peers, (2) family and friends, (3) experts, or (4) clients (Tough, 1975; Baskett, 1986), or to (ii) combined resources such as (1) networks (Danis & Tremblay, 1987), or (b) these resources and channels may be material and refer either to (i) separate resources such as (1) print or (2) different media (Tough, 1975; Baskett, 1986) or to (ii) combined resources such as multimedia aids (Penland, 1988).
3. SOCIAL AND ORGANIZATIONAL STRUCTURES that intervene at higher hierarchical levels and that may influence the individual or collective learners (Baskett, 1986).

Further research into this component's constituents could shed light on more interactive, increasingly complex aspects of the individual or collective learners' environment.

Within the proposed framework, the Context component (V) has a direct impact on the Strategies component (I), and is, in turn, directly affected by this same component (I) (see Figure 4.1.c). In order to be specific to the self-directed learning field of research, investigations should therefore take into account the link between this component (V) and the learners' self-regulated ways of proceeding (component I). For instance, investigations could focus on the interrelation between prevailing facilitating or inhibiting conditions (V,1) and the learner's repertoire of meta-strategies (I,B,1), or study the link between the origin of given self-regulated learning strategies (I,A,2) and the use of complex multimedia technology (V,2,b,ii).

Figure 4.1
Essential Relationships Among the Five Components of the Proposed Framework

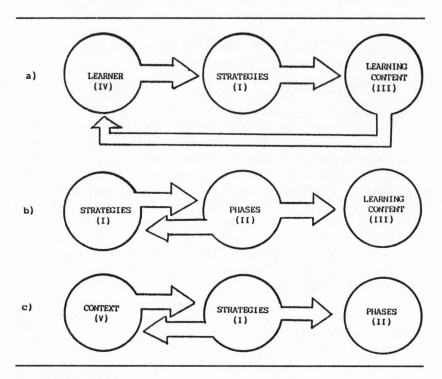

CONCLUSION

In a theory-building perspective, the proposed "map of the territory" could not only be used by researchers in order to describe the main components of the self-regulated learning phenomenon, but also in order to explain how these components act and interact (de Winter Hebron, 1983; Spear, 1988; Danis & Tremblay, 1988).

The use of different theoretical and methodological approaches as well as a broadening of the actual self-directed learning research base in order to include more findings provided by other closely related areas of investigation could greatly enrich the analysis of the complex and simultaneous adult self-regulated learning processes involved.

Furthermore, a redistribution of research priorities may be required in order to take into account a greater number of essential elements or notions, such as, for instance, the role of meta-strategies in the monitoring of the self-regulated learning processes (I), the transfer of specific self-regulated learning strategies to various tasks (I) and the corresponding competencies that are required (IV), the dynamics of the self-regulated integration of new knowledge (II), the efficient assessment of the quality of the self-regulated learning outcomes (III), the impact of cultural and social factors (IV) on the self-regulated learning processes of both individual and collective learners (IV), as well as the impact of increasingly complex multimedia channels (V) on the self-regulated mode of learning.

REFERENCES

Baskett, H.K. (1986). Knowledge utilization in social work practice: Toward a substantive theory of professional learning, Adult Education Research Conference Proceedings, (pp. 13-18). Syracuse, NY: University of Syracuse.

Baskett, H.K. (1991). Processes involved with developing autonomous learning competencies. In H.B. Long (Ed.), Self-directed learning: Consensus & conflict (pp. 245-272). Norman, OK: Oklahoma Research Center for Continuing Professional and Higher Education of the University of Oklahoma.

Brookfield, S.M. (1988). Conceptual, methodological, and practical ambiguities in self-directed learning. In H.B. Long (Ed.), Self-directed learning: Application and theory (pp. 11-37). Athens, GA: Adult Education Department of the University of Georgia.

Caffarella, R.S. & O'Donnell, J.M. (1988a). Research in self-directed learning: Past, present, and future trends. In H.B. Long (Ed.), Self-directed learning: Application and theory (pp. 39-61), Athens, GA: Adult Education Department of the University of Georgia.

Caffarella, R.S. & O'Donnell, J.M. (1988b). Self-directed learning: The quality dimension. In Adult Education Research Conference Proceedings (pp. 31-36). Calgary, Alberta: The University of Calgary.

Danis, C. (1980). Les modèles d'intervention en éducation populaire extra-institutionnelle dans le Québec actuel [Models of out-of-school, informal adult education in Quebec]. Unpublished doctoral dissertation, University of Montreal, Canada.

Danis, C. (1988a). Relationship between learning strategies/meta-strategies and experiential learning styles of self-taught adults. In Adult Education Research Conference Proceedings (pp. 85-90). Calgary, Alberta: University of Calgary.

Danis, C. (1988b). Revision of self-directed learning models in the light of self-taught adults' learning experiences. In Trans-Atlantic Dialogue (pp. 120-125). Leeds, England: Standing Conference on University Teaching and Research in the Education of Adults.

Danis, C. & Tremblay, N.A. (1984). Manifestations de méta-apprentissage en situation d'autodidaxie [Characteristics of meta-learning found in self-directed learning situations]. In Canadian Association for the Study of Adult Education Conference Proceedings. Guelph, Ontario: University of Guelph.

Danis, C. & Tremblay, N.A. (1985). Principles d'apprentissage des adultes et autodidaxie [Adult learning principles and self-directed learning]. Revue des sciences de l'éducation, 11, No 3, 421-439.

Danis, C. & Tremblay, N.A. (1987). Propositions regarding autodidactic learning and their implications for teaching. Lifelong Learning - An Omnibus of Practice and Research, 10, No. 7, 4-7.

Danis, C. & Tremblay, N.A. (1988). Autodidactic learning experiences: Questioning established adult learning principles. In H.B. Long (Ed.), Self-directed learning: Application and theory (pp. 171-197). Athens, GA: The Adult Education Department of the University of Georgia.

Danis, C., Tremblay, N.A., Brouillet, M.I., Theil, J.P., & Mvilongo-Tsala, A. (1989). Analyse interdisciplinaire des principales caractéristiques de la situation d'autodidaxie - Symposium [Interdisciplinary analysis of the main characteristics of the self-directed learning experience - Symposium]. In Canadian Association for the Study of Adult Education Conference Proceedings (pp. 100-104). Quebec, Canada: The University of Ottawa.

Dansereau, D. (1978). The development of a learning strategies curriculum. In H.F. O'Neil (Ed.), Learning Strategies (pp. 1-29). New York: Academic Press.

de Winter Hebron, C. (1983). Can we make sense of learning theory?. Higher Education, 12, 443-462.

Fox, R.D. & West, R.F. (1983). Personality traits and perceived benefits associated with different approaches of medical students to self-directed learning projects (pp. 210-215).

Guglielmino, L. (1978). Development of the self-directed learning readiness scale (Doctoral dissertation, University of Georgia, 1977). Dissertation Abstracts International, 38, 6467A.

Guglielmino, L. & Guglielmino P. (1988). Self-directed learning in Business and Industry: An Information Age imperative. In H.B. Long (Ed.), Self-directed learning: Application and theory (pp. 125-148). Athens, GA: Adult Education Department of the University of Georgia.

Hrimech, M. (1990). Stratégies d'apprentissage utilisées par des adultes universitaires [Learning strategies used by adult university students]. Unpublished doctoral dissertation, University of Montreal, Canada.

Jarvis, P. (1987). Meaningful and meaningless experience: Towards an analysis of learning from life. Adult Education Quarterly, 37, 164-172.

Jones, B.F., Sullivan Palincsar, A., Sederburg Ogle, D., & Glynn Carr, E. (1987). Learning and thinking. In B.F. Jones and associates (Eds.), Strategic teaching and learning: Cognitive instruction in the content areas (pp. 3-32). Alexandria, VA: ASCD Publications.

Kasworm, C. (1983). Self-directed learning and lifespan development. International Journal of Lifelong Education, 2, No. 1, 29-46.

Kasworm, C. (1988). Self-directed learning in institutional contexts: An exploratory study of adult self-directed learners in Higher Education. In H.B. Long (Ed.), Self-directed learning: Application and theory (pp. 65-97). Athens, GA: Adult Education Department of the University of Georgia.

Knowles, M.S. (1981). Preface. In D. Boud (Ed.), Developing student autonomy in learning (pp. 7-9). New York: Nichols Publishing Company.

Long, H.B. (1990). Changing concepts of self-direction in learning. In H.B. Long (Ed.), <u>Advances in research and practice in self-directed learning</u> (pp. 1-7). Norman, OK: Oklahoma Research Center for Continuing Professional and Higher Education of the University of Oklahoma.

Long, H.B. & Agyekum, S.K. (1988). Self-directed learning: Assessment and validation. In H.B. Long (Ed.), <u>Self-directed learning: Application and theory</u> (pp. 253-266). Athens, GA: Adult Education Department of the University of Georgia.

Martin, J. (1984). Toward a cognitive schemata theory of self-instruction. <u>Instructional Science</u>, <u>13</u>, 159-180.

Marton, F. & Saljo, R. (1979). On qualitative differences in learning: Outcome and process. <u>British Journal of Educational Psychology</u>, <u>46</u>, 4-11.

Mayer, R.E. (1988). Learning strategies: An overview. In C.E. Weinstein and associates (Eds.), <u>Learning and study strategies - Issues in assessment, instruction, and evaluation</u> (pp. 11-22). San Diego, CA: Academic Press.

Meichenbaum, D., Burland, S., Gruson, L., & Cameron, R. (1979, October). <u>Metacognitive assessment</u>. Paper presented at the Conference on the Growth of Insight, Wisconsin Research and Development Center.

Mvilongo-Tsala, A. (1990). <u>Le mode d'intervention autodidactique de l'Esuan camerounais</u> [The Cameroonian Esuan's use of the self-instructional mode of learning]. Unpublished doctoral dissertation, University of Montreal, Canada.

Oddi, L.F. (1986). Development and validation of an instrument to identify self-directed continuing learners. <u>Adult Education Quarterly</u>, <u>36</u>, 97-107.

Palmer, D.J. & Goetz, E.T. (1988). Selection and use of study strategies: The role of the studier's beliefs about self and strategies. In C.E. Weinstein and associates (Eds.), <u>Learning and study strategies - Issues in assessment, instruction, and evaluation</u> (pp. 41-61). San Diego, CA: Academic Press.

Penland, P.R. (1981). <u>Towards self-directed learning theory</u>. ERIC Document Reproduction Service No. ED 209 475.

Penland, P.R. (1988). Self-directed learning and natural language processing. In H.B. Long (Ed.), Self-directed learning: Application and theory (pp. 223-251). Athens, GA: Adult Education Department of the University of Oklahoma.

Peters, J.M. (1981). Adult problem-solving and learning. ERIC Document Reproduction Service No. ED 200 758. Rossing, B.E. (1988). Learning from experience - An examination of contributions and limitations of two promising theories. In Trans-Atlantic Dialogue. Leeds, England: Standing Conference on University Teaching and Research in the Education of Adults.

Schmeck, R.R. (1988). Individual differences and learning strategies. In C.E. Weinstein and associates (Eds.), Learning and study strategies - Issues in assessment, instruction, and evaluation (pp. 171-191). San Diego, CA: Academic Press.

Sexton Hesse, C.A. (1984). Assuming responsibility for self-directed learning in professional practice: The contribution of psychosocial factors. Adult Education Research Conference Proceedings (pp. 202-207).

Singer, R.N. (1978). Motor skills and learning strategies. In H.F. O'Neil (Ed.), Learning strategies (pp. 79-106). New York: Academic Press.

Smith, S.L. (1982). Learning strategies of mature college learners. Journal of Reading, 26, No.1, 5-12.

Spear, G. (1988). Beyond the organizing circumstance: A search for methodology for the study of self-directed learning. In H.B. Long (Ed.), Self-directed learning: Application and theory (189-221). Athens, GA: Adult Education Department of the University of Georgia.

Spear, G. & Mocker, D. (1984). The organizing circumstance: Environmental determinants in self-directed learning. Adult Education Quarterly, 35, No 1, 1-10.

Theil, J.P. (1984). Les styles d'apprentissage d'adultes autodidactes [The learning styles of self-taught adults]. Unpublished master's thesis, University of Montreal, Canada.

Thomas, J.W. & Rohwer, W.D. (1986). Academic studying: The role of learning strategies. Educational Psychologist, 21, No.1 and No.2, 19-41.

Tough, A. (1975). The adult's learning projects. Toronto: The Ontario Institute for Studies in Education.

Tremblay, N.A. & Theil, J.P. (1991). A conceptual model of autodidactism. In H.B. Long (Ed.), Self-directed learning: Consensus and conflict (pp. 29-51). Norman, OK: Oklahoma Research Center for Continuing Professional and Higher Education of the University of Oklahoma.

Van Rossum, E.J. & Schenck, S.M. (1984). The relationship between learning conception, study strategy, and learning outcome. British Journal of Educational Psychology, 54, 73-83.

Weinstein, C.E. (1987). Fostering learning autonomy through the use of learning strategies. Journal of Reading, April, 590-595.

Weinstein, C.E. & Mayer, R.E. (1986). The teaching of learning strategies. In M.C. Wittrock (Ed.), Handbook of Research on Teaching (pp. 315-327), third edition. New York: MacMillan Publishing Company.

Weinstein, C.E., Zimmerman, S.A., & Palmer, D.R. (1988). Assessing learning strategies: The design and development of the LASSI. In C.E. Weinstein and associates (Eds.), Learning and study strategies - Issues in assessment, instruction, and evaluation (pp. 25-46). San Diego, CA: Academic Press.

Wilson, V.L. (1988). Evaluation of learning strategies research methods and techniques. In C.E. Weinstein and associates (Eds.), Learning and study strategies - Issues in assessment, instruction, and evaluation (pp. 263-274). San Diego, CA: Academic Press.

Zimmerman, B.J. & Martinez Pons, M. (1986). Development of a structured interview for assessing student use of self-regulated learning strategies. American Educational Research Journal, 23, No.4, 614-628.

CHAPTER FIVE

WHAT'S IN A NAME? THE LANGUAGE OF SELF-DIRECTED LEARNING

Lorraine S. Gerstner

> Language is, without a doubt, the most momentous and at the same time the most mysterious product of the human mind.
>
> Susanne K. Langer

Self-directed learning is increasingly being appreciated as a variegated activity. As we continue to explore and refine our understanding of the phenomenon of self-directed learning, we also have come to appreciate the diversity which attends this undertaking. While the notion of self-directed learning is not a new one, it has in the last two decades been receiving a significant and sustained amount of attention from scholars, researchers, and practitioners. Why then does the concept of self-directed learning cause continuing difficulties both philosophical and practical?

One important reason for our difficulties is that the linguistic functions of self-directed learning are as varied as the phenomenon they describe. Thus, there have appeared a multitude of phrases and terms associated with the idea of self-directed learning. All of these many phrases are now familiar in the sense that they appear in books, research studies, and amongst educators and learners alike. These terms, such as self-planned learning, independent study and autodidactism, are often intoned and used interchangeable such that they have become comfortable and habituated. After all, one might argue, these terms all basically mean the same thing. However, if language is to have any explanative value, it is necessary to reject such a casual grouping of ideas and to proceed to discuss the various referents which words denote and thereby clarify some of the distinctions amongst these terms.

To understand more fully the concept of self-directed learning, we need more than a definition of the term, we need to understand how the concept relates to a host of others, such as the self and direction. This paper will provide a linguistic analysis of the terms and referents of self-directed learning with the idea of revealing ambiguities, meanings, and values. A case will be made for a rewording of the concept from self-directed learning to learner self-directedness.

ORIGIN OF THE TERM SELF-DIRECTED LEARNING

There is a little doubt that Knowles has focused attention on self-directed learning and indeed can be credited with popularizing the concept through his many writings, but most particularly with his book, <u>Self-directed learning: A guide for learners and teachers</u>, (Knowles, 1975). Nonetheless, the first mention of this idea in the adult education literature dates to Bryson (1936). He observed that the most characteristic quality of adulthood is that of self-directed learning. Bryson then goes on to equate adult education with self-education. And here, we have one of the earliest examples of the semantic confusion which would plague future discussions of self-directed learning. Over four decades later, Gibbons (1980) continues this confusion when he offers a theory of self-directed learning and then shifts his terminologic focus to the process of self-education.

DEFINING THE PROBLEM

A concise, universally accepted definition of self-directed learning continues to elude us. Table 5.1, in Appendix A presents a sampler of some of the definitional diversity associated with the term self-directed learning. Such diversity has prompted Brookfield (1987, p. 7) to observe that "it is now past the point where the most often used word in our professional vocabulary and the concept which is most central to our research activities, is still befuddled by confusion and definitional ambiguity." Notwithstanding the range of philosophical opinion surrounding the term self-directed learning, per se, the definitional issue is only one side of the problem. The other side of the problem concerns the abundance of terms related to or associated with self-directed learning. I have encountered twenty phrases which are linked with the idea of self-directed learning. All of these terms have been used at one time or another to mean more or less the same thing.

One way to clarify the terminologic and semantic confusion is to understand that language is not simply the confirmation of the ways in which the world is experienced, but rather that it represents the imposition of borders within what is experienced. In the field of semantic analysis, the term onomastic refers to the process of identifying a concept and then indentifying the various words that can be used in connection with it (Baldinger, 1980). Figure 5.1 graphically represents the onomasiological field of self-directed learning. Table 5.2, in Appendix A identifies the sources for the various terms associated with self-directed learning.

On the one hand, all of these phrases reflect a rich and varied semantic environment. Conversely, there is now such an abundance of terms that the literature on the topic of adult self-directed learning seems more like a cacophony of confused words and phrases distorting rather than clarifying the concept.

Figure 5.1
Onomastic Field of Self-Directed Learning

	Autonomous		
Self-	Self-	learning	Self-	
study	mastery		organized	Self-
			learning	instruction
Self-				
education				Self-
				directed
				change
Independent				
self-				Individual
education				learning
Independent				Self-
learning				propelled
learning				
	SELF-DIRECTED			
	LEARNING			
Independent				Independent
scholarship				study
Self-				Self-
planned				initiated
learning				learning
Self-				Self-
teaching				directed
				education
	Autotelic		Self-	
	inquiry	Autodidactism	directed	
			inquiry	

DIFFERENCES WITH DISTINCTION

A review of the self-directed learning onomasiologic field (Figure 5.1) reveals six referents we need to consider. They are the self, direction, teaching, education, independence and learning. It is important to examine these referents in order to explore the boundaries they establish in order to demarcate the inferred meanings of these phrases.

Self

The idea of self is a pivotal one for self-directed learning because it gives primacy and potency to the self as a paragon for initiation and agency especially with regard to the learning process. Whether the self be understood as a synonym for the individual organism, or as an intrinsic force common to the human species, yet unique to each person, it is assumed to represent an infinite capacity for growth, development, and actualization. It is belief and faith in the individual human potential, which is a hallmark of western cultural values, that bond the self to learning. This is considered to be so, for the self strives to learn to become competent in its environment as well as to express and discover itself. The concept of self-directed learning simply cannot exist, in any meaningful sense, without a concept of self which embraces and values the self as a proactive agent capable and desirous of not only learning, but of directing its own learning for its own ends.

This conceptualization of the self represents a pro forma argument in support of self-directed learning. This is so because the self needs to learn and this need is thought to provide evidence of the positive, proactive aspects of the self which make it worthy of acting on its own behalf and of directing its own learning. This view of individual supremacy is embodied in democratic ideas which laud the freedom to think, speak, and act. The very concept of democracy, in its broadest sense, enshrines the view that individual freedom is the ultimate value. Individual critical thinking and expression describes the democratic approach and democratic adult education requires self-directing capacities and activities in which the person expresses his/her potential with a maximum of freedom and a minimum of restraint (Cherrington, 1939; Wriston, 1940).

While such a view is immensely appealing, it begs the question why self-direction should be more highly valued than other direction? For it is not simply a matter that self-direction is good and other-direction is bad, or that self-direction represent freedom while other-direction represents restraint. In addition to being inaccurate, this is also much too simplistic an explanation. In the real world, the issue is not one or the other, but rather what means affords the best possible expression of the human potential. While other-direction is often necessary and desirable at different stages of the human experience, it is the belief that enlightened self-choice and self-determination permit one to explore and achieve new, progressive levels of humanness. The idea of progress reflects a concern with the growth of people as humans and thus suggests the capacity for transcendence, a surpassing of one's self and one's society (Maslow, 1971). If we wish to advance towards our own potential we must do it ourselves. For it is not possible for another person to know and then actualize anyone else's human endowment, it is the vocation of the self.

Direction

In some cases, the word self is linked to the word directed or direction. Direction implies that the self guides the learning (Webster, 1979). However, it is necessary to press this issue further. What does it mean to direct or guide one's learning? Or to pose this issue another way, to what extent does directing the learning process imply control and/or choice? Some writers use the word directed to refer to the learner's control of the learning effort (Gelpi, 1979; Cheren, 1983; Brookfield, 1986). Other writers use the word directed to refer to the learner's choice in the learning effort (Watson and Tharp, 1983; Rogers, 1983).

The notion of locus of control suggests that some people experience perceptions of having greater control over the environment than do others. Control refers to a situation in which there is thought to be a relationship between one's behavior and the outcome achieved. That is to say, behavior can determine the outcome or desiring a certain outcome can determine behavior (Deci and Ryan, 1985). The formulating of learning objectives is an example of control over the learning process by predetermining the outcome.

However, it is not sufficient to say that a person can or does have control over his or her learning efforts. An essential ingredient in the process of self-directed learning is whether the individual chooses to be a self-directed learner, and if so, whether that individual chooses to be controlled by specific outcomes. If self-direction implies an absence of dependency, as Knowles (1975) and others have suggested, then an individual also needs to be free from dependency on outcomes. Control does not ensure self-determination, it simply permits self-control. Choice permits self-determination and a broader context within which to appreciate self-directed learning.

Teaching

A number of terms suggest that self-directed learning be understood as a method of self-teaching. The terms self-instruction, autodidactism, self-organized learning, and self-planned learning all reflect this orientation.

Teaching refers to the act of instruction whereby an individual intentionally arranges and manages the activities necessary to acquire established skills and knowledge (Houle, 1980; Menges, 1981). This view posits that self-directed learning is a sequence of instructional activities in which an individual acts as both teacher and learner (Kidd, 1973; Knowles, 1975), deciding what to learn, and then engaging in the planning, designing, and evaluating of the instructional process and learning outcomes (Tough, 1979; Penland, 1979).

One is forced to ask whether this is actually possible? In order to teach or instruct, it is necessary to have knowledge of the subject or skills one wishes to acquire. The very need or desire to learn suggests an absence of such knowledge or skills. For one does not seek to learn what one already knows. If a person does not know about electricity, for instance, how can that same person teach him or herself about rewiring a house? Even if one were to buy a how-to-book on electrical repair, this is not self-teaching but rather other-directed instruction. It is the author of the book who is actually teaching or demonstrating the skills necessary for electrical repair. This example also raises questions as to whether this is the most efficient way to learn about electricity. A person with little or no knowledge of residential electrical wiring needs to know about currents, amps, and voltage as well as appropriate techniques for handling and installing electrical wires. The allotment of time and energy necessary for the selection of materials and the comprehension of self-instructional manuals is substantial. This certainly can be done, but it might not be the most timely way to accomplish the task.

Nonetheless, the self-teaching view of self-directed learning represents a management model of instruction. That is, an individual wants to learn something, and then manages (by controlling, planning, directing, and organizing) the learning sequence that he or she believes will bring about the desired knowledge and skills. While it might be the case that some individuals proceed in this fashion, there is reason to doubt that most people self-direct their learning in this way. Leean and Sisco (1981) have reported that their subjects did not engage in a highly organized teaching process, but were instead guided by a diffuse pattern of knowledge gathering. Similarly, Danis and Tremblay, (1985) found that adult learners proceed in a heuristic manner, discovering as they go along rather than learning in a linear, lock stop manner.

Education

The term education can be understood in two ways, the first is a literal interpretation. The word education derives from the Latin word educare, meaning to teach or instruct (Webster, 1979). Therefore, education might be thought of as a synonym for teaching. The word education, though, implies more than just a process of teaching. It suggests the existence of subject matter to be taught.

Another way to understand the word education is as a social invention; that is, a formal, organized structure of provision intended to promote and transmit worthwhile knowledge, information, and skills (Peters, 1966; Good, 1973; Darkenwald and Merriam, 1980).

Education, then, must be understood as a purposeful activity undertaken to acquire a certain kind of knowledge. Knowledge which is considered to have social utility and value and which, thereby, meets public standards of worthiness. Worthiness is meant to ensure the validity and replicability of the acquisitions, operations, and measures of various forms of knowledge (Lawson, 1975; Paterson, 1979). Thus, education is something which occurs outside the individuals and is intended to promote learning.

This view of education presupposes a method of tutelage to assist a student in the educational process since the student does not yet know the subject, as well as to offer a criteria for evaluating the education which has taken place.

From this vantage point, the term self-education and self-directed education should be understood to refer to an individual's decision to acquire a certain body of public knowledge. Accepting this meaning of the terms, there remains the question of how the student can know what he or she does not yet know? It is the role and function of the tutor or facilitator, human or otherwise, to introduce the educant to those things which he or she is not aware of. Therefore, while a person engaging in self-education or self-directed education can choose the public knowledge to be acquired and the books, teachers, or computer assisted program that will provide the assistance, it does not ipso facto introduce the educant to those things he or she is not aware of. Furthermore, the evaluative criteria used to determine the successful accomplishment of the education remains external to the learner. Evaluative criteria, in this case, are to be found within the subject matter or particular form of knowledge. In choosing to learn such material, the student accepts certain predetermined measures of accomplishment.

Independence

Independence is generally understood to refer to freedom from the influence or control of others (Webster, 1979). Thus, when the word independence is associated with the ideas of study, learning, or scholarship it can be thought of as a "wholly self-guided way of designing and controlling an educational activity" (Houle, 1972, p. 91). In this context, then, independence requires unconditional liberty in the educational endeavor by the learner.

Neither freedom nor control can usefully be thought of as absolute or even appropriate states or conditions for learning. It is simply not possible to be free from the influence or control of others while learning. Learning is itself an interactive process. Whether a learner interacts with books, people, television, computers, or a teacher, that learner is controlled by the form of that interaction. That is, the learner is both informed and restrained by print, peers, vision, sequencing, or dialogue. The learner is also influenced by the information and message which is received through a particular medium. It is not feasible to be free of either the medium or the message. It is, however, desirable to be aware of and alert to the various forms and functions of learning.

If we consider this term in the context of formal education, the concept of independent study is found to have a long and respectable heritage which traces its origins to the tutorial tradition established in English universities (Brown, 1968). The essence of this model involves an educational engagement in which a student and a teacher are in a one to one relationship (Gruber, 1965). Independence in this case can be understood in several ways. In one instance, it refers to the learner's release from regularly scheduled class meetings, examinations, and assignments. Such release allows the learner to proceed at his or her pace and to negotiate learning requirements with the teacher. This approach is prevalent in most colleges and universities (Gleason, 1967).

In another instance, independence refers to the separation of the learner from the teacher. Thus, independence is a function of physical separation between teacher and learner. This model of independence study is representative of distance learning system such as the British Open University (Wedemeyer, 1972; Moore, 1973).

In a third instance, independence refers to the separation of the learner or scholar from institutional control or constraint. Here, the learner is not bound or tied to any academic institution (Brookfield, 1982; Gross, 1982).

Notwithstanding the various inferences conveyed by the term independence, it is important to note that independence does not necessarily ensure self-direction. Neither self-pacing nor separation of the student from a teacher or a researcher from an institution necessarily results in choice or freedom. In fact, the vast majority of what is referred to as independent study in educational institutions is closely prescribed and evaluated by a teacher. Even when workbooks and computer assisted instruction are available, so that the student can work on his or her own, this does not represent self-directed learning but rather self-paced instruction.

To this writer, the idea of independent learning is a misnomer. In the first place, it assumes that influence and control are negative and harmful. If it is wrong for the teacher to influence and control the learning, then why is it right for the learner to do so? Clearly, influence and control, in and of themselves, are not undesirable aspects of learning. The issue is what degree of influence or control is appropriate and in what contexts.

In the second place, independent learning insists on an unattainable condition in which an individual is free from influence or control. Such a suggestion is naive and undesirable. It is naive because freedom from influence is impossible to achieve; and it is undesirable because any such isolated learning would be narrow and shallow. Neither the self nor its need for learning can develop in isolation, both require interaction. Since no one can be free of influence and control, it is necessary to bring into consciousness the form and degree of such influence so that one can mediate its effect.

Learning

Human learning is a universal, yet highly individualistic process. While it is generally agreed that humans have the capacity to learn, just how that learning occurs is not clear. Thus, learning must be understood as an inferred concept. Since we don't know the precise manner in which learning happens, we must look instead for evidence which is believed to demonstrate that learning has taken place (Lawson, 1975). As a result, ideas about learning are based on assumptions about what takes place within the individual when he or she learns, and which in turn influences both how we encourage learning and how we determine when and if learning has occurred (Coleman, 1977).

Learning is often presumed to have occurred when change is manifest. Whether the change is in consciousness (Brookfield, 1986), physiology (Little, 1979), or behavior (Good, 1973), it is commonly assumed that learning results in an observable change in the individual. These views posit a cause and effect model of learning. This is, learning is casually linked to change. Given that we don't know exactly what learning is, it seems unduly restrictive to limit learning to a change function. While change might be a necessary external measure of learning, it need not be a necessary condition of internal learning. That is, in setting standards or objectives, it might be necessary to establish verifiable, uniform measures of accomplishment. Learning, then, is being used in a restrictive sense. However, when learning is considered from the point of view of the individual (which is the case with self-directed learning), change need not be a result of learning. One might learn from reading a magazine, for example, that the state of New Jersey has decided to divest itself of any economic interests in South Africa, as well as reasons for this decision. Such learning, though, need not result in observable change. It does, however, result in an expanded state of awareness. If learning is life (Lindeman, 1926), that is, if learning is such a broad, inclusive, diverse capacity, that it is coterminous with life itself, then the word learning should not be used in a restrictive manner.

It is certainly possible to differentiate between kinds of learning such as random or planned learning or insight and discovery learning. But what is common to all of these learning encounters is not change, but that the individual has a heightened state of awareness and knowledgeability. As Greene has commented:

> The point is that learning must be a process of discovery and recovery in response to worthwhile questions rising out of conscious life in concrete situations. And learning must be in some manner emancipatory, in the sense that it equips individuals to understand the history of knowledge structures they are encountering, the paradigms in use in the sciences, and the relation of all these to human interests and particular moments of human time.
>
> (Green, 1973, p. 19)

Learning is used also to refer to both a process and a result. When learning is used as a verb, it refers to the process or range of activities the learner engages in. When used as a noun, learning refers to a product reflecting change or awareness which has occurred in the learner (Clayton, 1965; Brookfield, 1986).

SUMMARY AND CONCLUSIONS

Thus, it will come as no surprise to find that there are myriad meanings associated with self-directed learning. The possible meanings of self-directed learning include a state of awareness (Mezirow, 1981), an internal change of consciousness (Brookfield, 1986), the ability to actualize one's values (Watson and Tharp, 1977), the freedom to choose (Rogers, 1983), the enhancement of learning skills (Cheren, 1983), an internal process of continual human development (Kasworm, 1983), a transformation of outlook (Green, 1973), and the external planning and management of instructional events (Knowles, 1975; Dave, 1975; Penland, 1979; Tough, 1979; Skager, 1978; Smith, 1982; Brookfield, 1986).

This review of the language of self-directed learning leaves us with two questions. What is the status of the term self-directed learning? Where do we go from here?

The term self-directed learning has been used so often, in so many ways, and in so many contexts, that the phrase itself is a labyrinth of confusion and contradiction. For all of the reasons previously discussed, the term self-directed learning has been rendered both normatively and functionally ambiguous. In acknowledging the complexity and diversity of ideas and activities associated with this concept it then becomes necessary to adopt a phrase which conveys the open-ended conceptual potential of this idea. Cheren (1983) has suggested that we use the term self-direction in learning, implying that learner control operates on a continuum which varies in different learning situations. This phraseology, however, remains rooted in a control orientation and thus falls short of providing an adequate context from which to appreciate the multiplicity of perspectives which this concept can afford.

CODA

The term "learner self-directedness", for this writer, offers a focusing as well as a recording of the concept of self-directed learning allowing for a broader interpretation of the concept.

Learner self-directedness is considered preferable to that of self-directed learning for several reasons. Fist, the term is focused on the learner. This accent is an important one for the field of adult education because self-directedness is an amorphous idea unless it is seen in conjunction with the learner. It is the learner who represents the common melody which resonates across all and every perspective. Further, a learner-centered approach allows for individual variation in terms of readiness and capacity for such learning, while encouraging an expanding understanding of the self as a learner. Second, it suggests that there is a range of forms and options available to an adult learner who elects to be self-directed. As I have discussed previously (Gerstner, 1990) there are several variations on the theme of self-directed learning. Thus, a learner can choose to engage in self-directed learning for self-knowledge, self-management, or instrumental learning. Third, it allows the learner to choose the degree of self-directedness that individual wants to engage in. This point is significant because the initial emphasis is on informed choice not merely control. An initial emphasis on choice is an important distinction to clarify because the idea of learner control is thought by many educators to be central to the concept of self-directed learning (Garrison, 1989; Long, 1988). The point being made here, however, is not whether the learner should control the content and methods of a specific learning engagement, but rather whether the learner had authentic options and choices regarding the mode of learning he/she is participating in. The salient issue is that if the learner does not have a real choice as to whether to be a self-directed learner or not, the crucial decision has already been pre-determined and other-directed. Such a lack of choice can result in a forced participation resulting in a tyranny of self-directed learning (Frewin, 1976). Learner self-directedness is grounded in the belief that adults have the ability and the right to choose for themselves how they want to learn based on needs, circumstances, and appropriateness.

The idea of learner self-directedness is not merely convenient semantic contrivance designed to patch over the troublesome issues associated with the term self-directed learning. Or even worse, just one more term adding to the confusion. On the contrary, learner self-directedness emerges from an analysis of a variety of data which reveals the legitimate and important linguistic and conceptual difficulties inherent in the phrase self-directed learning. What this rewording seeks to accomplish is to acknowledge all of these difficulties which bedevils current discussions of self-directed learning. By so doing, it provides an opportunity to eliminate the inclination to polarize the concept of learning as an either/or phenomenon, that of either self-directed or other-directed learning into opposite extremes. It will also, I believe, produce over time models of learner self-directedness with wider explanatory power than currently exist under the rubric of self-directed learning.

I should say that I am not seeking a precise definition of learner self-directedness. Rather, I am inclined to think that it is not possible to say absolutely or definitely what learner self-directedness is anymore than it is possible to say wholly and precisely what knowledge or learning is. What I hope this rewording will lead us to is a broadened vision of what sort of thing learner self-directedness is and can be, so we can be more secure in recognizing and promoting it, even if we are unable to capture it in speech. Learner self-directedness is meant to be understood as an architectonic concept. That is, a term which is more inclusive and seeks to unify these myriad of ideas into a more realistic and meaningful concept which allows for cultural and circumstantial influences and also for learner choice and options across a variety of learning engagements and purposes.

REFERENCES

Apps, J. W. (1981). The adult learner on campus: A guide for instructors and administrators. New York: Cambridge.

Baldinger, K. (1980). Semantic theory: Towards a modern semantics. New York: St. Martin's Press.

Bartkus, E. P. (1973). The two-hours-a-week self-study plan. Continuing Education, 657-659.

Boud, D. (Ed.) (1987). Developing student autonomy in learning. Kogan Page.

Brookfield, S. D. (1987). Conceptual, methodological and practical ambiguities in self-directed learning. In H.B. Long (Ed.), Adult self-directed learning: Application and theory. Athens: Adult Education Department, University of Georgia Press.

Brookfield, S. D. (1986). Understanding and facilitating adult learning: A comprehensive analysis of principles and effective principles. San Francisco: Jossey-Bass.

Brookfield, S. D. (Ed.) (1985). Self-directed learning: From theory to practice. San Francisco: Jossey-Bass.

Brown, C. (1983). Confessions of an autodidact. Adult Education Quarterly, 56, 227-232.

Bryson, L. (1936). Adult Education. New York: American Book Company.

Candy, P. C. (1990). The transition from learner-control to autodidaxy: More than meets the eye. In H. Long and Associates Advances in research and practice in self-directed learning. University of Oklahoma: Oklahoma Research Center for Continuing Professional and Higher Education.

Cheren, M. C. (1978). Facilitating the transition from external direction in learning to greater self-direction in learning in educational institutions: A case study in individualized open system post secondary education. Dissertation Abstracts International, 39, 1362A.

Cherrington, B. M. (1939). Democratic versus authoritarian adult education, Journal of Adult Education. 11, 242-245.

Coleman, J. S. (1976). Differences between experimental and classroom learning. In M. T. Keeton and Associates, (Eds.), Experimental learning: Rationale, characteristics, and assessment. San Francisco: Jossey-Bass.

Danis, C., and Tremblay, N. (1985). Critical analysis of adult learning principles from a self-directed learner's point of view. Adult Education Research Conference Proceedings, No. 26. Tempe, AZ: Arizona State University.

Dadswell, G. (1978). The adult independent learner and public libraries: A new perspective for library service. Adult Education (UK), 51, 5-11.

Dave, R. (1975). Reflections on lifelong education and the school. Germany: UNESCO Institute for Education.

Deci, E.L., and Ryan, R. W. (1985). Intrinsic motivation and self-determination in human behavior. New York: Plenum Press.

Dickinson, G., and Clark, K. M. (1975). Learning orientations and participation in self-education and continuing education. Adult Education, 26, 3-15.

Dill, W. R., Crowston, W. B., and Elton, E. J. (1965). Strategies for self-education, Harvard Business Review. 43, 119-130.

Frewin, C. (1976). Individualized goal setting in informal education settings. Ontario Institute for Studies in Education.

Garrison, D. R. (1989). Facilitating self-directed learning: Not a contradiction in terms. In H. Long and Associates Self-directed learning: Emerging theory and practice. Norman, OK: Oklahoma Research Center for Continuing Professional and Higher Education, University of Oklahoma, 53-63.

Gelpi, E. (1979). A future for lifelong education (Vol 1-2; No. 13), Manchester Monographs. England: University of Manchester.

Gerstner, L. S. (1990). On the theme and variation of self-directed learning. In H. Long and Associates Advances in theory and practice in self-directed learning. Norman, OK: Oklahoma Research Center for Continuing Professional and Higher Education, University of Oklahoma.

Gibbons, M., and Phillips, G. (2982). Self-education: The process of lifelong learning. Canadian Journal of Education, 4, 67-86.

Gleason, G. T. (Eds.) (1967). The theory and nature of independent learning. PA: International Book Company.

Good, C. V. (Ed.) (1973). Dictionary of education (3rd ed.). New York: McGraw Hill.

Greene, M. (1973). Teacher as stranger: Educational philosophy for the modern age. Belmont: Wadsworth.

Gross, R. (1982). The independent scholars handbook. Boston: Addison-Wesley.

Hamm, C. (1982). Critique of self-education. Canadian Journal of Education, 7, 87-106.

Harri-Augstein, E. S., and Thomas, L. F. (1983). Developing self-organization learners: A reflective technology. In R. M. Smith (Ed.) Helping adults learn how to learn: New directions for continuing education (No. 19). San Francisco: Jossey-Bass.

Houle, C. O. (1984). Patterns of learning: New perspectives on life span education. San Francisco: Jossey-Bass.

Houle, C. O. (1972). The design of education. San Francisco: Jossey-Bass.

Johnstone, J. W. C., and Rivers, R. J. (1965). Volunteers for learning: A study of the educational pursuits of American adults. Chicago, IL: Aldine.

Kasworm, C. (1983). Self-directed learning and lifespan development. International Journal of Lifelong Education, 2, 29-46.

Knowles, M. S. (1975). Self-directed learning: A guide for learners and teachers. Chicago, IL: Follett.

Knox, A. B. (1973). Lifelong self-directed education. Project continuing education for health manpower: Fostering the growing need to learn. Syracuse, NY: Syracuse University.

Kolb, D. A., and Winter, S. K. (1968). Self-directed change: Two studies. Journal of Applied Behavior Science, 4, 453-471.

Leean, C., and Sisco, B. (1981). Learning projects and self-planned learning efforts among undereducated adults in rural Vermont. Final Report. Washington, DC: National Institute of Education.

Lindeman, E. C. (1926). The meaning of adult education. New York: New Republic.

Little, D. (1985). Self-directed education: A conceptual analysis. Proceedings of Adult Education Research Conference. Tempe, AZ.

Long, H. (1988). Self-directed learning reconsidered. In H. Long and Associates, Self-directed learning: Application and theory. Athens, GA: Adult Education Department, University of Georgia, 1-10.

Long, H. (1983). Adult learning: Research and practice. New York: Cambridge.

Martens, K. H. (1981). Self-directed learning: An opinion for nursing education. Nursing Outlook, 2, 18-21.

Maslow, A. H. (1970). Motivation and personality. New York: Harper and Row.

Mearns, H. (1940). The creative adult: Self-education in the art of living. New York: Doubleday and Company.

Menges, R. J. (1982). Freedom to learn: Self-directed study in a required course. Journal of Teacher Education, 23, 32-39.

Mezirow, D. (1985). A critical theory of self-directed learning. In S. D. Brookfield (Ed.), Self-directed learning: From theory to practice. San Francisco: Jossey-Bass.

Miller, W. J. (1964). Teaching and learning in adult education. New York: Macmillan.

Moore, M. G. (1983b). Self-directed learning and distance education. Zentrales Institut fur Fernstudienforschuug.

Paterson, R. W. K. (1979). Values, education, and the adult. London: Routledge and Kegan Paul.

Peddler, M. (1972). Teaching students to learn. Adult Education (UK), 45, 87-91.

Penland, P. (1979). Self-initiated learning. Adult Education, 29, 170-179.

Penland, P. (1977). Self-planned learning in America. Pittsburgh, PA: University of Pennsylvania.

Peter, R. S. (1966). Ethics and education. London: George Allen and Unwin, Ltd.

Redwine, J. A., Krauss, K., and Joray, P. A. (1980). Self-studies of teaching: Am I doing what I meant to do? Lifelong learning: The adult years, 4, 18-19.

Rogers, C. R. (1983). Freedom to learn for the 80s. OH: Merrill.

Selby, D. (1973). Towards self-education. Adult Education (UK), 46, 245-249.

Skager, R. (1984). Organizing schools to encourage self-direction in learners. Oxford: Pergamon Press.

Smith, R. M. C. (1982). Learning how to learn: Applied theory for adults. Chicago, IL: Follett.

Spear, G. E., and Mocker, D. W. (1984). The organizing circumstances: Environmental determinants in self-directed learning Adult Education Quarterly, 35, 110.

Swanson, R. W. (1973). Self-study in system analysis. Continuing Education, 6, 4-6, 8.

Tough, A. (1979). The adult's learning projects: A fresh approach to theory and practice in adult learning (2nd ed.). TX: Learning Concepts.

Watson, D. L., and Tharp, R. G. (1977). Self-directed behavior: Self-motivation for personal adjustment. CA: Brooks/Cole.

Webster, C. A. (1971). Independent study. In L. C. Deighton (Ed.), The encyclopedia of education. Journal of Adult Education, 12, 237-243.

APPENDIX 5A

Table 5.1
Selected Definitions of Self-Directed Learning

Author	Definition

Brookfield, 1986   Self-directed learning as the mode of learning characteristic of an adult who is in the process of realizing his or her adulthood is concerned as much with an internal change of consciousness as with the external management of instructional events.   This consciousness involves an appreciation of the contextuality of knowledge and an awareness of the culturally constructed form of the value frameworks, belief systems, and moral codes that influence behavior and the creation of social structures. The most complete form of self-directed learning occurs when process and reflection are married in the adult's pursuit of meaning.

Cheren, 1983   To achieve greater self-direction in learning is to achieve control over one or more aspects of a learning situation.

Dave, 1975   Self-directed learning refers to the planning and management of learning by individuals (either individually or collectively) to accomplish their personal, social, and vocational development by recognizing specific learning needs from time to time and fulfilling them through suitable techniques, resources, and learning opportunities.

Gelpi, 1979   Self-directed learning means individual control of the ends, contents, and methods of education.

Greene, 1973   ...learning is a mode of individual cognitive action.   On a fundamental level, learning is self-directed, whether it culminates in mastery or a principle, reconstruction of some

Kasworm, 1983   I posit that self-directed learning must be considered not just as an externally-defined or self-perceived process. It also must be considered as an internal process of continual development grounded in a framework of both cognitive and human developmental psychology.

93

Author	Definition
Knowles, 1975	Self-directed learning describes a process in which individuals take the initiative, with or without the help of others, in diagnosing their learning needs, formulating learning goals, identifying human and material resources for learning, choosing and implementing appropriate learning strategies, and evaluating learning outcomes.
Mezirow, 1981	A self-directed learner must be understood as one who is aware of the constraints on his efforts to learn, including the psycho-cultural assumptions involving reified power relationships embedded in institutionalized ideologies which influence one's habit of perception, thought, and behavior as one attempts to learn.
Mocker/Spear, 1982	Self-directed learning represents the ultimate state of learner autonomy, i.e., the learner exercises control over the major responsibility for choosing both the goals and the means of the learning.
Page/Thomas, 1977 (International Dictionary of Education)	That of the learner's own choosing and not provided by a formal educational system.
Rogers, 1983	Self-directed learning refers to the freedom to learn or choose.
Skager, 1978	Individuals who set their own goals, plan and carry out their own learning, and evaluate the results are self-directed learners.
Smith, 1982	Self-directed learning involves carrying out personal learning projects. This requires assuming overall control of a learning effort by the individual learner. For success in self-directed learning, one needs planning skills for deciding what, when, how, and where to learn; for setting realistic goals, for finding learning resources, and choosing and implementing learning strategies. Also central to learning on one's own are overcoming personal blocks to learning, sustaining motivation, estimating progress, and assessing results.

Table 5.2
Self-Directed Learning Terminology and Source

Term(s)	Proponents
Self-Directed Learning	Brookfield, 1985; Dave, 1975; Gelpi, 1979; Gibbon et al, 1980; Harrison, 1977; Kasworm, 1983; Knowles, 1975; Martens, 1981; Mezirow, 1985; Moore, 1983; Penland, 1981; Skager, 1984; Smith, 1982; Spear, 1984
Autonomous Learning	Boud, 1981; Houle, 1961; Miller, 1964; Moore, 1977; Pedler, 1972; Smith, 1976
Self-Organized Learning	Harri-Augstein & Thomas, 1983
Self-Instruction	Johnstone & Rivera, 1965; Smith et al, 1976
Self-Directed Change	Kolb & Winter, 1968
Individual Learning	Smith, 1976
Self-Planned Learning	Penland, 1977; Tough, 1971
Independent Scholarship	Gross, 1982
Independent Self-Education	Johnstone & Rivera, 1965
Self-Education	Dickinson & Clark, 1975; Dill et al, 1965; Gibbons et al, 1982; Hamm, 1982; Mearns, 1940; Selby, 1973; Smith, 1976; Snedden, 1930
Self-Study	Apps, 1981; Bartkus, 1973; Redwine & Knauss, 1980; Swanson, 1973
Self-Mastery	Lindeman, 1926

Term(s)	Proponents
Self-Propelled Learning	Miller, 1964
Independent Study/Independent Learning	Brookfield, 1980; Dadswell, 1978; Gleason, 1967; Jourard, 1967; Moore, 1973; Smith, 1976;
Self-Initiated Learning	Penland, 1976
Self-Directed Education	Knox, 1973; Little, 1985
Self-Directed Inquiry	Long, 1976
Autodidactism	Brown, 1983; Candy, 1990; Danis & Tremblay, 1985
Autotelic Inquiry	Dye, 1980
Self Teaching	Tough, 1965

CHAPTER SIX

FREE-WILL, FREEDOM AND SELF-DIRECTED LEARNING

Peter Jarvis

No existentialist philosopher claims anything other than human beings are free to act in whatsoever way they wish. Indeed, freedom is a condition of authentic humanity, whatever the moral constraints imposed upon it by such thinkers as Buber (1961) and Marcel (1976). However, according to Macquarrie (1973, p. 177) when it comes to deciding precisely what freedom is there is a certain elusivity about existentialist writings, and such a charge could justly be leveled at adult educators who frequently employ the synonym, self-directedness, with the same degree of imprecision. This, they well recognize (Brookfield, 1988; Caffarella and O'Donnell, 1988; Long, 1988, inter alia)! During the course of this paper the concept is fully discussed in relation to self-directed learning, one of the most frequent themes to occur in the adult education literature in recent years.

Self-direction implies something of this highest human state although, paradoxically, the concept of self-directed learning need not actually have the same connotations. Additionally, it is recognized that on occasions the inhibition of freedom also produces learning, but of a more incidental kind (Marsick and Watkins, 1990).

It is apparent in much of the adult education literature that adults are assumed to be free, although a rigorous analysis of the concept is lacking, and the type of freedom implied is unclear. Knowles, (1980, pp. 45-46), for instance, when discussing the point at which adults define themselves as adults, writes: Adults acquire a new status in their own eyes

97

and in the eyes of others, from.(their) non-educational responsibilities. The self concept becomes that of a self-directing personality. They see themselves as being able to make their own decisions and face the consequences, to manage their own lives. In fact, the psychological definition of adulthood is the point where individuals perceive themselves to be essentially self-directing. And at this point people also develop a deep psychological need to be seen by others to be self-directing.

This claim, repeated in his more recent writings (Knowles, 1989, pp. 91f), is perhaps more ideological than empirical, since the possibility for self-direction occurs much earlier in life, for children can be very self-willed! By contrast, however, it will also be recalled that Riesman (1950) actually discovered that many adults are 'other-directed' and Fromm (1984) suggested that there is a fear of freedom, so that not all adults appear to have this deep psychological need to be self-directing. Indeed, these contradictions both point to some of the conceptual problems surrounding the idea of autonomy and also to the fact that there is not one psychological definition of adulthood. Indeed, many existentialist writers seem elitist when they suggest that the mass of people do not value freedom (Macquarrie, 1973, p. 181).

The reason for this might lie in the difference between free-will and freedom to act - an interior freedom, an exterior one and the interaction between the two - and while many people may know that they have free-will they also know that they do not always have freedom to act. Nevertheless, the fact that, for Knowles, the theory of adult education assumes the self-directedness of adults is significant for this discussion, even though he neither discussed the concept with any rigor, nor drew any distinction between the will and the action.

By contrast, Chene (1983) did expand on the idea of autonomy, which she regarded as synonymous with self-directing (Chene, 1983, p. 39). She returned to the Greek roots of the word and pointed out that it refers to individuals setting their own rules, although it is possible to conceptualize the situation of autonomous people being free to act within already agreed rules. She (1983, p. 40) went on to suggest that in autonomous learning there are three elements: independence in the leaner, the learner's creation of norms and the learner's ability to foresee and choose. Thereafter, she placed her discussion within an adult education framework and related it to the pedagogical context, the teacher-learner relationship and the learning activity. It is perhaps significant that Long (1989, pp. 8-10) also brought the dimension of pedagogical control into his discussion. He did recognize, however, that low degrees of pedagogical control are essential to self-directed learning. Tough (1979, pp. 18-19), however, noted that less than 1% of all the self-directed learning projects discovered in his research were undertaken for credit. Hence, it is perhaps wise to exclude education from the initial consideration of self-directed learning, since learning and education are not synonymous concepts, and the significance of Tough's work lays in the fact that he discovered so much self-directed learning occurring outside of education.

Educationalists have to be aware that there is a danger of seeking to claw back the theories of learning into the confines of education rather than recognizing the breadth of the phenomenon and that learning is of interest to scholars from a variety of disciplines. Even so, the pedagogical context is an important element for later aspects of this discussion.

The aims of this paper are, therefore: to discuss fully the concept of free-will; thereafter to discuss freedom of action; finally, to discuss self-directed learning in relation to these concepts.

FREE-WILL

Thus far distinction has been drawn between interior freedom and exterior freedom, and self-directed learning appears to combine the two. In the first instance, however, it is important to distinguish between them and this initial discussion will concentrate upon the former. Moreover, interior freedom is regarded as that form of freedom whereby the thinker could have reached decisions to act other than those which were reached. At first sight this could be claimed to be self-evident, and were it so philosophers would not have perhaps spent so much time considering free-will. The decision to act otherwise is really the essence of planning, something which everybody does during their lifetime but if there is not some element of free-will in decision making planning is no more than a facade. In addition, the existence of free-will is also implicit in the many discussions that occur in adult education about problem solving. It is now necessary, therefore, to investigate whether planning is really free and rational, or in some way predetermined.

As the human essence emerges from existence it is continually being affected by previous experiences. Hence, it is possible to claim that those previous experiences embedded in individuals' biographies determine future decisions to act and, thereby, inhibit free-will. Consequently, it could be claimed that individual plans occur as a result of a very sophisticated computer-like program in the mind, and that any decision has, therefore, been predetermined by prior biographical experiences. Logically, then, it is possible to claim that people do not really have free-will and that their thought processes are habitualised as a result of their learning and socialization and that they are really no more than computer programs in operation, and the apparently planned behaviors are the logical and predetermined outcome.

On the surface this position does appear to be quite straightforward, even if it is not very attractive when expressed in these terms - but surely that is what learning from experience implies! People have learned to cope with situations in specific ways and they can, therefore, presume upon the world. In fact, they do not have to think very much about them, they can decide to act almost unconsciously and monitor their actions at a very low level of consciousness. Their decisions are determined by their social situation and their actions follow. Such a position can account for the fact that individuals' decisions to act in similar circumstances might diverge greatly since their biographies are unique.

Hence their biographical programs are their own and the outcome of their operation is individuality, but not freedom! But such a position does not appear to account for the fact that, at different times, many people appear to act out of character; for instance, individuals who have had unfortunate or unhappy experiences at school as children actually decide to further their learning and return to school, even without the incentive of getting credit for it! Study is undertaken for the enjoyment of learning (Houle, 1988, pp. 24ff.). That people do not always act in accordance with their apparent biographical programs at least suggests the possibility that there is actually some degree of freedom, even if many people do not apparently exercise it on all occasions.

Indeed, this can be developed further since it was pointed out that throughout life people are confronted with alternatives - they have to choose, because this is the nature of pluralist society. Hence the human essence emerging from existence is itself continually confronted with choice and decision and so the human biography is itself full of conflicting possibilities. However, it might be argued that this merely means that the computer program is much more sophisticated. But it still does not account for people acting out of character, unless the argument runs that when they do so, it is because the biographical program in the mind has utilized a number of conflicting possibilities from the past experiences, evaluated the decisions that were made then and decided quite rationally that a new approach is required. Hence, the question that needs to be posed now is: is this apparent acting out of character still determined by previous experiences and therefore merely the result of a more sophisticated program or is it as result of rationality or, perhaps, is rationality merely a more sophisticated program learned throughout life?

Certainly the recognition of the proximity of rationality and computer programs is recognized through the use of language such as 'computer logic'. In addition, it is clear that different cultures at different times in history have disagreed as to what is self-evident truth. Hence, rationality might be regarded as relative and culturally specific and there are many anthropological research reports that tend to suggest this to be the case (Evans-Pritchard, 1936). In addition, it is clear from all the previous discussion about learning, that there is a sense in which every learning experience is adding to human biography and, therefore, it could be seen as producing an increasingly sophisticated program which determines future planning. In the very least, it can be claimed that any one choice, if such exists, is likely to affect the available choices in any subsequent planning situation, and so on, so that there appears to be a degree of predetermination in every choice. However, this would only appear to be the case if there were a restricted number of possibilities as a result of any previous choice. But this does not occur for while any one choice closes some future doors, it can also open others to a multitude of new possibilities, and so the computer analogy might be flawed at this point. However, the outcome of new choices might still be viewed as the result of predetermined dispositions, whether they be rational or not, and so the idea of free-will is still not demonstrated.

The logic of this position is that either rational or irrational planning can be related to the sophistication of the biographical program, and therefore people are not totally free from their previous experiences. Now this does appear to be a logical result of learning - that whatever is learned by people as individuals is bound to affect their future choices. Hence, a paradox emerges, at least on the surface, that every learning situation appears to restrict the possibility for future choices since, for the greater part of the time, individuals do reach decisions which are in accord with the own individual characters. This appears to be logical - people do appear to act in accord with their own biographies and, indeed, society is based upon patterns of consistent behavior. Freedom does appear to be restricted and it might be possible to claim that, therefore, people only think and feel that there are times when they are free, because they do not introspect sufficiently to be aware of the processes through which they have gone. But such a position is contrary to that held by the majority of people and by many scholars. Dennis Wrong (1977), for instance, attacked it in his well known paper on the oversocialized conception of man (sic). People, themselves, claim to know that they are free and, more significantly, that the plans that they make are not necessarily predetermined. They know that they could have reached another decision to have acted otherwise and even though their decisions may be predictable they are still responsible for them. Hence, once again the computer analogy appears to be a weak one, since the computer cannot think or reflect upon its own processes. People claim to know that they are free and to know that what they learned in certain situations may not be applicable in others. Indeed, human beings would hardly be capable of authenticity if they were no more than sophisticated computers. But, still the argument for autonomy of will appears unproven, despite these feelings and assertions that people do have free-will.

But the fact that people claim to know that they could have easily reached a different decision when confronted with a very difficult choice has to be taken seriously in itself. Either all people who make such a claim are continually deluding themselves, or there is a conspiracy by people to delude the human race that it is does not have the free-will that it thinks it has, or else they are actually free in some situations.

People can delude themselves some of the time, but it is inconceivable that human beings should go through life seeking to delude themselves all the time, claiming that they are free when they know that they are not. Likewise, it is total nonsense to think that there should be a plot by humanity to deceive itself that it is free. Consequently, there must be some situations when the freedom of choice is possible. If this is true, then is the whole of the preceding argument false? Clearly, this is not so. There are many times when previous experience guides decisions that are made and many such decisions do not have to be thought about a great deal because experience guides the thought processes and allows for presumption to occur. By contrast, there are times when people cull from the depth of their experience in order to make conscious decisions based upon past experiences. Clearly there are also times when those past experiences have affected the present situation unconsciously as a result of suppressed or repressed or even unrecalled memories. But there also are times when specific situations leave persons in some doubt and that any decision that they make is not self-evident; there are other times when the moral duty to do something may be contrasted with the desire to act in a different manner; there are times when what was learned in one situation has to be rejected in another; there are other times when the desire to conform to previous learning experiences conflict with the possibility to introducing change and experiment. There are times when people make decisions knowing that there were a variety of alternatives and even when their decision to act in one direction is deliberate and deliberately out of character. There are times when people deliberately loose the reins of constraint and seek to create totally new situations rather than follow the apparent rules of rationality. These choices, and the claims made by the actors that they do feel free to make the decisions that they made and that there were other decisions that they could have made, have to be taken seriously.

Indeed, the person who always acts in accord with the rules and regulations, who can always be relied upon to act 'rationally' in accord with previous learning experiences, is often regarded as rigid and inflexible, uncharacteristic in some ways of humankind in general. Often no emotion and no affection, and even a restricted form of morality, is to discovered in that form of behavior. It is rather like the animal, programmed to respond to stimuli but unable to learn from situations where decisions are not self-evident. It is here also that the analogy of the computer program breaks down, for while it makes sense in many circumstances, it is possible to find others where people seem to exercise a degree of discretion and act independently and in these instances the computer program appears to be a weak analogy. Freedom appears at the points where decisions have to be made and where it is possible to make other ones, where the outcome of a decision is not necessarily known, and where the human being is like the scientist experimenting with life. (Kelly, 1963).

Classical philosophers have not been quite so concerned about the decision making process, although they have claimed that it should be based upon rational thought. The nature of that rationality has, to some extent, been assumed but their concern has been the relationship between the will and the act. In Lindley's (1986) discussion on autonomy, he summarizes three classical positions and his analysis is used here for the sake of convenience. Kant based the whole of his argument upon the idea that acts of free-will are performed from a basis of pure rational thought, but such an argument falls down at the points where rational ideas conflict and emotion, affection and morality. Additionally, there is no logical reason why an apparently rational decision should be acted upon. Hume, by contrast, argued that it is a combination of rationality and the affect that underlie autonomous acts, although there is a problem here when desires appear to be irrational. By contrast, Mill has argued that autonomy is a vital interest in human activity but it must be combined with respect for persons. Clearly this view is in accord with the position of Buber and Marcel which were mentioned earlier but for them, respect for persons emerges from the belief that people are autonomous. However, it can be seen that the issues of the affect and of morality are all included in the above discussion. All of this points in the direction that humankind has free-will and while it cannot be proven beyond all logical doubt that people are autonomous, there is a great deal of circumstantial evidence that supports this contention.

It is at the point of free-will that new learning can occur rather that established patterns be reinforced. This then is a part of the paradox of learning, if actors seek only to act from previous learning rather than from present situations, the growth and development of the person is stifled and people become rigid and inflexible. If, on the other hand, they decide to act adventurously, looking forwards rather than backwards and not necessarily knowing what the outcomes will be, then they can learn new knowledge, skills and attitudes. In other words, criticality is but one part of the story of learning - creativity is the other, and one which may be even more important. Through creativity people grow and develop as persons - but new forms of behavior are not always acceptable within organized society and so the next section of this chapter examines the idea of freedom to act.

FREEDOM TO ACT

It is maintained here that no theory of learning is complete without a theory of action, a position that is being worked out more thoroughly in a forthcoming book (Jarvis, forthcoming). Implicit in the idea of planned action is the idea that the actor has some freedom to act as well as having a free-will. But planning also recognizes the contingencies of the situation, and even the wisdom of restricting free action in order to achieve future ends. Hence, it is important to elaborate upon the idea of freedom to act here.

No person lives in splendid isolation, everybody has been socialized and most people's actions occur at least some of the time in relation to other people, and this is frequently in an organized form. In other words, they act in time and space - be it public or private. In recent years, however, the distinction between the public and the private space has become a focus for analysis (Habermans, 1989), and the ownership or control of space is a significant feature in self-direction. There is a sense in which the idea of 'public space' refers to the apparatuses of state but, in addition, it also refers to that apparently public thoroughfare of everyday life where people interact with other people. Much of the following analysis of public space owes its origin to Habermans (1989), pp. 27-56), without necessarily following all of his analysis uncritically.

Everybody acts in space, often space which they have little or no control or ownership, so that their freedom to act may be curtailed by those who do have that power and, as the existentialist philosophers claim, restrictions upon people prevent them becoming authentic persons. Traditionally, analyses of space have started from the distinction between private and public space and, while this is a useful starting point, it is necessary to extend the analysis as a result of the structural changes in contemporary society.

Public space has a long and significant history: clearly it is the space in which the state exercises power through law and regulation. People are expected to obey these laws and conform; if they fail to do so they risk formal or informal punishment either by the state or by the people with whom they interact. Hence individuals tend to conform to what is expected of them. Likewise, the state insures that its laws are kept by a number of mechanisms, through which the majority of the people consider the state to be legitimate. The existence of law and the power to insure conformity means that, although people have the free-will to think that the law is wrong, illogical and so on, for the most part they feel constrained by those perceived external forces to conform, to act repetitively and to recognize that their freedom to act is limited.

During the development of modern society there emerged mechanisms for critical public debate about society - in England these were the coffee houses and in France the salons provided the same function, when private persons created a public sphere and endeavored to subject the law to reason. It is, as if, in these situations of debate and discussion the participants could view the law objectively from their enlightened perspective. These were early self-directed learning processes where people taught and learned through public debate in an equal and democratic environment - it was the emergence of the third estate. Public debate became a significant feature in the emergence of contemporary society for while these new bourgeoisie could not exercise power, they were in a position to reason about it. However, a feature of present-day society is that the public sphere in this sense has ceased to be of significance. Public space remains that controlled by the state and, depending upon the way that government employs the mechanism of state, people do not always feel free to act in accordance with their free-will or planning. In these situations individual freedom to act is curtailed.

However, many actions are performed in the private sphere, where liberty of action has always resided. But society has undergone tremendous changes in recent years. Now private property is hardly the basis of freedom of action, although that is often the claim, for much action is carried out in space not owned by the actors. For instance, the large industrial and commercial organizations are private, in as much as they are technically owned by persons other than the state. But the question of ownership need not be a concern of this study, while the question of the control of space does! Those who control that private space may be free to act within certain limits specified by, or act on behalf of, those who actually own the space. This is the age of managerialism! But those who have no control over the private space of their life or their work are less free. Hence, the point made by some existentialists about the mass of people not being concerned about freedom: they may know that they have a free-will but they also know that they do not control a great deal of the space in which they act, so that they decide that discretion is the better part of valor, and conform to the patterns or expectations decreed by those who do control it. In contemporary managerial society, those who control private space have freedom to act in it, but those who do not control it have only that freedom granted to them by those who exercise power. This, then, is a matter of managerial style, with authoritarianism inhibiting the authenticity of the workers and facilitation enhancing it.

Since people appear to have a free-will and the ability to think and to plan, they do not always succumb to the exercise of power meekly nor unquestioningly; there are many examples of negotiation between those who have power and those who do not. Individuals and groups of individuals negotiate for the opportunity to put their own ideas into action. Indeed, in education, for instance, the idea of the negotiated curriculum reflects the fact that learners often know what they want to learn, even if their knowledge is neither as full nor as sophisticated as those who teach. Naturally, there are also situations where the people rebel, knowing that they have free-will they seek also the freedom to exercise that will. Disobedience, rebellion and revolution are symbols that there is free-will without freedom to act - and, paradoxically, they are positive signs about the nature of humankind.

Without entering a debate about where educational space comes in this argument, it is clear that it might be considered to be either public space or organized private space, but in both cases it is controlled by those who exercise office within it - that is the teachers and lecturers. Hence, there is a sense in which educational space is not controlled by learners, although they may be granted certain control by those who have the power, and upon this point hinges a crucial definitional point about the nature of self-directed learning. The same argument may be made for human resource developers working within industrial and commercial corporations - they may be in a position to grant, or gain for, learners control over learning space in the course of their activities, or in obtaining some release from those who do exercise this control in order that they might become self-directed for a while.

However, there is some space that most people own - private, or privatized, space. This has traditionally been the intimate space of the family. Indeed, the structure of private homes reflects the demise of public space within family life - once homes had a great public hall but now the hall has become relegated to a small entrance-way from which the private rooms of the family lead. However, the family has itself undergone even more transformation and so the home no longer has many family rooms, but rooms for individual members of the family. Here in privatized space, individuals are more free to act! However, those internal constraints discussed in the first section of this chapter still exercise some power over the actors and so they are far from totally free. And, in addition, even within the family freedom is still constrained for some members - children and, often, wives are constrained by the father and the male 'head of the household', who might perhaps seek to control that space, so that family members seek even more privatized space within the recesses of their own rooms and, in some cases, their own minds.

Not only does this freedom exist in the privatized space, it also exists in time, when people are free of the constraints of their work and so the ownership of private space may be exercised in leisure time. Here people have control over aspects of their private space, whether they be managers or workers. Having control of the space, however, does not mean that people are necessarily going to use it freely. Indeed, many people may act repetitively or presumptuously upon their world, and they also build up obligations that restrict their freedom. In these instances, when a life crisis, even a small one, occurs some of these obligations may be destroyed and individuals appear free again to act in new ways (Aslanian and Brickell, 1980). Other people may not wish to use their leisure time in making relationships and for them then there are other ways of spending time or being entertained whilst time passes.

Privatized space, however, is not totally free of the influences of those who control either the state or the large corporations. The media penetrate even this privatized world and individuals are open to the incideous influence of those who control or own these. People are exposed to social pressures to conform even in the most privatized space in contemporary society. Indeed, it could be claimed that from childhood onwards there are always pressures to conform - not to the world of nature but to the created social and cultural world and that there are only limited opportunities to be free and also to know that they have the space to exercise that freedom occurs only some of the time. However, people do not necessarily feel any loss about not having freedom, for it was Fromm (1984) who argued that there is a certain fear of freedom, since conformity helps produce a sense of security for many people. Not all individuals feel a great deep-seated need to be free and, indeed, probably do not necessarily consider this to be of significance since their actions are of a presumptive nature.

110

From this analysis it is possible to conclude that while people do have free-will, if they wish to exercise it, the freedom to act is disproportionately distributed throughout the population, with those who have more control of private space having more opportunity to be free. Many, especially from the working classes, have fewer opportunities to act freely, even though they may have free-will. However, the psychological constraints on freedom are considerable, so that many people appear to have a propensity to conform to the prevailing social pressures, even a desire not to appear different. But sometimes conformity creates problems for the conformist, since it goes against the individual's conscience. Hence, while Freud has demonstrated the significance of conscience, it is sometimes through conformity that people feel that they have betrayed their own biography. These conclusions, therefore, have now to be applied to an analysis of self-directed learning.

SELF-DIRECTED LEARNING

As it was suggested at the outset of this paper, self-directed learning is one of those amorphous terms that occur in adult education literature, but which lacks precise definition. Knowles (1975, p. 18) described self-directed learning as:

> a process in which individuals take the initiative, with our without the help of others, in diagnosing their learning needs, formulating learning goals, identifying human and other resources for learning, choosing and implementing learning strategies, and evaluating learning outcomes.

Knowles goes on to criticize some of the other labels to describe this process as implying that they suggest that the learning occurs in isolation, whereas he (1975, p. 18) claims that 'self directed learning usually takes place in association with various helpers, such as teachers, tutors, mentors, resource people, and peers'. This claim indicates that he is not really focused about self-direction per se but rather a non-formal approach to learning which approximates to his formulation of andragogy. At the same time, the beliefs about humankind accepted in this paper are in accord with those espoused by Knowles throughout his work, for he is concerned both about the authenticity and mutuality of humankind. However, he is not really using the term 'self-directed' with sufficient conceptual rigor, as an analysis of the above definition suggests, since it is so broad as to be almost meaningless. Indeed, Long (1988, p. 2) rightly claimed that 'conceptualization about what adult self-directed learning is, or is not, varies from weak to non-existent.' Thus far this paper has endeavored to analyze some of the issues that underlie the debate about freedom. It has been concluded that humankind does have free-will, although much of the time previous learning experiences have provided behavior patterns that preclude the necessity for thought prior to action, and so on. Additionally, it has been argued elsewhere (Jarvis, 1987), that only when there is disjuncture between biography and experience is there the possibility of learning. Hence, it is necessary to apply this analysis of free-will and freedom to act to learning itself in order to understand the extent to which self-directed learning is possible.

In the study by Jarvis, referred to above, it was shown that there are nine different types of learning and non-learning and it is clear from this discussion that different forms of learning are possible in different situations. For instance, it does not matter whether actors control space if their learning does not involve any action, and in these situations memorization and contemplation can occur. In these situations people are free to dream dreams, have fantasies and perform feats of memory. But, paradoxically, non-learning can also occur wherever free-will is exercised because, by definition, free individuals have the freedom not to consider or to reject the opportunity to learn. Additionally, if individuals do not wish to exercise their free-will then they can be other-directed or tradition-directed, that is doing what others tell them or doing what they have always done. They find it difficult to be creative or innovative; indeed, they probably also find it difficult to exercise any aspect of criticality.

However, different forms of learning occur when action, as well as thinking, is an integral part of the learning process and in these instances, the control of the space affects the learning that occurs. When the space is controlled by others, it is often only possible to practice and repeat skills learned which are acceptable to those who exercise power, but only possible to experiment if there is a degree of freedom granted to individuals. Teachers of adults do control educational space and the style by which they manage that space may be more significant than the teaching method that they use. The more they seek to control the space the more they will determine the forms of learning that can occur.

It follows from this self-directed learning, in forms other than memorization and contemplation, occurs when people feel that they have some control over the space in which they act, be it delegated or owned. The following diagram summarizes this position.

FREEDOM AND THE CONTROL OF SPACE

Figure 6.1
Free-Will and the Control of Space

Control of Space	Free-will	
	Desire to exercise free-will	No desire to exercise free-will
Controlled by Others	Alienating (1)	Other/tradition (2)
Delegated control to actor	Limited autonomy (3)	Tradition (4)
Actor controls space	Autonomy (5)	Anomic (6)

In only three of the situations described by these six boxes (3, 4 and 5) is self-directed learning possible but since the nature of the control of space differs, it is most unlikely that the forms of self direction will be the same, a point which is pursued further below. By contrast, incidental learning may occur in almost all situations. Incidental learning refers to unintended learning, often occurring in tacit and unintended situations (Marsick and Watkins, 1990, p. 127), so that when actors are in positions where they are unable to act presumptively, then they are forced to think and learn from the experience. Incidental learning and self-directed learning can occur simultaneously but they are at different ends of the spectrum - the one is planned and intended whereas the other is tacit and unintended. Unintentional learning is reactive and reflective but self-directed learning is pro-active and covers all aspects of learning - it can be creative or critical, cognitive or psychomotor.

However, the different type of control of space in the three situations in which self-direction is possible means that it is impossible to regard them as similar. Candy (1990) makes this point clearly when he distinguishes between learner controlled instruction and autodidaxy: the former occurring in situations where teachers delegate control to learners and the latter where the learners have absolute control of the space where the learning occurs. Long (1989, p. 9) also discusses the significance of pedagogical control. Candy's use of the term autodidaxy epitomizes the position of those learners who both have the desire to utilize their free-will and who also control their own space, but he also recognizes that there is a variable degree of control in the other two situations. A teacher, or a manager, for instance, may grant almost total control to a student or an employee to pursue a learning project but, by contrast, those who do not wish to exercise their free-will may have to be urged to become even the least self-directed. Even in the former situation, however, vestiges of control remain, often in the use of language itself, and they subtly influence the learners' choices 'and even the criteria used to make those choices'

(Candy, 1990, p. 18), whereas in the latter, paradoxically, control has to be exercised in order to assist individuals to become more self-directed. Candy (1990, 14) correctly suggests that 'an indiscriminate application of the term self-direction to both phenomena has done much to blur the distinction between the two'. Candy's argument is important and it relates closely to the position assumed here that delegated control of space is not the same as absolute control, for in the former learners usually have a responsibility for learning to those who have delegated control whereas in the latter they have responsibility to themselves alone.

This distinction recognizes the reality of the control of private and public space, but perhaps more significantly, it must be seen how subtle control is exercised. Sometimes that control may not be fully recognized by the ones who exercise it, since they genuinely desire to encourage the learners to be totally self-directing - this may often be true in the educational setting. In the teaching and learning situation, which is a form of delegated control, it is clear that self-directed learning is a teaching technique rather than a form of self-initiated self-directed learning and, as such, it should be treated as a separate phenomenon from it.

CONCLUSION

Implicit in the concept of self-direction has been the idea of power, either ownership or control of space. That individuals do not all control a great deal of the space of their everyday life means that totally self-directed learning can only occur in those situations where the control is delegated. By contrast, where people control their own private space, then self-directed learning, in the autodidactical sense, becomes more of a possibility. Perhaps, therefore, it is not surprising that with the growth of the leisure-oriented society, where people have more free time and, therefore, control more of the space of their own lives, that self-directed learning has become of greater interest to scholars. However, there is a dangerous rhetoric in the term self-direction, if it is used where the control of space is delegated rather than actual, since it gives the misleading impression that the learners are free to control their own space.

It is, therefore, incumbent upon adult educators to recognize the reality of the situation and to make adequate demarcation in their own terminology and analysis in order to reflect accurately the way by which power and control actually operate within society.

REFERENCES

Aslanian C. & Brickell H (1980). Americans in Transition: Life Changes as Reasons for Adults Learning. New York: College Entrance Examination Board

Brookfield, S.M.(1988). Conceptual, Methodological and Practical Ambiguities in Self-Directed Learning. In H. B Long & Associates, Self-directed learning: Application & theory (pp. 11-37). Athens, Georgia: Adult Education Department, University of Georgia.

Buber, M. (1961). Between man and man. London: Fontana.

Caffarella, R. & O'Donnell, J. M.., . (1988). Research in Self-Directed Learning: Past, Present and Future Trends in H. B. Long & Associates Self-directed learning: Application & theory (pp. 3 -64). Norman, Oklahoma: Oklahoma Research Center for Continuing Professional and Higher Education, University of Oklahoma.

Chene, A.(1983). The concept of autonomy: A philosophical discussion in Adult Education Quarterly, Vol. 34, No. 1, pp. 38-47.

Evans-Pritchard E.E. (1936). Witchcraft, oracles and magic amongst the Azande Oxford: Clarendon Press.

Fromm, E.(1984). Fear of freedom. London: ARK Paperbacks.

Habermans, J. (1989) The structural transformation of the public sphere. Oxford: Polity Press.

Houle, C. O.(1988). The inquiring mind. Norman, OK: Research Center for Continuing Professional and Higher Education. (Original work published 1961)

Jarvis, P.(1987). Adult learning in the social context. London: Croom Helm.

Jarvis, P. (forthcoming). The paradoxes of human learning. San Francisco: Jossey-Bass

Kelly, G. A.(1963). A theory of personality: The psychology of personal constructs. New York: W. W. Norton.

Knowles, M. S.(1975). Self-directed learning. Chicago: Follett.

Knowles, M. S.(1980). The modern practice of adult education (rev. ed.). Chicago: Association Press.

Knowles, M. S. (1989). The making of an adult educator. San Francisco: Jossey-Bass

Lindley, R.(1986). Autonomy. London: MacMillan.

Long, H. B.(1988). Self-directed learning reconsidered. In H. B. Long and Associates, Self-directed learning: Application & theory (pp. 1-9). Norman, Oklahoma: Oklahoma Research Center for Continuing Professional and Higher Education, University of Oklahoma.

Long, H. B.(1989). Self-directed learning: Emerging theory and practice in H. B. Long & Associates, Self-directed learning: Emerging theory and practice (pp. 1-11). Norman, Oklahoma: Oklahoma Research Center for Continuing Professional and Higher Education, University of Oklahoma.

Long, H. B.(1990). Changing Concepts of Self Direction in Learning in H.B. Long and Associates. Advances in research and practice in self-directed learning. (pp. 1-8). Norman, OK: Oklahoma Research Center for Continuing Professional and Higher Education.

Long, H. B. and Associates(1988). Self-directed learning: Application and theory. Athens, GA: Univ. of Georgia. Department of Adult Education.

Macquarrie, J.(1973). Existentialism. Harmondsworth: Pelican.

Marcel, G.(1976). Being and Having. Glos Mass: Peter Smith.

Marsick, V. J. and Watkins, K. (1990 Informal and incidental learning in the workplace. London: Routledge.

Riesman, D.(1950). The lonely crowd: A study of changing American character. New Haven: Yale University Press.

Tough, A. (1979). The adult's learning projects. Toronto: Ontario Institute for Studies in Education.

Wrong, D. (1977). Skeptical Sociology. London: Heinemann.

117

CHAPTER SEVEN

RESEARCH IN SELF-DIRECTED LEARNING: SOME CRITICAL OBSERVATIONS*

Rosemary S. Caffarella

Since Tough's work on adult learning projects published in 1971, the area of self-directed learning has captured the imagination of researchers and writers both within and outside of the field of adult education. Although learning on one's own has been the primary mode of learning in adulthood throughout the ages, serious study of this phenomena has only been undertaken in the last twenty-five years, and even that work has been fairly limited in its scope. Why this apparent dichotomy of the prevalence of this learning mode and the lack of serious in-depth study? One response has been that only learning which took place in formal institutions was important and relevant to adult educators (Verner, 1964; Houle, 1988). Studying learning within the natural environment of how adults learn, grow, and change as part of their everyday life was not considered useful by some. Tied in with this perspective was the question of our role as educators of adults (Hiemstra, 1980, 1988; Brookfield, 1981). Did we have any business working with learners outside of the formal institutional environment? From an even more critical perspective, others have questioned whether self-directed learning as a distinct concept actually exists (Boshier, 1983; Little, 1979; Brookfield, 1986; Candy,

---

* Portions of this chapter were previously published in Chapter 11 of S. B. Merriam and R. S. Caffarella, <u>Learning in Adulthood: A Comprehensive Guide</u>, (Copyright 1991 by Jossey-Bass, Inc., Publishers), and have been reprinted here with permission.

1987). Despite these concerns and criticisms, the study of self-directed learning has become more prevalent and one of the more salient strands of research to emerge in adult education over the last two decades. As it appears, this line of research is "here to stay", what is needed now is continued critical reflection both on where we have been with this research agenda and where we should be going, as exemplified by authors such as Brookfield (1984, 1985), Candy (1987, 1989b), and Long and Associates (1988). Therefore, the purpose of this paper is to make some critical observations concerning the building of future research in self-directed learning.

My first observation is that building a sound theoretical base for self-directed learning is critical to the future of self-directed learning research. Model building is one way to embark on this effort. The journey on this path has already begun in earnest with the work of such writers as Long (1989), Brockett and Hiemstra (1991), and Grow (1991). Long proposes that "adult self-directed learning has a number of conceptual dimensions," including sociological, pedagogical and psychological elements. The sociological dimension captures the ideas of the social isolation of the learner (i.e., adults learning independently on their own), while the pedagogical dimension emphasizes the procedure carried out by the learner (e.g., diagnosing needs, identifying resources). The psychological dimension refers to the degree "which the learner, or the self, maintains active control of the learning process" (Long, 1989, p. 3). Long believes that we have given the least attention to our work to the psychological dimension which he views as the most critical dimension in self-directed learning. He goes on to propose a theoretical framework for studying self-directed learning in situations where the learner is involved in group activity. As of yet, Long's framework has not been empirically tested.

Brockett and Hiemstra (1991) suggest an alternative model for capturing and integrating the various elements of self-directed learning. Their model, the Personal Responsibility Orientation (PRO) model, is grounded in a definition of what they term "self-direction in learning," which for them is "an umbrella concept" that refers to two distinct but related dimensions. The first of these dimensions, self-directed learning, centers on the instructional processes of learning whereby learners assume the primary responsibility for planning, implementing, and evaluating their learning experiences. "An educational agent or resource often plays a facilitating role in this process" (p. 13). The second dimension, referred to as learner self-direction, "centers on a learner's desire or preference for assuming responsibility for learning" (p. 13). In the PRO model, Brockett and Hiemstra provide a framework for linking these two major dimensions of self-direction (self-directed learning as an instructional methods and learner self-direction as a personality characteristic) "through the recognition that each emphasized the importance of learners assuming personal responsibility for their thoughts and actions" (p. 27). Although they agree that the individual learner is central to the idea of self-direction, they also see the context, or social milieu in which that learning activity transpires, as important in gaining a full understanding of self-direction in adult learning. The PRO model appears to have a great deal of promise in helping researchers formulate a more holistic concept of self-directed learning.

Grow (1991) also proposes a model, the Staged Self-Directed Learning (SSDL) model, that suggests "how teachers can adequately equip students to become more self-directed in their learning (p. 1) within the formal educational process. Grounded in the situational leadership model of Hersey and Blanchard (as cited in Grow, 1991), the model describes four distinct stages of learners:

Stage 1 Learners of low self-direction who need an authority figure (i.e., a teacher) to tell them what to do.

Stage 2 Learners of moderate self-direction who are motivated and confident, but are largely ignorant of the subject matter to be learned.

Stage 3 Learners of intermediate self-direction who have both the skill and basic knowledge base and view

	themselves as being both ready and able to explore a specific subject area with a good guide participants in their own education . . . [who] are ready to explore a subject with a good guide") or facilitator.
Stage 4	Learners of high self-direction who are both willing and able to plan, execute, and evaluate their own learning, "with or without the help from experts" (p. 134).

Within each of these stages, Grow outlines possible roles for the teacher or facilitator of the learning experience, depending on the stage of the learners involved in the learning experience. He goes onto both highlight and describe the problems that may arise in a learning situation when there is a mismatch between the role or style of the teacher and the learning stage of the participants. Grow emphasizes that good teaching matches the student's stage of self-direction, and it allows the student to progress toward greater self-direction, and therefore is situational in nature. His sentiments on integrating the notion of self-direction into the formal instructional situations are very similar to those of Pratt (1988), Hiemstra and Sisco (1990), and Brockett and Hiemstra (1991).

My second major observation is that we need to firm up our methodological act in research on self-directed learning. Three issues emerge here which, although they have been addressed in part, still need further consideration. The first is we need to frame our research from a number of different paradigms, depending on the problems being addressed and not the availability of "tried and true" research designs and instruments or the latest research "fad". Candy (1987, 1989a, 1989b), for example, has suggested one way for us to restructure our studies from a constructivist or interpretive approach, such as those used in earlier studies of Houle (1961) and Tough (1967) and the more recent work of Danis and Tremblay (1987) and Caffarella and O'Donnell (in press). Within this approach, "examining the attitudes and the intentions of learners is essential" (Candy, 1989b, p. 28).

Caffarella and O'Donnell (1988), on the other hand, suggest that certain types of questions, such as those focusing on self-direction in learning as a personality construct, call more often for the quantitative paradigm, with a greater emphasis on quasi-experimental and experimental designs. Still other designs, which have had limited use, such as historical studies, case study approaches (Houle, 1984), and policy analysis (Hiemstra, 1980) need also to be included in the repertoire of possible ways of conducting research in self-directed learning.

In a similar vein, the second methodological issue relates to a need to be able to defend to both ourselves as adult educators and to the wider educational community that we have valid and reliable instruments that measure variables important to understanding self-directedness in learning. Currently the two most widely used instruments (the Self-Directed Learning Readiness Scale - SDLRS (Guglielmino, 1977) and the Oddi Continuing Learning Inventory - OCLI (Oddi, 1986) are both undergoing some serious scrutiny. Major questions have been raised about the SDLRS by Field (1989), among others (Brookfield, 1984; Brockett, 1985b, 1985c), as to its basic validity and reliability. Field contends, based on a thorough examination of the instrument, that "the problems inherent in the scale are so substantial that it should not continue to be used" (1989, p. 138). In addition to methodological concerns, he highlights conceptual flaws as the fundamental problem with the scale. In a tripartite response to Field, Guglielmino, Long and McCune (1989) dismiss most of Field's arguments due to the "errors of omission and commission" in Field's research. More specifically, they criticized Field's analysis of the SDLRS on three major grounds: incorrect interpretation of sources cited, the limited nature of his subject pool for a study of this type, and the statistical procedures used. Only further well conceptualized and executed studies on the SDLRS will put to rest these major differences of opinion.

The OCLI, which has had less exposure than the SDLRS, has also undergone some recent scrutiny (Six, 1989) and is in current revision by the author. Six indicated that the three underlying major dimensions of the inventory (e.g., Ability to be Self-Regulating) did remain stable under different study conditions. He cautioned that before using this scale with populations other than those which have been included in the major validation studies (i.e., adult undergraduate and graduate level college students) that further validation studies need to be completed. In addition, he suggested that further efforts be initiated to improve the measurement properties of the OCLI, such as analysis that might lead to "simpler and more meaningful factor solutions" (p. 50).

The third methodological issue is related to the populations being studied. Although other types of groups have been included (Brockett, 1985a), subjects for research projects on self-directed learning seemingly have been primarily middle-class (Brookfield, 1984, 1985). Yet McCune (1988), in a recent meta-analytic study of self-directed learning which include both descriptive and quantitative studies, disagrees with that observation by stating that information about "socioeconomic status is sparely reported in the adult self-direction in learning studies so definite conclusions" (p. 120) cannot be drawn. The same is true for the ethnicity of the subjects. McCune goes on to say that the data available do suggest that the population studies have consisted primarily of middle-aged, educationally advantaged females. McCune's findings are in agreement with earlier observations by Caffarella and O'Donnell (1987, 1988) that many times only sketchy descriptions of the subjects have been given. Caffarella and O'Donnell (1988) suggest that in reporting out a study "at least five major demographic variables should be highlighted: age, gender, ethnic origin, socioeconomic status, and educational level" (p. 47). Unfortunately, complete reporting of these types of variables is still not being done when describing studies which have been completed. In addition, we must continue to research for subjects who have not been widely included in research on self-directed learning. These populations included, but are not limited to, people with a high school education or less, those from lower socioeconomic groups, and subjects from a variety of ethnic backgrounds.

My third major observation is we need to better integrate our findings from the self-directed learning research with that which we know about learning in adulthood in general. What we know about self-directed learning might assist us in rethinking other arenas of research such as adult intelligence, cognition in adulthood, and cognitive development. For example, there may be a very usable data source within many of the completed descriptive studies of self-directed learning (e.g., Houle, 1961; Tough, 1979; Brookfield, 1981; Spear and Mocker, 1984; Danis and Tremblay, 1987; Berger, 1990) through which different questions about learning in adulthood could be answered. Might this data give us some insights into: the differences between novice and expert learners (Chi, Glaser and Farr, 1988); how adults develop in their thinking over the life of a project, especially those projects of a long-term nature (Perry, 1981; Rybash, Hoyer and Roodin, 1986); and what kinds of intelligence are these adults exhibiting? (Gardner, 1983; Sternberg, 1988).

Jarvis (1990) and Sisco (1990) have recently made similar observations that our work is self-directed learning should be tied more closely with other arenas in adult learning. Jarvis made his comments within the sociological framework, stressing that you cannot separate individual self-directed learning from the environment in which it is bounded. Examples of specific questions he posed were: What social constraints are there "upon individuals which exhibit the development of self-directed learning?" (P. 1). Are there periods in history when people are more likely to understand learning of a self-directed nature? Sisco, on the other hand, focused on the notion of moving from self-directed learning to self-directed thinking, with the emphasis on studying the thinking processes involved in the learning act. He discussed the concept of "self-regulation", defined as an individual being "aware of how he or she processes information, controls stressful situations, maintains optimum motivation, effectively and efficiently manages time, successfully copes with ambiguity, and generally knows how to think and learn (p. 1)," as a key to future study of self-directed thinking.

My final observation is that we should not forget the important why questions--why are we into this line of research anyway? Is self-directed learning really a needed area for educators to understand more fully or are we hanging onto it merely because it gives us as adult educators something "unique" that most other educational researchers have ignored? My own response to these questions is there is a very practical consideration to why adult educators should continue to study self-directed learning--being self-directed in one's learning is critical to surviving a world of constant personal and societal change. On the personal side, adults often find themselves in life situations (e.g., a serious illness, a new job, being a first-time parent) in which major decisions and actions must be made around issues they may know little about. For example, in the case of a serious illness, many adults have to make life or death decisions about alternative treatments within very short time frames, often with minimum information. This minimal informational level could be transformed if these adults and members of their personal support systems accepted the responsibility to learn as much as possible about the disease and the treatment. This learning process often requires an enormous combination of fairly sophisticated strategies from questioning medical specialists to combing library shelves and data bases to some deep soul searching. Likewise, in societal events it is becoming even more critical to stay informed of major issues and changes facing our nation states, both internally and on a more global basis. In the last year alone, the faces of Germany, The United Soviet Socialist Republic, and the Middle East have changed drastically, changes which have for the most part been accepted as either "good or bad" by the general population. Most adults have not seriously considered from a critical perspective the many implications these changes have on both their personal and collective lives.

In summary, four critical observations have been made concerning the building of future research agendas in self-directed learning: constructing a sound theoretical base; using a variety of methodological approaches which match the problems being addressed; integrating this work into general adult learning theory; and fostering a continued value that practical applications of this research should always be a vital part of our work as researchers. Of these four, I believe the last observation, the practical implications of our research, has been the one that has most often been lost and should be recaptured as a major focus of our work in self-directed learning.

REFERENCES

Berger, N. A. (1990). A qualitative study of the process of self-directed learning. (Unpublished doctoral dissertation, Virginia Commonwealth University, 1990).

Boshier, R. (April, 1983). Adult learning projects research: An alchemist's fantasy. Invited address to American Educational Research Association, Montreal.

Brockett, R. G. (1985a). A response to Brookfield's critical paradigm of self-directed adult learning. Adult Education Quarterly, 36, 55-59.

Brockett, R. G. (1985b). The relationship between self-directed learning readiness and life satisfaction among older adults. Adult Education Quarterly, 35, 210-219.

Brockett, R. G. (1985c). Methodological and substantive issues in the measurement of self-directed learning readiness. Adult Education Quarterly, 36, 15-24.

Brockett, R. G. & Hiemstra, R.(1919). Self-direction in adult learning: Perspectives on theory, research, and practice. London & New York: Routledge & Kegan Paul.

Brookfield, S. (1981). Independent adult learning. Studies in Adult Learning, 13, 15-17.

Brookfield, S. (1984). Self-directed learning: A critical paradigm. Adult Education Quarterly, 35, 59-71.

Brookfield, S. (1985). Analyzing a critical paradigm of self-directed learning: A response. Adult Education Quarterly, 36, 60-64.

Brookfield, S. (1986). Understanding and facilitating adult learning. San Francisco: Jossey-Bass.

Caffarella, R. S. & O'Donnell, J. M. (1987). Self-directed learning: A critical paradigm revisited. Adult Education Quarterly, 37, 199-211.

Caffarella, R. S. & O'Donnell, J. M. (1988). Research in self-directed learning: Past, present, and future trends. In H. B. Long and Associates (Eds.), Self-directed learning: Application and theory, Athens, GA: Adult Education Department of the University of GA.

Caffarella, R. S. & O'Donnell, J. M. (1989). Self-directed learning. Nottingham, England: Department of Adult Education, University of Nottingham.

Caffarella, R. S. & O'Donnell, J. M. (in press). Work related, self-directed learning: An exploratory look at the learner's perceptions of the quality dimension. Adult Education Quarterly.

Candy, P. C. (1987). Reframing research into 'self-direction' in adult education: A constructivist perspective. Unpublished doctoral dissertation, University of British Columbia.

Candy, P. C. (1989a). Constructivism and the study of self-direction in adult learning. Studies in the Education of Adults, 21, 95-116.

Candy, P. C. (1989b). The transition from learner-control to autodidaxy: more than meets the eye. Paper presented at the Third American Symposium on Adult Self-Directed Learning, University of Oklahoma Center for Continuing Education, Norman, OK.

Chi, M.; Glaser, R.; & Farr, M. J. (Eds.) (1988). The Nature of Expertise. Hillsdale, N.J.: Erlbaum, 1988.

Danis, C. & Tremblay, N. A. (1987). Propositions regarding autodidactic learning and their implications for teaching. Lifelong learning: An omnibus of practice and research, 10, 4-7.

Field, L. (1989). An investigation into the structure, validity, and reliability of Guglielmino's self-directed learning readiness scale. Adult Education Quarterly, 39, 235-245.

Field, L. (in press). Guglielmino's self-directed learning readiness scale: Should it continue to be used. Adult Education Quarterly.

Gardner, H. (1983). Frames of Mind. New York: Basic Books.

Grow, G. (1991). Teaching learners to be self-directed: A staged approach. Adult Education Quarterly, 41, 125-149.

Guglielmino, L. M. (1977). Development of the self-directed learning readiness scale. (Doctoral dissertation, University of Georgia, 1977). Dissertation Abstracts International, 38, 6467A.

Guglielmino, L. M.; Long, H. B.; and McCune, S. K. (1989). Reactions to Field's investigation into the SDLRS. Adult Education Quarterly, 39, 235-245.

Hiemstra, R. (1980). Policy recommendations related to self-directed learning. Occasional Paper No. 1. Syracuse, New York: Syracuse University.

Hiemstra, R. (1988). Self-directed learning: Individualizing instruction. In H. B. Long and Assoc., Self-directed learning: Application and theory. Athens, GA.: University of Georgia.

Hiemstra, R. and Sisco, B. (1990). Individualizing instruction for adult learners: Helping adults take responsibility. San Francisco: Jossey-Bass.

Houle, C. (1961). The inquiring mind. Madison: The University of Wisconsin Press.

Houle, C. (1984). Patterns of learning. San Francisco: Jossey-Bass.

Houle, C. (1988). The inquiring mind, (2nd ed.). Madison: The University of Wisconsin Press (Published by the Oklahoma Research Center for Continuing Professional and Higher Education, University of Oklahoma, Norman, OK).

Jarvis, P. (1990). The future of self-directed learning research. Paper presented at the Commission of Professors of Adult Education, Salt Lake City, Utah.

Little, D. (1979). Adult learning and education: A concept analysis. In P. Cunningham (Ed.), Yearbook of adult and continuing education, 1979-1980. Chicago: Marquisa Academic Press.

Long, H. B. and Associates (1988). Self-directed learning: Application and theory. Athens, GA.: University of Georgia.

Long, H. B. (1989). Self-directed learning: Emerging theory and practice. In H. B. Long and Assoc., Self-directed learning: Emerging theory and practice. Norman, OK: Oklahoma Research Center for Continuing Professional and Higher Education, University of Oklahoma.

McCune, S. N. (1988). A meta-analytic study of adult self-direction in learning: A review of research from 1977-1987. (Unpublished doctoral dissertation, Texas A & M University, 1988).

Oddi, L. F. (1986). Development and validation of an instrument to identify self-directed continuing learners. Adult Education Quarterly, 36, 97-107.

Pratt, D. D. (1988). Andragogy as a relational construct. Adult Education Quarterly, 38, 160-181.

Perry, W. (1981). Cognitive and ethical growth: The making of meaning. In A. W. Chickering (Ed.), The modern American college. San Francisco: Jossey-Bass.

Rybash, J. M., Hoyer, W. J. and Roodin, P. A. (1986). Adult cognition and aging. New York: Pergamon.

Sisco, B. (1990). Self-directed thinking and the year 2025. Paper presented at the Commission of Professors, Salt Lake City, Utah.

Six, J. E. (1989). The generality of the underlying dimensions of the Oddi Continuing Learning Inventory. Adult Education Quarterly, 40, 43-51.

Spear, G. E. and Mocker, D. W. (1984). The organizing circumstance: Environmental determinants in self-directed learning. Adult Education Quarterly, 35, 1-10.

Sternberg, R. J. (1988). The triarchic mind: A new theory of human intelligence. New York: Viking Press.

Tough, A. (1967). Learning without a teacher. (Educational Research Series No. 3). Toronto, Canada: The Ontario Institute for Studies in Education.

Tough, A. (1979). The adult's learning projects: A fresh approach to theory and practice in adult education, 2nd Ed. Toronto, Canada: Ontario Institute for Studies in Adult Education.

Verner, C. (1964). Definition of terms. In G. Jensen, A. A. Liveright, and W. Hallenbeck (Eds.), Adult education: Outlines of an emerging field of university study. Washington, D.C.: Adult Education Association of the U.S.A.

CHAPTER EIGHT

VALIDATION STUDY OF THE SELF DIRECTED LEARNING READINESS SCALE WITH UNIVERSITY AND COMMUNITY ART STUDENTS

Jean Ellen Jones

Artists are concerned with expression of their personal vision, often at great sacrifice. The starving artist image, while a stereotype, recognizes the artist's single minded dedication to reaching personal goals. The art making enterprise, so driven by the artist, is a model of self-directed learning. Confessore (1990) reported that a select group of 23 artists from many fields scored unusually high ($X=244$) on the Self-Directed Learning Readiness Scale for adults (SDLRS), the most widely used instrument for measuring self direction in learning. In view of the repeated calls for closer examination of both the construct of self directed learning (Long, 1988, 1989) and the SDLRS (Brockett, 1985; Field, 1989), I have taken a closer look at SDLRS data I gathered during recent test development projects with art students.

I have extended Confessore's work by examining evidence of SDLRS validity with 276 visual art students. The larger size and more typical nature of the sample allowed for a more extensive analysis. In the process, by using subjects from both college and community visual art settings, I was able to describe adult students in two different adult learning domains. This description provided new information to aid in the still-young theory building process for the self directed learning.

First, more needs to be said about the use of art students in the study and their characteristics. Even though they are not yet professional artists, art students are likely to exhibit high levels of self direction. Both their educational attitudes and art classroom teaching practice predict it. For example, art students value their subject highly. A study of college art majors by Getzels and Csikszentmihalyi (1968) revealed that the art majors "seem to be dedicated to the values of their profession more single mindedly than most other groups to the values relevant to their profession" (p. 8). For example, art majors valued the aesthetic more than business majors valued the economic and more than social workers valued the social. Further, learning art offers more intrinsic rewards than learning in some other subjects. Csikszentmihalyi (1989) studied learning attitudes of gifted adolescents studying a variety of subjects. He found that students involved in the arts found pleasure in the activity for its own sake and found it early in the process. Students in math and science actually lost motivation and became depressed the longer they were involved with their subjects. Proposing causes to lie both in the nature of math and science as subject matter and the ways it is taught, he pointed to the arts and similar enterprises as offering special contributions to an individual's quality of life. This benefit also seemed to be present among adults he studied.

Art classroom teaching practice promotes self direction. Even at beginner levels of formal instruction, students get practice in making choices, solving open-ended problems, and looking to their personal vision and experience. For example, Eisner (1972) in a widely used art education text, describes the traditional and appropriate dynamic of art teaching to be one in which a "high priority has been placed...on encouraging student-specific learning" (p. 185). His diagram of this teaching dynamic is pictured in Figure 8.1. By encouraging through the diagram, "increased opportunities for choice," Eisner is also encouraging increased student control of the learning environment. Such student control has been singled out as central to the concept of self directed learning (Long, 1989; Garrison, 1989; Candy, 1991). A comparison of diagrams below from Eisner (1972) and Candy (1991) reveals the strong similarity between descriptions of learning in art education and descriptions of self directed learning.

Figure 8.1
Diagrams of Teacher and Student Control of Learning

---

imposed conditions
opportunities for choice

Art Instruction
Eisner (1972, p. 188)

teacher direction
learner control

Self-directed Learning
Candy (1991, p. 10)

PURPOSE

Given the characteristics of art students and art teaching, one would expect that 1) art students would score high on a measure of self directed learning such as the SDLRS, 2) there would be a high correlation between the SDLRS scores and measures of art related attitudes and behaviors, and 3) there would be a high correlation between the SDLRS and level of art study. These general hypotheses were investigated in this study. If support could be found for them, then the validity of the SDLRS as a measure of self directed learning would also be supported. Each of these propositions is expanded below.

The general hypothesis that art students would score unusually high on the SDLRS was investigated by testing the proposals that a) art student scores would be higher than the SDLRS norm of 214 and b) that art student scores would be higher than the mean score of 227.7 from a meta-analytic study conducted by McCune, Guglielmino, & Garcia (1990). The meta-analytic mean was determined through the analysis of 29 research projects that used the SDLRS. Discovery of significantly higher scores by the visual art students would add to the criterion validity of the SDLRS.

The second part of the study focused on the Art Self Efficacy Test and the Art Practices Test, both of which were under development. The Art Self Efficacy test was designed to measure self confidence in art; the Art Practices Test was to describe, in part, the inquisitive nature of the artist. Both of these characteristics have been isolated by factorial analysis (West & Bentley, 1990) as important in the SDLRS construct.

The Art Self Efficacy Test was developed from the self efficacy theory of Albert Bandura and was modeled very closely on a general self efficacy test developed by Sherer et al.(1982). Students rated their level of agreement using a five-point Likert scale on such questions as, "I don't work well with my hands," and, "I give up easily as I attempt art," (both scored in reverse).

The Art Practices Test was developed from statements of studio art-related working habits and attitudes. Items were developed from statements to which least 70% of a national sample of professional artists agreed. The total Art Practices Test was intended to tap the attitudes and learning practices associated with successful problem solving in art. Subjects marked their agreement or disagreement on a five-point Likert scale to such questions such as, "I like to try new techniques" and "I think about my art outside of class and studio working time."

A medium to high degree of correlation between the two tests and the SDLRS was expected. Scores on the Rosenberg Self-esteem Scale, a measure of general feelings of self worth, were collected as part of the Art Self Efficacy Test development. Though less theoretically tied to the SDLRS, the Rosenberg test was also compared to the SDLRS. It was hypothesized that there would be a small correlation between the SDLRS and the Rosenberg test.

If the expected relationships could be found between the three tests and the SDLRS, then its concurrent validity would be supported.

If art students have been educated in a system that encourages and rewards self direction, then it might be expected that students with different amounts of study and commitment would make corresponding high or low scores on the SDLRS. A third group of hypotheses proposed the following: a) that students committed to a college art major and career would be more self directed than persons taking art in a community recreational setting; and b) that for college art students and for community art students, the number of art courses they had taken would be a significant predictor of SDLRS scores. Examination of the influence of art study on SDLRS scores was combined in a multiple regression analysis with age, sex, and education level to describe differences that might be important to emerging self directed learning theory.

A final focus of the study was to look for evidence that the SDLRS was more valid for academic learning than art learning. Brockett (1985b) has suggested that the SDLRS may have limited utility with artists. He noted that the instrument contains a number of items referring to books and schooling that are not appropriate for persons, including artists, for whom "learning by doing" is an important component of their education. This study looked for poor item-total score correlations on SDLRS book-oriented and school-oriented questions.

SAMPLE AND PROCEDURES

Two different samples of art students took the SDLRS-A, a 58 item Likert scale (Guglielmino, 1977). One group was from the community and the other, from local college visual art departments. A demographic description is presented in Table 8.1. Only about 6% of the total sample were of a race other than Caucasian.

Table 8.1
A Demographic Description of Art Students Used in This
Study and Subjects in a SDLRS Meta-analytic Study

Groups	N	Mean Age	Mean Educ	Gender % Male	% Female
Comm. art students	127	46.5	15.4	15%	85%
College art students	149	25.0	13.8	31.3%	68.7%
Total art students	276	35.0	14.6	23.5%	76.5%
Meta-analytic study	4596	37.5	14.4	33.8%	66.2%

Community art students took evening and day classes at three art centers in metropolitan Atlanta, Georgia. They were enrolled in 8 to 10-week classes in drawing, painting, clay modeling, jewelry, watercolor painting, portrait painting with acrylics, and pottery. Due to the nature of another project subjects were solicited from classes that were advertised as beginner level and that were likely to contain at least some older adults. Even so, no class contained more than two persons over age 55.

In consultation with each teacher, the investigator visited the first or second session of each class, explained the project, and asked for volunteers. Students were offered a gift of a small sketchbook or blank watercolor paper note cards in exchange for their time. Students stayed after class to fill out a brief demographic questionnaire and to take the Art Self-Efficacy Test, the Rosenberg Self-Esteem Inventory, and the SDLRS. The majority of students in each class volunteered to participate.

College students came mostly from a school of art and design within a large urban university. A few of the students, 36, attended a two-year college specializing in the applied arts, a kind of art technical school with minimum liberal arts requirements. All 149 college subjects were enrolled in courses required for the art major and all had declared or were considering an art major. Most were in the beginning levels of art study, with 57% still taking foundation level art courses, having had 5 courses or fewer, and only 34% having taken advanced work, defined as 12 or more art courses.

Students were approached at the beginning of the term and asked to volunteer to take the Art Practices Inventory, the SDLRS, and the Myers-Briggs Type Indicator. Results and interpretation from the Myers-Briggs were used as an incentive for participation and were not part of the data for this study. The majority of each class volunteered to participate.

RESULTS

The first phase of the analysis compared SDLRS scores of all art students with the SDLRS norm and with the average score from a meta-analytic study (McCune, Guglielmino, & Garcia, 1990). The mean score of all the art students (N=276) was 237.2, higher than the normed mean of 214 reported in the SDLRS manual and higher than the mean of 227.7 reported in the meta-analytic study of the SDLRS. Table 8.2 presents means from the art students and the two comparison groups.

An analysis of means procedure was used to compare the norm of 214 and the art student mean of 237.2. The resulting z score of 15 was significant at the .001 level and beyond. A comparison of the meta-analytic mean with the art student mean using a one sample t test yielded a t of 6.95, which was significant at the .01 level. The hypotheses that SDLRS scores for art students would be higher than the population of adult students at large and higher than those used in SDLRS research projects was supported.

Table 8.2
A Comparison of SDLRS Means: Two Non-art Groups with Art Students

Group	Mean	SD	N	t or Z
SDLRS norm	214	25.59		Z of 15**
Meta-analytic study	227.7		4596	t of 6.95*
Art Students	237.2	22.7	276	

* p< .01
**p< .001

The difference between the meta-analytic and art student means is especially noteworthy because subjects in the two groups were similar demographically. Table 8.1 compares the two groups of subjects.

The correlation of the SDLRS with two art-related attitude tests and the Rosenberg Self Esteem Scale revealed the expected relationships. The Art Self Efficacy Test, administered to the recreational art students, correlated r =.58 with the SDLRS. The Art Practices Test, administered to the college art students correlated r =.60 with the SDLRS. These relationships were significant at the p < .01 level. Coming from applied psychology fields, they can be considered very large. Cohen (1977) notes that "when a investigator anticipates a degree of correlation between two different variables "about as high as they come," this would by our definition be a large effect, r =.50." There was a moderate correlation (Cohen (1977) between the Rosenberg Self Esteem Scale and the SDLRS, r = .39. This relationship was also significant at the p < .01 level. The

SDLRS appears to have strong concurrent validity, but the experimental nature of the two art tests must be taken into account in interpreting the result.

The third analysis centered on the ability of the SDLRS to distinguish students of different levels of commitment and art study. High commitment was determined by enrollment as a college art major and lower commitment as enrollment as a community recreational art student. Contrary to expectations, an examination of scores reflected a higher mean by the community artists (X = 241.7) than by the college students (X = 233.4). Table 8.3 describes this difference, which is significant at the .01 level.

Table 8.3
T-test of SDLRS Scores of College and Community Art Students

Student Group	N	SDLRS Mean	SD	t
College	149	233.4	22.27	3.07**
Community	127	241.7	22.58	

** p < .01

Since the community artists were much older (X = 46.5) than the college students (X = 25.0), and age has been noted as an important variable in SDLRS scores (McCune, Guglielmino, & Garcia, 1990; and Long and Agyekum, 1983), scores of the groups were analyzed with age as a covariate. This analysis revealed that, with the influence of age controlled, there was not a significant difference between the college and community art students.

College and community groups were examined separately for art study level influence. Measures of study level were different for each group. Level of study for the college students was determined by the number of college and community recreational art courses they had taken. Because the length of college art courses was not comparable between the technical school students and the university art students, only the larger university group (N = 113) was used in this analysis. Level of study for community art students was determined by adding their subjective description of how many courses and equivalent experiences they had taken in a variety of media. For this description students used a four-point Likert type scale ranging from "none" to "a lot" to rate experience in such areas as painting, ceramics, and needlework.

An examination of studies with the SDLRS and in adult education suggested that a number of variables were likely to contribute to SDLRS scores. The meta-analytic study mentioned earlier (McCune, Guglielmino, & Garcia, 1990) noted that both age and sex were important. Education attainment level also required attention. It was an important SDLRS correlate in a study of older adults by Brockett (1985a), and it is often the most important demographic variable in studies of adult student attitudes and behaviors. For the younger college students a survey of research suggested that after art study, SDLRS scores could be predicted by these variables in descending order: age, sex, and education level. For the older community art students, research suggested that after art study, SDLRS scores could be predicted by these variables in descending order: education, sex, and age. Hierarchical multiple regression allowed examination of the relative strength of the four variables.

For the university art students (N = 110), art study accounted for .0% of the variance. Age, entered next, accounted for 10.4% of the variance. Sex accounted for .3%, a non-significant amount, and education, the last variable to be entered, accounted for .0% of the variance. The four variables together accounted for 10.7% of the variance. The hypotheses that study level would be an important predictor of scores on the SDLRS was not supported with the university art student group. Instead, age was found to be the only predictor of any strength.

Table 8.4
SDLRS Regression: Influence of Art Study, Age, Sex, and Education

University Group (N=110)		Recreational Art Group (N=127)	
Variable	Variance Accounted For	Variable	Variance Accounted For
Art Study	.0%	Art Study	4.2%
Age	10.4%	Education	5.3%
Sex	.3%	Sex	2.7%
Education	.0%	Age	.3%
Total	$\overline{10.7\%}$	Total	$\overline{12.5\%}$

For community art students (N = 126), art study accounted for 4.2% of the variance, education accounted for 5.3%, and sex, entered third, accounted for 2.7%. All were significant changes at the .05 level. Age, in contrast, accounted for .3% of the variance when it was entered into the equation last. The four independent variables accounted for 12.5% of the variance, with age being the only variable not operating as a significant predictor. For the recreational art group the hypothesis that art experience level would be an important factor in performance on the SDLRS was supported, at least relative to other variables. Table 8.4 describes relative importance of the variables for the college and the recreational groups.

To summarize findings concerning level of art study, for community art students, art study predicted performance on the SDLRS, with education being a slightly better predictor. For college students, however, it was not a significant predictor. Age was the only important variable among the four in predicting performance on the SDLRS for college students.

The next analysis examined Brockett's (1985) observation that SDLRS items would likely show evidence of being invalid for arts students, who spend considerable time actively engaged in non-academic studio problems. He suggested that confusion over school- and book-oriented test items would show up through a reliability test of internal consistency. Thus, a low reliability could also reflect a low content validity for the test. However, Coefficient Alpha analysis yielded a very high SDLRS reliability (.94) with art students in this study. The median correlation was .4769. Correlations of individual items to total score revealed no items with a correlation below .2. Only 2 items, numbers 16 and 20, were correlated below .3 with total scores. Both of these were problematic negative statements and not school- or book-oriented. At this level of analysis, no evidence was found that the SDLRS functions less well for art students than other groups.

SUMMARY AND CONCLUSIONS

Art students scored higher than others on the SDLRS, and tests that measure art related attitudes and behaviors correlated highly with SDLRS scores. There seems to be a strong relationship between constructs measured by the SDLRS and characteristics of art students. The SDLRS seems to be sensitive to constructs often attributed to self directed learning. Its basic approach still appears to be sound and to have utility in research settings.

SDLRS scores did not correlate with amount of art study for college art students nor with level of professional commitment. Educational attainment level and not art study level was the strongest correlate with SDLRS scores of community artists. The SDLRS does not appear to be strongly related to the student centered pedagogy of studio art classes. Or, it may be that strategies that promote self direction in art classes are not as wide-spread as was thought, at least at the beginner levels represented by most of the students in this study.

Age was found to be a strong correlate to SDLRS scores for the mostly young, college art students, and to be inconsequential for post college students. For the latter, general educational attainment level and level of study in a valued domain such as art seemed to be more important as predictors of SDLRS scores. This may be the result of an increase in learning self-confidence over a lifetime. The younger college age students in this study may have simply needed more time for their learner self confidence to develop. College instructors interested in promoting self directed learning may find that a student's age will provide the most helpful cue in how to proceed.

Recent theorists (Long, 1989; Garrison, 1989; Candy, 1991) have proposed that psychological control is the central issue in developing the self-directed learning construct. Candy's conception is especially useful here. He proposes that there are two types of self-directed learning domains, the instruction-driven and the autodidactic. A main difference is in who "owns" the learning questions, the teacher or the student. Candy's theoretical distinction is supported by the results of this study. Predictors of performance on the SDLRS were very different for the college and community art students. Differences in self-direction between the two settings, which could embody Candy's two domains, appear to go beyond those of degree as reflected in test scores to differences in kind.

Further research is indicated for both the issue of age and self-direction and self-directed learning as an issue of control. A more detailed analysis of SDLRS scores and age may reveal more information about self directed learning from a developmental perspective. Candy's (1991) description of two very different self directed learning situations appears to be very important. Research that examines those differences and ways for adult educators to operate within them would be highly fruitful to the field.

REFERENCES

Brockett, R. G. (1985a). The relationship between self-directed learning readiness and life satisfaction among older adults. Adult Education Quarterly, 35(4), 210-219.

Brockett, R. G. (1985b). Methodological and substantive issues in the measurement of self-directed learning readiness. Adult Education Quarterly, 36(1), 15-24.

Candy, P. D. (1991). Self-direction for lifelong learning. San Francisco: Jossey-Bass.

Cohen, J. (1988). Statistical power analysis for the behavioral sciences, Hillsdale, New Jersey: Lawrence Erlbaum Associates.

Csikszentmihalyi, M. (1990). Triangulation #5: New voices on evaluation and DBAE Teaching Effectiveness: Art and the quality of Life (Summary). In A. L Walsh & P. Sharp (Eds.), Inheriting the Theory: New Voices and Multiple Perspectives on DBAE. (Report of a national invitational seminar published by the Getty Center for Education in the Arts.)

Confessore, G. J. (1989, February). Human behavior as a construct for assessing Guglielmino's self-directed learning readiness scale: Pragmatism revisited. Paper presented at the Fourth International Symposium on Adult Self-Directed Learning, Norman, Oklahoma.

Eisner, E. W. (1972). Educating artistic vision. New York: Macmillan.

Garrison, D. R. (1989). Facilitating self-directed learning: not a contradiction in terms. In H. B. Long & Associates (Eds.) Self-directed learning: emerging theory and practice (pp. 53-62). Norman, Oklahoma: Oklahoma Center for Continuing Professional and Higher Education of the University of Oklahoma.

Getzels, J. W. & Csikszentmihalyi, M. (1968). The value-orientations of art students as determinants of artistic specialization and creative performance. Studies in Art Education, 10(1), 5-16.

Guglielmino, L. M. (1977). Development of the self-directed learning readiness scale (Doctoral dissertation, University of Georgia, 1977). Dissertation Abstracts International, 38, 6467A.

Long, H. B. (1989). Self-directed learning: Emerging theory and practice. In H. B. Long & Associates (Eds.) Self-directed learning: emerging theory and practice (pp. 1-11). Norman, Oklahoma: Oklahoma Center for Continuing Professional and Higher Education of the University of Oklahoma.

Long, H. B. & Agyekum, S. K. (1984). Teacher ratings in the validation of Guglielmino's self-directed learning readiness scale. Higher Education, 13 709-715.

McCune, S. Guglielmino, L. M., & Garcia, G. (1990). Adult self-direction in learning: A meta-analytic study of research using the self directed learning readiness scale. In H. B. Long & Associates (Eds.) <u>Advances in research and practice in self-directed learning</u> (pp. 145-156). Norman, Oklahoma: Oklahoma Center for Continuing Professional and Higher Education of the University of Oklahoma.

Sherer, M., Maddux, J. E., Mercandante, B., Prentice-Dunn, S., Jacobs, B., & Rogers, IR. W. (1982). The self-efficacy scale: Construction and validation. <u>Psychological Reports</u>, <u>51</u> 663-671.

West, R. F., & Bentley, E. L. (1990). Structural analysis of the self-directed learning readiness scale: A confirmatory factor analysis using lisrel modeling, In H. G. Long & Associates (Eds.) <u>Advances in research and practice in self-directed learning</u> (pp. 157-180). Norman, Oklahoma: Oklahoma Center for Continuing Professional and Higher Education of the University of Oklahoma.

CHAPTER NINE

A DESCRIPTIVE INVESTIGATION OF THE CONSTRUCT OF SELF-DIRECTION

Terrence R. Redding & Lola Aagaard

Self-directed learning (SDL) literature is replete with attempts to quantify and apply the construct of self-directed learning or SDL readiness, yet basic agreement as to what is involved in that construct does not seem to exist. SDL has been considered variously as a learning style (Bonham, 1989), a personality construct (Caffarella & O'Donnel, 1988), a change of consciousness (Brookfield, 1986) and a manifestation of psychological control necessary and sufficient to cause SDL (Long, 1990).

According to Finestone (1984), this disagreement may be part of the natural progression of construct development. He maintains that a construct develops over time rather than being a fixed concept. If this is the case then the "emerging" nature of self-directed learning (Long, 1991, p. 2) should be accepted as normal with the maturing of the field.

Accepting that the construct of SDL is still under development, it becomes important to understand the different forms a construct can take. Borg (1989) discusses three kinds of constructs. (1) A theoretical construct is inferred from observed phenomena. (2) A constitutively defined construct is determined by referring to other constructs. (3) Finally, an operational construct can be identified by "specifying the activities used to measure or manipulate it (p. 26)." This investigation uses an instrument, and therefore an operational construct, to measure levels of SDL within a sample population thus permitting the researchers to describe the learners.

A Descriptive Investigation

The most widely used instrument for determining self-direction in learning is Guglielmino's (1978) Self-Directed Learning Readiness Scale (SDLRS) (McCune, 1989). A large number of studies have been designed to investigate the validity of the instrument as well as using it in research on self-directed learning (McCune 1988, 1989). A recent review of 173 SDL dissertation abstracts found 40 that used the SDLRS (Long and Redding, 1991).

Quantification of the construct the SDLRS measures has not clarified what is meant by self-directed learning or self-direction in learning. (Field, 1991; Bonham, 1991; Field, 1989; West and Bentley, 1989). Bonham (1991) approached the problem by assuming that self-direction in learning must have a polar opposite; she raised therefore the question of what is the opposite of self-direction. She proposed that there are two alternatives: other-direction, and lack of interest in learning in general. This study offers an alternative descriptive approach to the majority of SDL studies, which we hope will contribute to the research on the construct of self-direction itself, as well as help to determine what the SDLRS is measuring.

Our approach was based on the assumption that if a wide range of individuals were involved in discretionary, totally voluntary, goal oriented self-initiated acquisition of knowledge and skills, then as a group they could be described as self-directed, at least with regard to their specific topic of interest. These learner characteristics fit the following five of the factors associated with the SDLRS: (1) Love of Learning (2) Self-confidence as a Learner (3) Openness to a Challenge (4) Inquisitive Nature (5) Acceptance of Responsibility for Learning (Guglielmino, 1977). Given the previous research with the SDLRS, such a group would be expected to score above average on the SDLRS. Variability in scores across the group is of interest, because outlyers could be analyzed in depth to ascertain if there were qualitative differences between the low and the high groups. Could the difference between the high and low groups be thought of as opposites? These qualitative differences might help clarify and refine the construct of self-direction, and address Bonham's (1991) recent questions regarding what is signified by a low SDLRS score.

AMATEUR RADIO OPERATORS

Caffarella and O'Donnell called for additional verification studies using subjects from different socioeconomic, ethnic, and cultural backgrounds (Caffarella and O'Donnell, 1988). Their concern centered on the fact that many SDL studies used restricted populations (such as college students) and were therefore of limited use in terms of generalizing to larger more heterogeneous populations.   Amateur radio operators are a heterogeneous group in most respects (Redding, 1991). They vary greatly in age, educational level, income, geographic location, and occupation.   Additionally, their common commitment to their hobby, with its federally mandated requirement for self-training and increased skill acquisition through Incentive Licensing fits the descriptors used to describe highly self-directed learners (Long, 1987; Oddi, 1986) and Houle's (1988) description of continuing learners.

The investigators believe that in many ways the amateur radio operators (hams) of today represent Toffler's "Third Wave" (Toffler, 1981). By using packet radio, a form of digital communications developed by amateur radio operators, and by using artificial intelligence to manage data routing, hams communicate now in short blips. Toffler talks about them when he says, "Third Wave people, by contrast, are more at ease in this bombardment of blips ...they gulp huge amounts of information in short takes..... Rather than trying to stuff the new modular data in Second Wave categories ... they learn to make their own, to form their own 'strings'....(Toffler, 1981)." Further study of this unique group of individuals may provide insight into the nature of adult self-directed learning and how it might be used to address the information explosion.

PURPOSE

This study was a continuation of an ongoing study that explores the attributes of self-directed learners. In particular, the focus of this effort was to develop a descriptive picture of the self-directed nature of amateur radio operators in relation to their SDLRS scores. Additionally, the qualitative and descriptive data derived from this study should lend insight into the construct of self-direction especially as it relates to Bonham's questions.

METHOD AND SAMPLE

To date 213 Hams have completed a descriptive questionnaire and the SDLRS. Based on the distribution of SDLRS scores, the upper and lower quartiles were isolated for further analysis of the variables on the descriptive questionnaire. These variables included demographic as well as behavioral items related to hobbies and study habits.

A sample of convenience and self-selection was collected. Individuals sampled were licensed amateur radio operators or individuals that identified themselves as radio amateurs. The groups sampled and the number of subjects from each group are listed below.

1) Amateur radio club members (78)
2) Members of an amateur radio class (14)
3) Prior members of an amateur class (11)
4) Individuals invited to participate on the air (17)
5) Volunteer Examiners at a testing session (7)
6) Amateur radio church group (13)
7) Lawrence Kansas amateur radio operators (33)
8) Respondents to an invitation in an amateur radio journal (40)

RESULTS

In the total sample of 213 respondents, the mean SDLRS score was 239, with a standard deviation of 24.2. The median was 242, with a range from 166 to 283. The overall mean sample is higher than the mean reported by Guglielmino (1978) of 214. Indeed approximately 40% of the 213 respondents could be classified as high (>250), while only 8% fell in the low or below average categories (<202).

The first quartile point was 223.5 and the third quartile was 257.5. The means, standard deviations, minimum, maximum, and median scores for the groups in the third quartile (upper) and below the first quartile (lower) are reported in Table 9.1.

Table 9.1
Upper and Lower Group Statistics

Group	Mean	Std	Min	Max	Median
Upper	267.26	6.48	258	283	267
Lower	205.96	14.76	166	223	210

The variables used to compare the upper and lower groups included:

Gender	Ethnic group
Occupation	Study habits
License Class	Number of hobbies
Station location	Family Support
Statement of why they became a ham	Number of family licensed Level SDL

Gender and Ethnic Group

Approximately 90% of each group was male. There were only 12 females in the upper and lower groups combined: five and seven respectively. Given the demographic gender distribution within the USA (51.40% women), females are under represented within the amateur radio population.

Ninety-eight percent of each group was classified as White. There was one Native American in the lower group and one "Other" in the upper group. Given the demographic ethnic distribution of 80% White, 11% Black, 6% Hispanic, 2 Asian and 1% Native American other, Blacks and Hispanics are under represented.

Occupational Categories

Respondents listed their occupation, which was then categorized by the senior author as either nonprofessional, semiprofessional, professional, or research. A larger portion of the upper group were employed in occupations classified as professional (see Table 9.2).

Table 9.2
Percentage Distribution of Groups Across Occupational Categories

Group	Non-prof.	Semi-prof.	Prof.	Res.
Upper	9.43	41.51	45.28	3.77
Lower	30.19	50.94	15.09	3.77

Other Hobbies

The upper group has more hobbies than the lower group, with a mean of 2.68, compared to the lower group's mean of 2.25. The standard deviation of both groups was just slightly larger than 1.1. Table 9.3 shows the percentage of each group having differing numbers of hobbies. Nearly a third of the upper group have 3 or more other hobbies beside ham radio, compared to only about one-eighth of the lower group.

Table 9.3
Percentage Distribution of Groups Across Number of Other Hobbies

Group	No others	1	2	3	4+
Upper	24.53	15.09	30.19	28.30	1.89
Lower	29.41	33.33	23.53	9.80	3.92

License Class

The percentage distributions of the two groups across license classes are displayed in Table 9.4.

Table 9.4
Percentage Distribution of Groups Across License Classes

Group	Nov.	Tech	Gener.	Advan.	Extra
Upper	7.69	19.23	17.31	32.69	23.08
Lower	3.85	40.38	5.77	15.38	34.62

The requirements for advancement from class to class differ. To go from Novice to Technician requires additional "book learning" but no increased Morse Code proficiency, while advancement from the Technician to General class requires faster Morse code transmitting and receiving ability. Likewise, transition from General to Advanced class requires no extra coding ability, but faster coding ability is required to move up to the Extra class (the highest and hardest class of license). This Morse Code barrier explains why respondents in both groups tended to lump into Technician and Advanced classes in contrast to Novice and General classes.

Aggregating percentages into three class categories that are separated by coding requirements clearly shows a difference in the distributions of the upper and lower groups (see Figure 9.1).

Half of the upper group had advanced to the middle classes. However, the lower group was more bi-modal, with 40% in the lower classes and 34% in the Extras.

Number of Other Hams in Family

The respondents in the lower group tended to have more family members who also were licensed as amateur radio operators. The percentage distribution for group is displayed in Table 9.5.

Table 9.5
Percentage Distribution of Groups Across Number of Hams in Family Number of Other Hams

Group	None	1	2	3	4
Upper	46.15	40.38	7.69	0.00	5.77
Lower	50.94	24.53	11.32	7.55	5.66

Figure 9.1. The percent of Hams by class of license below the first and above the third quartile.

Station Location and Family Support

Approximately 70% of the respondents in each group said they had their radios set up in a spare room of their house. Another 16% in each group conducted their hobby in the family living area, while the remaining hams were set up in the garage or a separate building of some sort.

Figure 9.1
Percent of Hams by Class of License

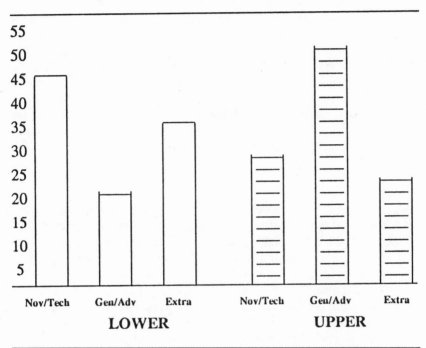

Seventy-five percent of each group felt their families were supportive or very supportive of their radio hobby. Of the upper group, 11% declared their families were not supportive of their hobby, in contrast to only 2% of the lower group.

Study Habits

Respondents were asked whether they preferred to study alone or in a group. No further clarification of the question was provided. Only 50% of the members of the two groups answered the question, and almost all of them said they preferred to study alone. Three respondents of the 25 in the lower cluster who answered the question indicated they like to study in a group.

Personal Assessment of Self-Direction

Respondents were asked whether they considered themselves self-directed or other-directed. No further clarification of the terms or question was given on survey. Approximately 70% of each group failed to answer the question, which may indicate a lack of understanding of the question. Of the answers that were received, only two people (one in each group) responded that they were other-directed.

Why Become a Ham?

Answers to an open-ended question concerning why respondents became amateur radio operators were read and jointly coded by the chapter authors. The four main categories that appeared in both the upper and lower groups were:

A. Long-time interest in ham radio, but only licensed recently;
B. To meet and communicate with people all over the world;
C. Technical interest in radio equipment and communication;
D. To please someone else.

The respondents in the upper group became amateur radio operators to satisfy a personal desire; either to communicate in general or because of their interest in technology. The respondents in the lower group primarily became amateur radio operators for someone else.

In the lower group, the primary reason (18 answers) for entering ham radio was to please someone else. Often the respondents mentioned that they had learned code "for my father" or "to please my husband," or because "my dad made me do it." Those persons who had become hams in order to communicate with one specific person were also included in this group, such as the women who said she needed to "communicate with my husband" or the person who wanted to "communicate with my brother in another state." Because these respondents indicated that they had become hams primarily to communicate with a specific other person, they were included in the group labeled "to please someone else."

The number of answers in the other three categories were clustered closely together with 12 in the "People/communication" area, 11 in "Technical interest," and 9 answers categorized as "Long-time interest." Other general answers such as "for an interesting hobby," "public service," and "because of the challenge" also appeared a few times.

The upper group said they were in it primarily for "People/communication" and "Technical interest," with 18 and 17 answers respectively. Ten answers indicated "Long-time interest," and only 8 responses were categorized as "for someone else." Even those 8 were not the "dad made me do it" type of response commonly found in the lower group, but were such answers as "my uncle showed me the magic of radio," or "my teachers and friends were hams." The general categories of "public service," "challenge," and "hobby" also appeared in the upper group a few times.

SUMMARY AND CONCLUSIONS

In summary, respondents in the upper group were more often in jobs classified as professional, had more hobbies, were more likely to be in the middle license classes, had fewer family members who were also hams, and were more likely to have become a ham due to an interest in the technical aspects or the intrigue of meeting people around the world.

Some of these findings make considerable sense when viewed jointly. For instance, self-directed people may advance in ham radio up to a certain level of satisfaction, but not push themselves to the extreme limits of the hobby, especially when they have other hobbies that they also enjoy. This could explain why the upper group, which tended to have more hobbies than the lower group, had more members who had advanced to the middle license classes and then stopped. The lower group, on the other hand, tended to either stay at the lowest levels (perhaps those who had only gotten their license to please someone else), or advance to the highest class, perhaps once again driven to meet an external standard.

Similarly, the less self-directed hams in the lower group were more likely to have family members who were also licensed, and more often reported beginning the hobby because of someone else. Thus, if someone became a ham because someone in their family wanted them to, then it would be very likely that families would generally have lower SDL.

In a sense, this approach combined the theoretical and operational approaches to construct development. The upper and lower groups were defined operationally by SDLRS scores, but then further observations were made to further amplify the constructs underpinning SDL.

The conjecture that amateur radio enthusiasts would tend to be highly self-directed as measured by the SDLRS was supported. However, the considerable variability in SDLRS scores across the group allowed for several qualitative comparisons of the respondents below the first quartile with those above the third quartile. Results of these comparisons indicated primarily that the upper group seemed to have taken more psychological control or initiative (Long, 1990) in becoming a ham, and that they were active in a number of other interest areas besides ham radio.

Our results are consistent with the general SDL literature, and support a psychological construct of self-directed learning. However, they are inconclusive with regard to Bonham's (1991) question about the opposite of self-directed learning. Considering the lower group members primarily were other-directed into the field of amateur radio, low SDLRS scores could indicate other-direction. Yet because the lower group had fewer other hobbies, low scores also might mean a lack of interest in learning in general. (Either that or they lacked people to direct them into other hobbies!) Another possibility is that low SDLRS score cannot be used to infer meaning as to what it means to be the opposite of a SDL. When you consider the definition of an operational construct, and the process by which the SDLRS was developed, it is not surprising that SDL opposites are not explicated by low scores.

It is important to note again that only 8% of the sample fell in the low or below average category on the SDLRS. Therefore the majority of respondents below the first quartile are not the low-scoring "opposites" that Bonham (1991) referred to for evaluating construct validity. Bonham's "opposite" construct is inferred (reference the Borg discussion at the beginning of this chapter) from Guglielmino's operational construct. However, because an operational construct is by definition based on what can be measured or manipulated, this descriptive study is helpful in gaining an appreciation for implications associated with the SDLRS. It should be recognized that, while the population of hams has the potential of being highly heterogeneous, and this sample reflects the heterogeneous nature of the population, in regards to self-directed learning hams are homogeneous.

RECOMMENDATIONS FOR FURTHER STUDY

To properly respond to Bonham's "opposites," the study population needs to exhibit a wider range of SDLRS scores than did ours. However, even with the widest possible range, it is likely that the SDLRS will not be able to measure a construct concerning the opposite of SDL as discussed. The fundamental concept of what low scores on the SDLRS indicate should be addressed in future studies of self-direction using a more general population.

There are also additional areas worthy of future study within the amateur radio population. Although the only barrier to becoming a ham is the requirement that the individual be able to receive mail through the U.S. Postal Service, our sample primarily was composed of white males. It would be of interest to search out and study various ethnic and female amateur radio operators. Because of the few barriers to the hobby, one might expect the ham population to be more representative of the U.S. demographics than revealed in this study. Why are white males so over-represented in the ham population, with women not choosing technical hobbies on their own, or other ethnic groups lagging in participation following their unofficial non-acceptance (perhaps due to racial bias) in the hobby prior to the 1970s? More studies of this population might contribute to our knowledge of self-direction, specifically the possibility of context-specific aspects of SDL.

REFERENCES

Bonham, L. A. (1989). Self-directed orientation toward learning: A learning style. In H. B. Long & Associates, Self-directed learning: Emerging theory and practice. Norman, OK: Oklahoma Research Center for Continuing Professional and Higher Education. pp. 13-42

Bonham, L. A. (1991). Guglielmino's Self-directed Learning Readiness Scale: What does it mean? Adult Education Quarterly, 41, 92-99.

Borg, W. R. & Gall, M. D. (1989). Educational research: An introduction. New York: Longman.

Brookfield, S. (1986). Understanding and facilitating adult learning. San Francisco: Jossey-Bass.

Caffarella, Rosemary S., and O'Donnell, Judith M. (1988). Research in self-directed learning: Past, present, and future trends. In H. B. Long and Associates Self-Directed Learning: Application and theory. Athens, GA: Adult Education Department, University of Georgia. pp. 39-61.

Courtney, B. C. & Long, H. B. (1987). New perspectives on the education of the elderly in the United States. In H. B. Long & Associates, New perspectives on the education of adults in the United States. London: Croom Helm.

Field, L. D. (1989). An investigation into the structure, validity, and reliability of Guglielmino's Self-directed Learning Readiness Scale. Adult Education Quarterly, 39, 125-139.

Field, L. D. (1991). Guglielmino's Self-directed Learning Readiness Scale: Should it continue to be used? Adult Education Quarterly, 41, 100-103.

Finestone, P. M. (1984). A construct validation of the Self-directed Learning Readiness Scale with labour education participants. (Unpublished doctoral dissertation, University of Toronto). Dissertation Abstracts International, 38, 6467A.

Guglielmino, Lucy M. (1977).   Development of the Self-Directed Learning Readiness Scale.   (Unpublished doctoral dissertation, University of Georgia, Athens). Dissertation Abstracts International, 38, 6467A.

Houle, Cyril O. (1988). The Inquiring Mind. Originally published in 1961, Norman, OK: Oklahoma Research Center for Continuing Professional and Higher Education.

Long, H.B. (1990).   Psychological control in self-directed learning. International Journal of Lifelong Education, 9 (4), 331-338.

Long, H. B. (1991). Self-directed learning: Consensus and Conflict. In H. B. Long & Associates, Self-directed Learning: Consensus and conflict. Norman, OK: Oklahoma Research Center for Continuing Professional and Higher Education. 1-9

Long, H. B. and Redding, T. R. (1991).   Self-directed learning dissertation abstracts 1966-1991.   Oklahoma Research Center for Continuing Professional and Higher Education of the University of Oklahoma, Norman, Ok.

McCune, S. (1988).   A meta-analytic study of adult self-direction in learning: A review of the research from 1977 to 1987. (Unpublished doctoral dissertation, Texas A&M). Dissertation Abstracts International, 49, 11A.

McCune, S. (1989). The validity generalization of Guglielmino's Self-Directed Learning Readiness Scale. Paper presented at the Third North American Symposium on Adult Self-Directed Learning, Norman, OK..

Oddi, L. F. (1986). Development and validation of an instrument to identify self-directed continuing learners. Adult Education Quarterly, 36, 97-107.

Redding, T. R. (1991). Spark-gap to space: A study of self-directed learning.   In H. B. Long & Associates, Self-directed Learning: Consensus and conflict.   Norman, OK: Oklahoma Center for Continuing Professional and Higher Education. 155-175

Toffler, A. (1981). The third wave. New York: Bantam Books.

West, R. F. & Bentley, E. L. (1989).   Structural analysis of the self-directed Learning Readiness Scale: A confirmatory factor analysis using Lisrel modeling. In H. B. Long and Associates, Advances in research and practice in self-directed learning.   Norman, OK: Oklahoma Research Center for Continuing Professional and Higher Education. 157-180

CHAPTER TEN

AN EXPLORATORY STUDY OF SELF- DIRECTED LEARNING READINESS AND FIELD INDEPENDENCE/DEPENDENCE AMONG STUDENTS IN ARCHITECTURAL DESIGN STUDIOS*

Michael A. Price, James Kudrna & Julie Flegal

This paper reports the preliminary findings of a longitudinal study concerning self-directed learning and student success in a college based architecture degree program.

The study focuses primarily on the potential value of the Guglielmino Self-directed Learning Readiness Scale (Guglielmino, 1977/78) as an indicator of self-directed learning among design students and as a predictor of their academic success.   A second area of interest concerns the construct of the SDLRS instrument and its relationship to the cognitive concepts of field dependence and independence.

An assumption was made at the outset of the study that a willingness and ability to engage in self-directed learning was necessary for success in an architecture curriculum and in later professional practice.   This was based upon the researchers personal experiences as both architectural practitioners and educators. One of the goals of the study is to determine whether students are being assisted in becoming self-directed learners or if less self-directed students are being weeded out by the demands of the curriculum.

The rationale for studying self- directed learning in schools of architecture is based upon three concurrent concerns in adult and architectural education.   First, there is general agreement that we live in a time of rapid technological and demographic change, information overload,

* This research was supported by the Oklahoma Research Center for Continuing Professional and Higher Education, University of Oklahoma, Norman, Oklahoma.

and paradigm shifts. Developing a self-educating work force is one way in which we can meet these challenges. This is not important only to increase economic productivity but also to effectively deal with complex environmental, social, and ethical questions.

Donald Schön (1990) has suggested that these challenges can only be met by individuals who possess a type of professional artistry that enables them to solve seemingly indeterminant problems and to think critically about their actions while solving them. Schön's studies of the architectural design studio has led him to conclude that it can foster these abilities and should, therefore, be used as a model for the development of "reflective practicums" in other educational settings. Schön further describes professional artistry as the ability to "reflect-in-action". This is both type of knowledge and a knowledge generating mechanism. The concept of reflection-in-action could be viewed as the ultimate form of self-directed learning. The relationship between self-directed learning and the architecture curriculum needs to be explored.

Second, within the architectural profession there is a persistent concern among both educators and practitioners as to the efficacy of the design studio as the primary method for pre-professional education. One study reported by Kay (1975) suggests that the average student spends 80% of his or her total academic time working on studio projects in the course of obtaining an architectural degree. Architecture instructors may have student contact hours in excess of three times that of instructors in lecture or seminar based curricula. In order to justify this seemingly inefficient method of instruction, architecture schools need ways to demonstrate that unique and desirable learning outcomes are being achieved through the studio method. The development of self-directed learning skills or behavioral patterns might serve as such a desirable end. Or on the other hand, schools wishing to increase the efficiency of studio courses may benefit by identifying the level of self-direction in students and adjusting learning strategies.

The third reason for conducting the study concerns the SDLRS instrument itself. Recently the validity and construct of the SDLRS have been the subject of debate among adult educators (see: Field, 1989; Long 1989a; Guglielmino, 1989; McCune, 1989). While it was not the intent of this paper to enter into this controversy, the study may help to clarify certain points concerning whether the SDLRS is a measurement of one's cognitive style, cognitive strategy, or simply motivation to learn.

SELF-DIRECTED LEARNING (SDL)

The term self-directed learning (hence referred to as SDL) is not easily defined and is used to describe a variety of activities (Bonham, 1989). Tough (1967) viewed SDL as the process in which individuals conduct intrinsically motivated learning projects separate from formal learning or social structures. Knowles (1980) broadened this concept of SDL to include formal situations in which the learner is directed or encouraged to use SDL as a learning methodology. In Knowles' model the learner is responsible for assessing their own learning needs, setting objectives, developing evaluative criteria, and conducting the learning project. The teacher acts as a facilitator during the learning process. According to Long (1989b) the critical dimension of SDL is not the social situation of the learners (i.e., whether they are isolated or within a formal group) or the pedagogical method employed but, rather, the degree to which the learner maintains psychological control over the learning process. Advancing this concept, Bonham (1989) has suggested that SDL may represent a learning style in which individuals not only use SDL as a cognitive strategy but also prefer to use it.

A useful framework for relating the various concepts of SDL is shown in Figure 10.1. In this illustration Long (1989) expresses SDL in terms of the interaction between two possible dimensions of SDL: the amount of learner control over the pedagogical process and the learners' own psychological control. Long places highly structured and other directed learning activities at one end of the pedagogical scale and nearly serendipitous learner directed activities at the other. He then combines cognitive strategy and personality into a single category of psychological control to form the vertical axis.

Figure 10.1
An Illustration of the Relationship Between Pedagogical and Psychological Control in Self-Directed Learning.

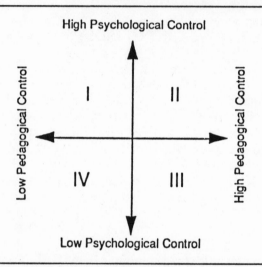

Theoretically any learning activity can be placed somewhere in Long's tetramorphic scale. His opinion is that learner satisfaction with a particular activity will be highest when there is a match between the two dimensions. That is, if an individual with high psychological control is involved in a low control learning activity or if an individual with low psychological control is involved in a high control learning activity. Long further suggests that highly self-directed learners may be able to do well in either pedagogical mode as long as they are willing to follow the imposed order of the high control methods. On the other hand, those learners less self-directed may not do well in a low control learning situation.

Although Long's conceptualization of SDL excludes a social dimension and does not differentiate between cognitive strategy and personality, it is useful in bringing order to an otherwise disorderly array of concepts. For this reason the authors have chosen to use it as a guide for this paper and adopt Long's definition of SDL, which is as follows:

> ...a personally directed purposive mental process usually accompanied and supported by behavioral activities involved in the identification and searching out of information. (Long, 1991a, p. 15)

THE SDLRS

The Self-Directed Learning Readiness Scale (form A) is a 58 item questionnaire with Likert type responses designed to indicate a persons readiness to engage in self-directed learning activities. As mentioned previously there is considerable concern over the validity of this instrument and confusion over what it actually measures. Nonetheless, the SDLRS is the most widely used instrument of this type and was therefore chosen for the study.

The basic factors said to underlie the construct of the SDLRS are as follows:

1. An openness to learning opportunities.
2. Self-concept as an effective learner.
3. Initiative and independence in learning: tolerance of risk, ambiguity and complexity in learning.
4. Acceptance of responsibility for one's own learning.
5. The love of learning.
6. Creativity; risk taking, skill in designing atypical solutions, and ability to conceive of multiple approaches to topics.
7. Future orientation; self-perception a lifelong learner.
8. Problem solving skills; skills for study and problem solving (Long, 1991b).

All of the above learner characteristics are thought to be necessary for success in the design studio with the possible exception of future orientation. If these assumptions about the design studio are correct and if the SDLRS is a valid measure of these characteristics, then the SDLRS may be useful in predicting which students are most likely to succeed academically.

THE DESIGN STUDIO

The protocol of design studios typically consists of a series of more or less related design problems (projects) that are assigned to the student by the studio instructor. Within the bounds of the problem statement (program) the student has a great deal of latitude in developing an acceptable solution. Variety and uniqueness are, in fact, encouraged.

One of the key features of the studio according to Schön (1990) is that often the students are asked to resolve design problems for which they do not yet possess the skills and may, in fact, be completely unaware of the existence of the skills. This requires a great tolerance for ambiguity and a confidence that some how the skills can and will be learned. Schön suggests that highly ambiguous problems in the design studio are resolved through reflection-in-action in which the learner creates their own knowledge during the act of designing. The learner may be helped by the studio instructor, but the learner's own actions are central to the learning process.

At a more immediate and practical level, students often must engage in self-directed and self-initiated learning projects in order to complete the primary objective of the project. They may learn new drawing techniques or gather information about building material and construction methods. Often their learning extends into the world of the client for whom the building project is intended.

The instructors' role in the design studios is more like that of a coach or facilitator than a teacher. They occasionally give short lectures on design issues, but most of their time is spent developing the project program, demonstrating, assessing student learning , counselling, motivating, and in general shepherding the students toward being an architect. They take full advantage of the teachable moment and try to elicit answers to problems from the students rather than tell them what to do.

The following learner characteristics are considered by the authors necessary for success in the design studio:

1. Visual and aesthetic sensitivity.
2. Spatial and environmental awareness.
3. Skills of both analysis and synthesis.
4. Willingness to make decisions on one's own.
5. Exploration beyond the parameters of the assigned project.
6. Natural curiosity, intrinsic drive to solve problems.
7. Creative problem solving abilities.

These factors have been empirically derived through personal experience and consultation with other studio instructors and were developed without prior knowledge of the SDLRS characteristics. Schön (1990) offers these additional characteristics:

8. The ability to deal with ambiguous and indeterminant problems.
9. The willingness to suspend judgement and attempt to do that which one has not yet learned.

Note that items 3 through 8 are very similar to all but future orientation from the SDLRS factors. Item 9 is difficult to interpret. It seems to be more compatible with other-direction rather than self-direction; however, a student that is tolerant of ambiguous situations may be willing to be directed by the instructor to some degree.

Items 1 and 2 are more related to perceptual orientation and cognitive style. The concept of field independence and dependence, which has many over lapping characteristics with self-directed learning readiness, was introduced into this study in order to enrich the researchers' understanding of student performance. A working hypothesis was formed that SDL and field independence combined may be more predictive than either taken separately.

FIELD INDEPENDENCE AND THE GEFT

Field independence and field dependence are cognitive styles which have been linked by some adult educators to self-directed learning. This linkage has, for the most part, been based upon the similarity between the description of field independent thinkers (hence referred to as FIs) and commonly held notions of SDL.

FIs are said to be socially independent, analytical, inner-directed, individualistic, and possessed of a strong sense of self-identity. Field dependent thinkers (hence referred to as FDs) are more extrinsically oriented, responsive to external reinforcement, aware of context, view things holistically, and are cognizant of the effects their learning has on others (Brookfield, 1986).

Research linking SDL with FI/FD thinking has been inconclusive. Bitterman (1988) found a small but statistically significant relationship between cognitive style and adult learners engaged in self-directed activities. Eisenman (1988) found no significant relationship between the SDLRS and cognitive style for a population of fifth grade students, while Carney (1985) did find a significant relationship in her study of gifted and talented fifth through eighth graders.

Newland, et. al. (1987) suggests that there is a link between designing and cognition and that architects tend to develop learning strategies as a means of creating and controlling their world. Creativity and the ability to impose structure on otherwise chaotic perceptions are characteristics of field independent individuals and architects. To verify that the study population was field independent, the Group Embedded Figures Test was selected. This instrument is designed to be used with large groups of subjects and is based upon the Embedded Figures Test developed by Witkin, et. al. (1971). Subjects are asked to find eighteen small shapes which have been "embedded" within slightly larger drawings with the intent to confound the subjects ability to see the shape. Those individuals who can find the shapes are said to be FI, while those that can not are said to be FD. Witkin found that the perceptual dimension measured by the embedded figures test acts as a "tracer" that indicates behavior at other levels and across the senses.

HYPOTHESES

The following working hypotheses were posed for the study:

1. SDLRS and/or GEFT should predict academic success in the design studio and/or overall architecture curriculum.
2. SDLRS scores should correlate to some degree with GEFT scores.
3. Student scores on SDLRS and/or GEFT should increase after long term educative intervention in the architecture curriculum.

METHODOLOGY

A quasi-experimental design was utilized to test the working hypotheses. During the fall of 1990 two groups of students from the University of Oklahoma College of Architecture were asked to voluntarily fill out the SDLRS and GEFT. The first group was selected from those students enrolled in the last required architecture design studio course, while the second group was selected from those students enrolled in the first basic design studio course. With the cooperation of the students' instructors, the tests were administered to entire sections of students during regular studio class time, thus improving the chance that the sample represented the possible range of subjects from this school. Approximately one-half of all upper level students and two-thirds of all lower level students were involved in the experiment. Only four students in each group declined to participate. All students were assured that their grades would not be affected by their scores on the tests or by their non participation in the experiment.

Nested within the lower level group were four subgroups representing those students declaring their major in either architecture, interior design, landscape architecture, or undecided. The policy of the College is to combine students during the first two design studios after which they are separated into specific studios by major. Of particular interest to the study was the group of lower level interior design students. In order to better understand the meaning of their scores relative to the architecture students, a small group (n = 4) of last semester interior design students was also administered the two tests. In all their were six groups of interest which were labeled as follows:

GROUP 1 Upper level architecture students
GROUP 2 Lower level architecture students
GROUP 3 Upper level interior design students
GROUP 4 Lower level interior design students
GROUP 5 Lower level landscape architecture students
GROUP 6 Lower level undecided students

Additional information gathered included the subjects age, gender, and overall grade point average. In order to derive a separate value for the treatment effect of the design studio, subjects were also asked to report the grade they typically receive on design studio projects. The reported letter grade (A+, A, A-, B+, B, etc.) was then converted to a numerical value (design grade) based upon the typical four point scale.

Analysis of the data was conducted using the SAS statistical program on an IBM main frame computer. Means and standard deviations were calculated for all six groups on all factors (see Table 10.1). Correlation tests were run for the following conditions:

1. SDLRS with GEFT for all subjects, for groups, and for gender.
2. SDLRS with GPA for all subjects, for groups, and for gender.
3. GEFT with GPA for all subjects, for groups, and for gender.
4. SDLRS with Design Grade for all subjects, for groups, and for gender.
5. GEFT with Design Grade for all subjects, for groups, and for gender.

ANOVA and multiple comparison tests were also run to detect differences between groups. All tests for significance were set at p ≤ .05.

FINDINGS

The following is a summary of the most significant findings. Refer to Table 10.2 for means and standard deviations.

1. ANOVA tests revealed no significant differences between groups, either across majors or over time.
2. No significant correlation was found between scores on the GEFT and those on the SDLRS for any of the groups.
3. SDLRS was positively correlated to Design Grade:
   All subjects ($r = .29796$, $p = .0039$)
   Group 1 & 2 males ($r = .35821$, $p = .0084$)
   Group 2 males ($r = .37730$, $p = .0255$)
4. SDLRS was positively correlated to GPA:
   Group 1 & 2 males ($r = .29832$, $p = .0300$)
5. GEFT was positively correlated to Design Grade:
   All subjects ($r = .24573$, $p = .0182$)
   Group 6 males ($r = .98359$, $p = .0004$)
6. GEFT was positively correlated to GPA:
   All subjects ($r = .23122$, $p = .0266$)
   Group 1 & 2 males ($r = .3024$, $p = .0268$)
   Group 1 & 2 males and females ($r = .33317$, $p = .0059$).
   Group 2 males and females ($r = .34168$, $p = .0216$)

The interaction effects of combinations of high and low SDLRS and GEFT scores are illustrated in Figure 10.2. The distribution of the combination scores are shown in Table 10.2. SDLRS scores were considered high if they fell in the upper quartile and low if in the lower quartile. GEFT scores were difficult to partition by quartile due to the extremely high overall mean and subsequent limited range. A high GEFT score was thus considered to be anything above the norm score for college undergraduates by gender (12 for males, 10.8 for females; Witkin, et al, 1971).

Figure 10.2
GPA and Design Grades Based on Interaction of SDLRS and GEFT.

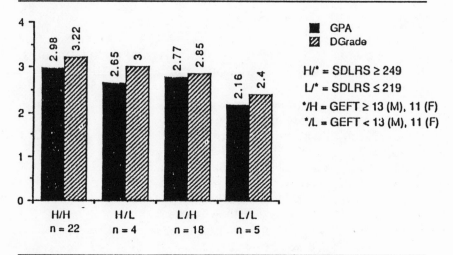

Legend:
- ■ GPA
- ▨ DGrade

H/* = SDLRS ≥ 249
L/* = SDLRS ≤ 219
*/H = GEFT ≥ 13 (M), 11 (F)
*/L = GEFT < 13 (M), 11 (F)

Table 10.1
Distribution of SDLRS/GEFT Scores by Groups.

GROUP	M/F	N	H/H	H/L	L/H	L/L
Group 1	M	18	4	-	6	-
Arch upper level	F	4	3	-	-	-
Group 2	M	35	1 0	1	7	1
Arch lower level	F	10	1	3	1	1
Group 3	M	0	-	-	-	-
ID upper level	F	4	3	-	-	-
Group 4	M	0	-	-	-	-
ID lower level	F	9	-	-	2	2

H/* = SDLRS ≥ 249
L/* = SDLRS ≤ 219
*/H = GEFT ≥ 13 (M), 11 (F)
*/L = GEFT < 13 (M), 11 (F)

174

Table 10.2
Mean Scores and Grades by Group and Gender

GROUP	Gend	N	SDLRS	StdDev	GEFT	StdDev	StdDev	DGrade GPA
GROUP 1 Arc Upper Lev	M	18	231.33	(21.41)	15.94	(4.41)	3.20	2.89 G
	F	4	245.00	(15.98)	16.25	(0.96)	2.87	2.59
Total		22	233.81	(20.90)	16.00	(3.99)	3.14	2.84
GROUP 2 Arch Lower Lev	M	35	233.34	(25.11)	15.00	(4.13)	3.15 S	2.84 S/G
	F	10	241.30	(24.10)	10.10	(6.28)	2.93	2.62
Total		45	235.11	(24.85)	13.91	(5.04)	3.10	2.79 G
GROUP 3 ID Upper Level	M	0	-	-	-	-	-	-
	F	4	251.00	(11.66)	12.50	(1.00)	3.27	3.07 G
GROUP 4 ID Lower Level	M	0	-	-	-	-	-	-
	F	9	223.00	(18.59)	11.44	(4.33)	2.72	2.90
GROUP 5 LA Lower Level	M	3	233.33	(8.50)	13.00	(1.00)	2.93	2.56
	F	0	-	-	-	-	-	-
GROUP 6 Undecided	M	6	220.00	(12.21)	15.00	(2.83)	2.89 G	2.08
	F	3	232.67	(28.11)	14.33	(0.58)	3.11	3.67
Total		9	224.22	(18.19)	14.89	(2.47)	2.96 G	2.61
Total Groups	-	92	233.18	(22.33)	14.17	(4.48)	3.06 S/G	2.80 G

175

DISCUSSION

The hypothesis that SDLRS and GEFT are correlated was not supported. The extremely high scores on the GEFT, especially those for the architecture students, may have obscured a possible correlation between GEFT and SDLRS. However, it is important to note that the interior design students had nearly normal GEFT scores, thus countering the argument that the GEFT lacked sensitivity due to the visual bias of design students. Another possible reason for a lack of correlation is the possibility that the SDLRS is biased toward reading. Architecture instructors typically complain that their students do not read. Nonetheless, based on the data, highly field independent architecture students exhibited a normal range of SDLRS scores; therefore, the SDLRS does not appear to correlate to their cognitive style.

The hypothesis that academic performance (GPA) is related to SDLRS is somewhat supported by the findings, at least for the male architecture students ($r = .29832$, $p = .0182$). The SDLRS also approached significance for all students ($r = .19459$, $p = .0631 > .05$); but, Pearson r values for all students were generally low and cast doubt as to the predictive value of the test.

SDLRS scores were better correlated to the design studio grades than to GPA. Because the design studio is central to both the architecture program and the students' career objectives, higher grades in the studio may be due to higher levels of student motivation. Perhaps the SDLRS is reflecting this motivation rather than driving it.

The SDLRS means for all groups were higher than the norm for all adults but consistent with those reported by Long (1991b) and Confessore (1991) which involved college students and creative artists respectively. The interesting points about the means is the lack of significant differences across the levels of the curriculum. The only effect of the learning intervention is a slight narrowing of the range of scores. Long has suggested that mis-matched levels of psychological and pedagogical control in learning activities may result in learner dissatisfaction and withdrawal, perhaps the academic experience was too structured for some and too unstructured for others. Without more qualitative information this point cannot be clarified.

The extremely high GEFT scores across the architectural curriculum are a curious phenomenon. High scores were expected for the upper level students, but a more normal distribution was expected in the lower level. Perhaps academic counselling and the image projected by the profession and of the profession have combined to guide only FI individuals into architecture degree programs. Females in the lower level had normal GEFT scores which may indicate that they have not been counselled in the same manner as the males. Since all the female students (n = 4) in the upper level were highly FI, it will be interesting to see if the FD females in the lower level will persist in the program.

The implications of the high GEFT scores for the architecture profession needs further study. Do all architects or architecture students need to be FI? Many of the tasks in architectural practice do not require field independent individuals and may actually be better done by field dependent individuals. Does the architecture curriculum actually teach creativity and problem solving as Schön implies, or does it merely provide a safe haven for field independent individuals to simulate practice situations? These are questions for future research.

The interaction of SDLRS and GEFT indicates that there is some advantage to being both FI and a self-directed learner. In Figure 10.2 the trend from high/high to low/low is obvious; however, it is interesting to note that the high/low students did slightly better in design than the low/high students. If SDLRS is actually a measure of motivation, then it would not be surprising to see motivated field dependent students trying harder than their less motivated field independent counterparts. In fact, the low/high students actually had slightly higher GPAs than the high/low students, which perhaps indicates that they were getting by on talent rather than hard work.

LIMITATIONS OF THE STUDY

Generalization of the study is not recommended without further research. The cross-sectional nature of the study introduces serious questions concerning between group variability due to differences in subjects and possible differences in treatments to subjects. A longitudinal study using the lower level design students is currently being planned.

Additional limitations concern the instruments used. The problems of the SDLRS test have already been mentioned. The GEFT is valid instrument but correlations between it and the more rigorous EFT vary with gender. Scores for females correlate as $r = .63$, while those for males correlate as $r = .82$. Therefore, conclusions based on scores for females should be carefully considered. On the other hand, most of the data collected was from male subjects.

CONCLUSIONS

Though the findings of this study are in general contrary to those expected by the researchers, they serve to redirect future research into potentially more fruitful areas. The usefulness of both tests as predictors of success in the design studio appears to be limited. The variety of teaching and learning activities present in the design studio and the latitude allowed in the evaluation of solutions to projects appear to give any reasonably intelligent and motivated individual a chance to succeed.

The primary significance of the extremely high field independent scores is that the profession may have a limited "gene pool" from which to draw its future members. Gutman (1988) has observed that too many architects are being trained as designers. The study indicates that the training may have less of an influence on selecting designer personalities than does the image that the school and profession projects to prospective students.

The reasonably high mean score for the SDLRS tends to support the assumption made by the researchers that self-directed learners are present in the design studios. Yet, there appears to be no measurable effect of the studio on the SDLRS scores. The instrument may be valid but its utility is questioned. Even though self-directed learning is difficult to define and measure, it remains a powerful and appealing concept. Researchers are encouraged to continue study in this area using more qualitative methods.

REFERENCES

Bonham, L. A. (1989). Self-directed orientation toward learning: a learning style. In H. B. Long & Associates, Self-directed learning: Emerging theory and practice. Norman, OK: Oklahoma Research Center for Continuing Professional and Higher Education. 13-42.

Field, L. (1989). An investigation into the structure, validity, and reliability of Guglielmino's self-directed learning readiness scale. Adult Education Quarterly, 39, 125-139.

Guglielmino, L. M. (1977/78). Development of the self-directed learning readiness scale. (Doctoral dissertation, University of Georgia) 1977. Dissertation Abstracts International, 38, 6467A.

Guglielmino, L. M. (1989). Reactions to Field's investigation into the SDLRS: Guglielmino responds to Field's investigation. Adult Education Quarterly, 39, 236-241.

Gutman, R. (1988). Architectural practice. Princeton, NJ: Architectural Press.

Kay, J. H. (1975). Architecture needs a new blue print. Change, June, 34-38.

Knowles, M. S. (1980). The modern practice of adult education (revised). New York: Cambridge, The Adult Education Company.

Long, H.B. (1989a). Reactions to Field's investigation into the SDLRS: some additional criticisms of Field's investigation. Adult Education Quarterly, 39, 241-244.

Long, H.B. (1989b). Self-directed learning: emerging theory and practice. In H. B. Long & Associates, Self-directed learning: Emerging theory and practice. Norman, OK: Oklahoma Research Center for Continuing Professional and Higher Education. 1-12.

Long, H.B. (1991a). Self-directed learning: consensus and conflict. In H. B. Long & Associates, Self-directed learning: Consensus and conflict. Norman, OK: Oklahoma Research Center for Continuing Professional and Higher Education. 1-10.

Long, H.B. (1991b). College students' self-directed learning readiness and educational achievement. In H. B. Long & Associates, Self-directed learning: Consensus and conflict. Norman, OK: Oklahoma Research Center for Continuing Professional and Higher Education. 107-122.

McCune, S. K. (1989). Reactions to Field's investigation into the SDLRS: a statistical critique of Field's investigation. Adult Education Quarterly, 39, 244-246.

Newland, P., Powell, J.A., & Creed, C. (1987). Understanding architectural designers' selective information handling. Design Studies. v.8, 1.

Schön, D. A. (1990, c1987). Educating the reflective practitioner. San Francisco: Jossey-Bass.

Tough, A. (1967). Learning without a teacher. (Educational Research Series No. 3) Toronto: The Ontario Institute for the Studies in Education.

Witkin, H.A., Oltman, P.K., Raskin, E., & Karp, S.A. (1971). A manual for the embedded figures tests. Palo Alto, CA: Consulting Psychologists Press.

CHAPTER ELEVEN

FAMILIAL RELATIONSHIPS IN READINESS FOR SELF-DIRECTED LEARNING

Lucy M. Guglielmino

Research in self-directed learning has proliferated rapidly over the past twelve years, and is expected not only to continue, but to increase. The primary reason behind this prediction is a sense that the ability to function as a self-directed learner is becoming increasingly necessary in an environment where change has become a constant (Caffarella, 1990; Guglielmino, 1990).

In such an environment, the most critical area of research in self-directed learning must be research which contributes to an understanding of the means through which the skills and attitudes involved in self-direction are developed. Research findings in this area would have potential for applications throughout our entire educational system, both formal and informal. This paper reports on the initial stage of a multi-phased study designed to explore possible origins of readiness for self-directed learning. The first phases of the study, focusing on the earliest potential influences, explore possible familial relationships in the development of readiness for self-directed learning. This phase explores the possibility of sibling relationships in levels of readiness for self-directed learning. No reference to such an investigation was found in the literature.

PURPOSE

The study is designed to investigate possible correlations between levels of readiness for self-directed learning among siblings as measured by the Self-Directed Learning Readiness Scale (SDLRS). A further purpose was to investigate the appropriateness of using the Adult Basic Education form of the SDLRS with elementary and middle school children.

HYPOTHESES

The hypotheses, stated in null form, are:

1. There will be no significant difference in the relationship of levels of readiness for self-directed learning between siblings and those between non-related individuals.
2. There will be no significant differences in SDLRS scores by age of subjects.
3. There will be no significant differences in SDLRS scores by sex of subjects.
4. There will be no significant differences in SDLRS scores by grade level of subjects.

SUBJECTS

The subjects were 214 students attending grades 4-8 of the Alexander D. Henderson University School (ADHUS), a university laboratory school which is a part of Florida Atlantic University in Boca Raton, Florida. The student population is balanced by gender within each grade and for the school as a whole. Eighty percent are Caucasian, 17% Black, and three percent Hispanic, Asian, and other minorities. Parents must register their students on a waiting list to attend the school (many are registered as soon as they are born); and parents must provide transportation to and from the school.

INSTRUMENTATION

A form of the Self-Directed Learning Readiness Scale that was originally developed for adult basic education students (SDLRS-ABE) was used in this study. It was theorized that the SDLRS-ABE might perform as well as or better than the SDLRS-E that has been used in prior research with elementary students for several reasons:

1. The SDLRS-ABE has fewer items than the SDLRS-E.
2. It has a low reading level: 3.7 on the Fry scale.
3. The SDLRS-ABE was carefully screened to eliminate idioms and sentence structures that might present difficulties for the non-native student.

The development of the SDLRS-ABE is described in <u>Self-Directed Learning: Emerging, Theory, and Practice</u> (Guglielmino, 1989). This study will examine its appropriateness for use with elementary students.

METHODOLOGY

Sibling Relationships

The SDLRS was administered to all students in grades 4-8 present on the designated test date by their regular classroom teachers. Any absent students having a sibling in the school were tested as soon as they returned to school. All teachers received information describing the study, and all were asked to read identical instructions to the students.

Testing was scheduled for early morning during an extended home-room period. Responses were recorded on answer sheets. All analyses were done on computer, using the Statistical Package for the Social Sciences (SPSS-X). T-tests were run on absolute differences between sibling scores as compared to randomly selected pairs of subjects from within one grade. In addition, correlations (Pearson's r) of sibling scores were compared with correlations of non-sibling scores. One-way analyses of variance were run on SDLRS scores by grade, gender, and age.

Use of SDLRS-ABE

Results of the testing were examined to determined the viability of the SDLRS-ABE for use with elementary and middle school students. The data were examined in terms of reliability estimate and item-test correlations. The Pearson's r split-half (odd-even) method was used to arrive at an estimate of internal reliability. The Spearman-Brown formula was then applied to arrive at an unbiased estimate of total test reliability (Thorndike & Hagen, 1977).

Item-test correlation coefficients were Pearson's r. The criterion for acceptable level of item-test correlation was set at .20, described as a "good" level by Nunnally (1978).

FINDINGS

Sibling Relationships

No significant relationship was found in the t-test on absolute differences in sibling and non-sibling pairs or in the correlations run on sibling and non-sibling scores.

Significant relationships were found between SDLRS scores and age, grade level, and gender. These findings are listed in Tables 1, 2, and 3. Total group means vary in these tables due to the failure of some subjects to record the demographic information requested.

Table 11.1
Grade Level Numbers and Mean Scores on the SDLRS

Grade	N	Mean
4	48	123.5
5	41	123.3
6	38	113.1
7	36	122.4
8	43	119.1
Total	206	120.4

An analysis of variance revealed the differences in mean SDLRS scores by grade level to be significant at the .03 level. By inspection, the mean score of the sixth graders was considerably lower than those of the other grade levels.

Table 11.2
Age Group Numbers and Mean Scores on the SDLRS

Age	N	Mean
10	22	124.0
11	40	124.7
12	37	113.2
13	41	118.4
14	39	120.8
15	12	114.2
Total	191	119.6

Analysis of variance revealed the difference in mean SDLRS scores by age group to be significant at the .04 level.

Table 11.3
Gender, Number, and Mean SDLRS Scores

Gender	Number	Mean
Males	105	117.9
Females	<u>105</u>	<u>122.9</u>
Total	210	120.4

Analysis of variance indicated that mean SDLRS scores by gender were significantly different at the .04 level. The mean score of females was higher than the males' mean score.

Use of the SDLRS

The examination of the functioning of the SDLRS revealed a mean score of 120.19 and a reliability estimate of .86, based on the Pearson split-half corrected by the Spearman-Brown formula. All items but question 2 met the criterion set for acceptable levels of item-test correlations (Nunnally's .20), and most exceeded it by a wide margin. Table 4 lists the item-test correlations for each item.

CONCLUSIONS AND DISCUSSION

The SDLRS-ABE appeared to function well for the elementary and middle school students. The reliability coefficient (.86) was quite good, and the item-test correlations of all items except item 2 were within the acceptable range (.20 or higher). This conclusion must be treated as preliminary, however. Although this study meets the criterion of sufficient numbers for a valid item analysis (a minimum of 5 subjects per item according to Nunnally, 1978); it represents a sample which, although representative in terms of gender and race, may be disproportionately composed of middle class students.

Table 11.4
Item-Test Correlation Coefficients for SDLRS-ABE

Item	Coefficient	Item	Coefficient
1	.46	18	.50
2	.15*	19	.51
3	.39	20	.52
4	.60	21	.40
5	.56	22	.57
6	.41	23	.48
7	.34	24	.49
8	.44	25	.45
9	.32	26	.49
10	.46	27	.35
11	.39	28	.60
12	.55	29	.58
13	.44	30	.36
14	.49	31	.45
15	.20	32	.55
16	.28	33	.46
17	.38	34	.47

*Did not meet Nunnally's .20 criterion.

Sibling relationships in levels of readiness for self-directed learning were no apparent in this study; in fact, although the findings were not significant, there were less difference between random pairs from the same grade than sibling pairs from different grades (with the exception of one pair of twins from the same grade). The significant relationships between SDLRS score and age, grade, and sex dictate further analysis of this data. In addition, since those types of analyses will significantly limit the pairs available for comparison, the subject pool must be enlarged. Exploration of other factors such as birth order, number of siblings, or the possibility of other familial relationships is also indicated. The next phases of the research involving parent-child and grandparent-grandchild relationships should be pursued as planned.

The SDLRS-ABE should be used on additional samples of elementary and middle school students in order to verify the preliminary findings of this study which indicate its appropriateness for use with students of that level. While the results are promising, the sample should be more broadly representative. The difference in scores by sex, age, and grade level, while small, were significant. Further examination with a larger and more representative group would be advisable.

REFERENCES

Caffarella, R. (1990, October). Self-directed learning: Moving beyond description. Paper presented at the national conference of the Commission of Professors of Adult Education, Salt Lake City, Utah.

Guglielmino, L. M. (1989). Development of an adult basic education form of the self-directed learning readiness scale. In H. B. Long & Associates, Self-Directed learning: Emerging theory and practice. Norman, Oklahoma: Oklahoma Research Center for Continuing Professional and Higher Education.

Guglielmino, L. M. (1990, October). Self-directed learning research in the next quarter-century. Paper presented at the national conference of the Commission of Professors of Adult Education, Salt Lake City, Utah.

Nunnally, J. C. (1967). Psychometric theory. New York: McGraw-Hill.

Thorndike, R. L., & Hagen, E. P. (1977). Measurement and evaluation in psychology and education. (4th ed.). New York: John Wiley & Sons.

CHAPTER TWELVE

AN ANALYSIS OF A MODIFIED FORM OF GUGLIELMINO'S SELF-DIRECTED LEARNING READINESS SCALE

Huey B. Long & Stephen M. Walsh

Studies of the of the Guglielmino Self-directed Learning Readiness Scale (SDLRS) have generally resulted in agreement concerning the validity of the instrument. However, several investigators (Brockett, 1985; Field, 1989, 1990; Long and Smith, 1989) have expressed some concern with the effect of reverse scored items. Following an acceptable instrument design procedure, Guglielmino (1977) developed 17 scale items that are reverse scored. The technique is used in scale construction to foil response set patterns adopted by some subjects. However, in some of the reported studies, as will be discussed in the literature review, reverse scored items were cited as having weak to nonsignificant correlations with total test scores. As a result, questions have been raised concerning the impact of the reverse scored items on the validity of the instrument.

This study was designed specifically to address the above problem. The purpose of the study was to determine if the subjects' performance differed on two versions of the SDLRS: the standard Form A that contains the 17 reverse scored items, and a modified Form AM. More is said about the two instruments later. The following research questions were explored:

1. Is there a significant correlation between A Form scores and AM Form scores?

2. What kind of test-retest results are obtained for the 47 items common to both forms?

3. How do the reverse scored items, including all the items to be modified, correlate with total test scores on Form A?

4. How do those items that were modified correlate with the total scores on Form AM?

REVIEW OF THE LITERATURE

The Self-Directed Learning Readiness Scale (SDLRS) was developed as a means to examine and explore the phenomenon of self-direction in learning (Guglielmino, 1977). The SDLRS has proven to be an immensely popular tool for measuring this qualitative construct. Inspired by Tough's (1966) and Knowles' (1970, 1975) interest in self-direction, Guglielmino developed the scale using a Delphi study, incorporating input from 14 experts in the field of adult education. Using Cronbach's alpha, a reliability coefficient of .87 was originally estimated for the scale (Guglielmino, 1977).

A review of the literature reveals that since its introduction in 1977, the validity of the scale has been debated. Construct validity has been the focus for much of this debate. Construct validity is concerned with the true correlation between an instrument (in this case the SDLRS) and some criterion (in this case self-directedness) (Howell, 1987). The question may be posed: Does the instrument measure what it purports to measure? Questions about the validity of the SDLRS have included such topics as: conceptual clarity regarding "readiness for self-directed learning" (Bonham, 1991; Field, 1989); correlation between SDLRS findings and other related constructs (Long and Agyekum, 1983); validity of the instrument when used with a particular sample (Brockett, 1985; Long and Smith, 1989); interpretation of items (Bonham, 1991); and, effects of reverse scored items (Brockett, 1985; Long and Smith, 1989; Field, 1989).

There is an abundance of research indicating that the SDLRS, taken in its entirety, is a valid instrument for measuring the construct "self-directedness" (McCune,

Guglielmino, & Garcia, 1989; West and Bentley, 1989; Long and Agyekum, 1983, 1984; Brockett, 1985; Long, 1987; Finestone, 1984). While one may take exception to Guglielmino's original validation studies which were conducted prior to test revision (Guglielmino, 1977; Field, 1989), it would be remiss to discount the numerous studies since that time. Though some researchers have raised questions concerning the validity of certain items on the instrument, or expressed doubts as to the usefulness of the instrument with certain groups (usually not groups on whom the SDLRS was originally standardized), there appears to be general consensus that the instrument is valid and reliable when employed in the fashion for which it was intended.

The term "self-directed" is qualitative, resulting in a variety of interpretations. There are, however, specific behaviors and abilities identified with self-directed learning. Based on her Delphi study findings, Guglielmino (1977) suggested the following characteristics as indicators of this construct: Initiative; independence; persistence; sense of responsibility for learning; curiosity; ability to view problems as challenges; goal-orientation; desire to learn or change; and, enjoyment from learning. Of these, initiative, independence, and persistence received the highest ratings.

The need for an instrument to effectively measure an individual's readiness for self-direction is confirmed in the literature (Knowles, 1975; Long, 1985). This need appears especially relevant in today's lifelong learning environment; an environment that finds individuals struggling to stay abreast of their changing society, and where an increasing number of colleges and universities offer self-paced degree, non-degree, and certificate programs. It would appear that Long (1988) has described the situation well by stating "The development of an instrument that can provide reliable and valid predictions of self-direction in adult learning is highly desirable. The SDLRS is the best instrument now available for this purpose" (p 255).

METHODOLOGY AND OBJECTIVES

This study examined both the original and modified versions of the Guglielmino Scale. The sample size of 105 observations consisted of 89 females and 16 males. Ethnicity of the sample was as follows: 91 Caucasians, 12 Native Americans, 1 Hispanic, and 1 Black. Two groups of undergraduate college students, from two separate locations, comprised this sample. Ages of test participants varied between 19 years and 50 years. Missing item responses on both forms were assigned a neutral score of three. Reverse scored items were correlated with the total scores on Form A to examine the relatedness of responses to these items with their total instrument scores. Of these 17 reverse scored items, 10 were modified on Form AM. An additional negatively phrased, positively scored item was also modified. The correlation of these 11 items with their respective total instrument scores was examined and compared to determine the effectiveness of the item modifications. A form correlation between the modified and original instrument was examined as well as test-retest analysis of the 47 items common to both versions of the instrument.

Instrumentation

Form A

The SDLRS Form A is a 58 item, self-report questionnaire, scored on a Likert-type scale. Each of the 58 items is structured as a personal descriptive statement. Examples include: "It takes me a while to get started on new projects" and "I'm better than most people are at trying to find out the things I need to know." The respondent's level of agreement or disagreement is registered using the following response pattern: 1) Almost never true of me; I hardly ever feel this way; 2) Not often true of me; I feel this way less than half the time; 3) Sometimes true of me; I feel this way about half the time; 4) Usually true of me; I feel this way more than half the time; 5) Almost always true of me; there are very few times when I don't feel this way.

Of the 58 items on the instrument, 17 are reverse scored in an attempt to reduce the impact of a response set. These 17 items are negatively phrased in one of two ways as discussed later. They require a low response selection to indicate a high level of self-directedness. The 41 remaining items are positively scored.

The original scale, developed by Guglielmino in 1977, was comprised of 48 items. The reliability coefficient of .87 was based on responses to these 48 items. A factor analysis conducted on the original test responses revealed eight factors. Guglielmino labeled these factors: Openness to learning opportunities; self-concept as an effective learner; initiative and independence in learning; informed acceptance of responsibility for one's own learning; love of learning; creativity; future orientation; and ability to use basic study skills and problem-solving skills.

Guglielmino used cluster sampling in her original research, and administered the instrument to 307 individuals; 304 of the results were usable. The sample was divided into three groups:

a)   high school juniors and seniors
b)   college undergraduates enrolled in daytime classes
c)   students enrolled in non-credit, evening enrichment courses

These groups were comprised of individuals from Georgia and Canada, and consisted of predominantly white, mid-socioeconomic level participants. This sample has provided the standard for the SDLRS.

Form AM

Ten of the seventeen reverse scored items in the Form A were modified, in addition to a single positively scored, negatively phrased item. The main effect examined is the impact of a negative term. The reverse scored items in Form

A seem to be of two kinds: (a) those items that are positively worded, but which describe a negative behavior or attitude regarding self-direction in learning; and, (b) items that contain a negative term. In each modified item a negative term or phrase was replaced by a positive one.

Item number 7 is an example of the former type of reverse scored item. It is worded as follows: "In a classroom, I expect the teacher to tell the class members exactly what to do at all times." Some items, such as item 3, were changed to limit the negative aspects. Item 3 reads: "When I see something that I don't understand, I stay away from it." As originally worded, item 3 has two negative dimensions: A behavior, e.g., staying away from something one doesn't understand, plus a negative term "don't understand." In the modified form, the behavior was expressed in a positive manner, e.g. "I am attracted to something that I don't understand." Item 33 is a positive statement, but in the original form contained a negative term, "I don't have any problem with basic study skills." Item 33 was changed to read: "I have good basic study skills." Item 9 is an example of the of the type of reverse scored item that contained a negative term and a negative behavior. Originally item 9 reads: "I don't work very well on my own." Modified, this item reads as follows: "I work very well on my own." Most of the modified items were of the latter type. Thus, of the 17 original reverse scored items, 10 of the items, numbers 3, 9, 12, 20, 22, 29, 32, 35, 44, and 56 were recast to eliminate negative terms or behaviors as noted above. Item number 33, which was not reverse scored, was also modified to eliminate a negative term. See Table 12.1 for a listing of the targeted items in their original and modified forms.

TABLE 12.1
Targeted Items: Original and Modified Versions

Item	FORM A (Original)	FORM AM (Modified)
3	When I see something that I don't understand, I stay away from it.	I am attracted to something that I don't understand.
9	I don't work very well on my own	I work very well on my own.
12	Even if I have a great idea, I can't seem to develop a plan for making it work.	I have no problem in developing a plan for making things work.
20	If I don't learn, its not my	If I don't learn, its my fault.
22	If I can understand something well enough to get a good grade on a test, it doesn't bother me if I still have questions about it.	Even if I can understand something well enough to get a good grade on a test, it bothers me if I still have questions about it.
29	I don't like dealing with questions where there is not one right answer.	I enjoy dealing with questions where there in not one right answer.
32	I'm not as interested in learning as some other people seem to be.	I'm more interested in learning than some other people seem to be.
33	I don't have any problem with basic study skills.	I have good basic study skills.
35	I don't like it when people who really know what they are doing point out mistakes that I am making.	I appreciate it when people who really know what they are doing point out mistakes that I am making.
44	I don't like challenging learning situations.	I enjoy challenging learning situations.
56	Learning doesn't make any diff- in my life.	Learning makes a difference in my life.

Assumptions

Assumptions that have implications for the interpretation and conclusions based on the study findings are as follows:

1) Individual respondents did their best on each exposure to the instruments.
2) Respondents were honest and truthful in their responses.
3) The order in which the forms were completed did not materially effect the results.
4) There were no differences between the subjects by location.

Limitations

Limitations that have implications for the interpretation and conclusions based on the study findings are as follows:

1) This is a pilot inquiry and the number of subjects participating is less than preferred for sound statistical assurance.
2) Volunteers administered the forms and there is no assurance that the instructions were consistent.

Data Collection Design

Two different groups, situated in different locations, participated in the research. A four-fold design was used to administer the two versions of the SDLRS. One-half of each group completed Form A while the other half completed Form AM during the first data collection. At the follow-up data collection, approximately three weeks later, the procedure was reversed with individuals who completed Form A earlier completing Form AM and visa-versa.

FINDINGS

Following general descriptive findings, data are presented in order of the four research questions. The questions that were addressed are:

196

1. Is there a significant correlation between A Form scores and AM Form scores?
2. What kind of test-retest results are obtained for the 47 items common to both forms?
3. How do the reverse scored items, including all the items to be modified, correlate with total test scores on Form A?
4. How do those items that were modified correlate with the total scores on Form AM?

General Descriptive Findings

Group One was composed of 60 subjects including: 11 males; 49 females. The distribution by race was: 9 Native Americans; 1 Black; and 50 Caucasians. The mean score for this group was 243.5 for Form A (standard deviation = 22) and 238.6 (standard deviation = 20) for Form AM. Group Two was comprised of 45 subjects including: 5 males; 40 females; 3 Native Americans; and 42 Caucasians. The mean score for Group Two was 241.0 (standard deviation = 19) for Form A, and 236.9 (standard deviation = 31) for Form AM.

Research Question Findings

1. A correlation of Form A and Form AM revealed a correlation coefficient of .563 at a significance level of .0001. The overall mean score for Form A was 241.9 with a standard deviation of 20. The overall mean score for Form AM was 237.8 with a standard deviation of 25. A t-test on the overall means was nonsignificant, indicating that differences in overall responses on the two instruments were not statistically significant. T-tests comparing the clustered scores of both reverse and positively scored items between Group One and Group Two were also nonsignificant.

   Using Chronbach's alpha, a reliability coefficient of .939 was indicated for Form A, and a coefficient of .958 was indicated for Form AM. Chronbach's alpha measures the individual's consistency of response from item to item (Thorndike et al., 1991). Theoretically, a coefficient that high, could allow one to predict, with some degree of accuracy, an individual's total test score based on the response to a single item. Guglielmino reported a coefficient of .87 in her original study.

2. Test/retest analysis on the 47 unchanged items resulted in a overall reliability coefficient of .564. Group One displayed a coefficient of .777, while Group Two's coefficient was .411.

3. The 17 reverse scored items, in addition to the single positively scored, modified item, generally reflected lower correlations with total scores on Form A than did the other items. The mean r value for these 18 items on Form A was .374. The mean r value for the remaining 40 items on Form A was .533. The mean response for these 18 items on Form A was 4.12. The mean response was 4.19 for the 40 positively scored items on Form A.

Two of the reverse scored items, numbers 7 and 35 failed to be significantly correlated with the total score on Form A (r =.015, p=.87; r=.172, p=.079 respectively). Two additional reverse scored items, numbers 6 and 22, were found to have low correlations with the total score on Form A (r=.212, p=.029; r=.287, p=.003 respectively). Significance was defined in this study at an alpha level of .05 and an r2 of . > .10 (greater than 10% shared variance, r = > .316).

4. Nine of the eleven items that were modified increased their level of correlation with the total score on Form AM. The mean r value for the 11 modified items prior to revision was .408. Subsequent to revision these eleven items reflected a mean r value of .545. The mean increase in correlation for these items was .136. The two remaining modified items, numbers 9 and 20, showed a slight decrease in association with total score on Form AM (-.048 and -.042 respectively).

Prior to modification, the mean response of the eleven targeted items was 4.08. Subsequent to modification (reflected on Form AM), the mean response of these items was 3.86.

The item-total score correlation for two of the eleven items modified on Form AM increased dramatically. Item 35 originally displayed an r value of .172 and a p value of .079. After revision, item 35 exhibited a significant correlation with total score on Form AM with an r value of .469 and a p value of .0001. Similarly, item 22, which displayed a low correlation with total score on Form A, r = .287 and p = .003, displayed a higher correlation with the total score on Form AM, r = .551 and p = .0001. See Table 12.2 for reverse scored item correlations and modified item correlations.

DISCUSSION

The following serves to provide discourse on the findings presented in the previous section. These findings are discussed in the following order. First, the discussion addresses the relationship between Form A and From AM. Second, comments concerning test-retest findings are presented. Third, findings concerning item-total-score correlations are discussed.

Form A and Form AM

The correlation coefficient of .563 indicates that there is a significant degree of association between Forms A and AM. This would be expected since 47 of the items remained unchanged.

As reported in the findings, the overall mean score for Form AM was somewhat lower than that of Form A. Although t-tests did not reveal the difference in total scores to be significant, it is interesting to note that the overall mean response for ten of the eleven modified items was lower on Form AM than on Form A, with a net raw score change of -.460. Item 33 reflected a slightly

TABLE 12.2
Reverse Scored Item Correlations and Modified Item Comparison

Item #	FORM A r	p	FORM AM r	p	Magnitude of Change +/-
* 3	.321	.0008	.468	.0001	+.140
6	.212	.0298	.069	.4906	-.143
7	.015	.8720	.229	.0214	+.214
* 9	.581	.0001	.533	.0001	-.048
*12	.431	.0001	.585	.0001	+.154
19	.389	.0001	.533	.0006	+.144
*20	.363	.0001	.321	.0011	-.042
*22	.287	.0030	.551	.0001	+.264
23	.382	.0001	.456	.0001	+.074
*29	.363	.0001	.486	.0001	+.123
31	.308	.0004	.433	.0001	+.125
*32	.435	.0001	.575	.0001	+.140
*33	.434	.0001	.643	.0001	+.209
*35	.172	.0092	.469	.0001	+.297
*44	.626	.0001	.758	.0001	+.132
48	.336	.0005	.212	.0330	-.124
53	.604	.0001	.504	.0001	-.100
*56	.475	.0001	.602	.0001	+.127

* Denotes a modified item

higher mean response after modification(+.135). This drop in the modified item's mean scores, coupled with the increased correlation of these items with their total instrument score (this latter point is discussed below), may be attributed to an increased understanding of the question. This greater understanding may have resulted in a more realistic interpretation of the question and, in turn, a more accurate, but not significantly different, response pattern for these items.

Test-retest

The test/retest analysis that was conducted on the 47 unchanged items reflected an overall reliability coefficient of .564. This is somewhat lower than may be desirable (Gronlund and Linn, 1990). It is also lower than the test-retest reliability discovered by Long (1986) with a sample size of N=45. That study indicated a coefficient of .79. It should be noted that both the original and modified versions of the test were administered to two groups of individuals. To reduce the possible effects of a learned response, the four-fold procedure noted earlier was used. The reliability coefficient for Group One was .776 while Group Two's reliability coefficient was .411. Thus a much higher degree of variability existed between the original and modified instruments for Group Two. T-Tests on the test procedure were not significant, indicating that the order in which the forms were completed did not affect total test scores. Thus, the dissimilarities in scores must be in some way associated with differences between the two groups. These differences can most likely be attributed to the interaction between the test and Group Two being substantially different than the interaction between Group One and the test. Possible explanations for this may be the lack of test standardization, membership composition of Group Two, or other possible unidentifiable differences in group composition.

In an attempt to address the relatively poor test/retest results of Group Two, item correlations were independently run on Group One. This was done to determine if the inconsistency exhibited by Group Two had negatively impacted the findings presented above. It was determined that the results remain virtually unchanged through the examination of data in this fashion. That is, the same trends existed with relation to those items that exhibited low to nonsignificant correlations.

Item-Total Score Correlations

Prior to modification, items 22 and 35 revealed low and nonsignificant correlations to the total test score on Form A. Subsequent to modification, both of these items increased their total test score relatedness, surpassing the criteria for significance as defined in this study.

Further examination of items 22 and 35 reveals they are characterized by relatively lengthy sentence structure (26 and 20 words per item respectively). Generally, the remaining modified items have between 6 and 13 words per item (exceptions are items 7 and 12, which consist of 18 words each, and item 48, which is comprised of 19 words). Taking into consideration the lengthy construction of items 22 and 35, coupled with the negative terminology in the original form, they may appear confusing to the test participant. Item 22 seems to have the potential for appearing especially ambiguous in this regard.

It appears that semantics, which relates to the meaning of a sentence, and syntax, which relates to sentence structure, are factors in the correlation of certain items with total instrument scores (Brown, 1983). The transition of items 22 and 35 from failing to display significant association with the total score on Form A, to displaying a significant correlation with the total score Form AM may be explained by both semantics and syntax. The lengthy sentence structure of items 22 and 35, coupled with the negative wording in each of these postulates, makes it difficult to estimate their actual reading level. The understandability of these items is questionable. Through the elimination of a negative component in each statement, readability and level of understanding may have been improved. This may account for the increased correlation of these items with the total score on Form AM. It should be noted that the sentence length of these postulates was not altered.

Another course of inquiry may be explored to determine why certain items fail to demonstrate significant correlations with their respective total test scores. This involves the interpretation of a particular item by the test participant, and the individual's cognitive reaction to that interpretation. Once again, this is related to semantics. There are several items which should be examined in this way.

Item number 35 was one of the items that was recast to eliminate a negative term. It reads: "I don't like it when people who really know what they're doing point out mistakes that I am making." One may presume that a highly self-directed individual may, or may not, be open to such constructive criticism as this item implies, but who is to say what is true in most instances? Item 35 may be a better indicator of self-confidence, ego level, or defensive posturing than that of self-directedness. Whereas item number 35 failed to be significantly related with total scale scores on the original form, it was shown to be significantly correlated on the modified form. Item 35 was changed from: "I don't like it when people who really know what they're doing point out mistakes that I am making" on the original form, to "I appreciate it when people who really know what they're doing point out mistakes that I am making" on the modified form. The replacement of the negative phrase "I don't like it" with "I appreciate it" was apparently an effective means of increasing the correlation of this item to the total scale score.

Two other reverse scored items, numbers 6 and 7 (it should be noted here that these two items were not modified) did not display significant correlation with the total scale score. Item number 6 reads: "It takes me a while to get started on new projects". Item number 7 reads: "In a classroom, I expect the teacher to tell the class members exactly what to do at all times". Once again, an individual's possible interpretation as to the meaning of these items should be considered.

Responses to item six may indicate one's readiness for self-direction in learning, as was intended. It may, however, be worded in a manner that does not allow for such conclusions to be drawn. An individual who responds positively to this item may indeed have some degree of difficulty in initiating new learning endeavors. Since initiative is one of three characteristics originally concluded in Guglielmino's Delphi study (1977) to be the most common indicators of self-directedness, this may be a valid indicator of self-directedness. However, it may be that highly self-directed learners do not devote themselves to new learning projects without considerable preparation and commitment. It may be that self-directed learners do not take "projects" lightly. If an individual expects to spend a considerable period of time committed to what their interpretation of a project is, then it is not difficult to understand that a decision of that magnitude may take some degree of time. It appears that item six has several ambiguous aspects to it. What is a "new project"? What does "it takes me a while" really mean? What is "a while"? Answers to these questions may reveal why this item failed to significantly correlate with the total score on either the original or modified forms.

Similarly, item seven can be interpreted several ways. While an individual may expect to be told what to do in a classroom, he or she may not necessarily desire this. It may be that response to this item reflects one's past experience in the classroom regarding the role of the teacher. It does not necessarily reflect one's self-directedness, nor one's preference regarding teacher role. Hence, as stated this item may not be a good indicator of motivation or one's readiness for self-direction in learning.

Finally, the modification of item 33, a positively scored but negatively worded item, provides a good test of the underlying assumption that negative terms may have affected the responses. By recasting the statement so that positive words reflect a positive belief, the item-total score correlation was raised from .434 to .643. These findings suggest that the use of a negative phrase, either in syntactical or semantic terms, may influence the way subjects respond to the scale items.

SUMMARY AND CONCLUSIONS

Based on the findings previously outlined in this study several conclusions were drawn. First, the original and modified forms of the SDLRS are significantly correlated as would be expected. Second, the test/retest reliability for the 47 unchanged items differs significantly between the two groups. Third, the 17 reverse scored items display lower correlations with total score data than their positively scored counterparts. Fourth, it appears that modifying certain reverse scored items on the SDLRS had a positive impact on the correlation of those items with their respective total test scores. Additionally, it is possible to offer reasonable, but not conclusive, explanations for the failure of certain items to be significantly correlated with the total instrument score.

IMPLICATIONS FOR FUTURE RESEARCH

Future research should explore the use of SDLRS Form AM as a means of overcoming possible questions associated with negatively phrased, reverse scored items. Specific areas that should be addressed include using the Form AM in a large scale study, and subsequently conducting a factor analysis to determine if factors may have been altered. Test construction analysis should be conducted to determine if modifying 10 of the 17 reverse scored items, in addition to a single negatively phrased, positively scored item changed the instrument response pattern. An attempt should be made to standardize test administration of the two forms in future studies. This may result in increasing test/retest reliability. Additional study of syntactic and semantic issues also may be beneficial.

REFERENCES

Bonham, L.A. (1991). Guglielmino's Self-Directed Learning Readiness Scale: What does it measure? Adult Education Quarterly, 41, 92-99.

Brockett, R.G. (1985). Methodological and substantive issues in the measurement of self-directed learning readiness. Adult Education Quarterly, 36 15-24.

Brown, D.A. (1982). Reading diagnosis and remediation. Englewood Cliffs: Macmillan.

Field, L. (1990). Guglielmino's Self-Directed Learning Readiness Scale: Should it continue to be used? Adult Education Quarterly, 41, 100-103.

Field, L. (1989). *A*n investigation into the structure, validity, and reliability of Guglielmino's Self-Directed Learning Readiness Scale. Adult Education Quarterly, 39, 125-139.

Finestone, P. (1984). A construct validation and substantive issues in the measurement of self-directed learning readiness scale with labor education participants. Unpublished doctoral dissertation, University of Toronto, Ontario.

Gronlund, N.E. and Linn, R.L. (1990). Measurement and evaluation in teaching. New York: Macmillan.

Guglielmino, L. M. (1977). Development of the self-directed learning readiness scale (Doctoral dissertation, University of Georgia, 1977). Dissertation abstracts international, 38, 6467A.

Howell, D.C. (1987). Statistical methods for psychology. Boston: PWS-Kent.

Knowles, M.S., (1975). Self-directed learning: A guide for learners and teachers. Chicago: Association Press.

Knowles, M.S. (1970). Self-directed learning. Chicago: Follett Publishing Co.

Long, H. B. (1988). Self-directed learning: Assessment and validation. In H.B. Long and Associates, Self-directed learning: Application and theory (pp. 253-266). Athens: University of Georgia.

Long, H. B. (1987). Item analysis of Guglielmino's self-directed learning readiness scale. Journal of Lifelong Education, 6, No. 4, 331-336.

Long, H. B. (1986), Test-retest reliability of Guglielmino's Self-Directed Learning Readiness Scale: A summary report. Unpublished manuscript.

Long, H. B. (1985). Contradictory expectations? Achievement and satisfaction in adult learning. Journal of Continuing Higher Education, 33(3), 10-12.

Long, H. B., and Agyekum, S.K. (1983). Guglielmino's self-directed learning readiness scale: A validation study. Higher Education, 12, 77-87.

Long, H. B., and Agyekum, S.K. (1984). Teacher ratings in the validation of Guglielmino's self-directed learning readiness scale. Higher Education, 13, 709-715

Long, H. B., and Smith, S. (1989). Older adults' performance on the SDLRS: An item analysis. Educational Gerontology, 15, 221-229.

McCune, S.K., Guglielmino, L.M., and Garcia G. (1989). Adult self-direction in learning: A meta-analytic study of research using the Self-Directed Learning Readiness Scale. In H. Long & Associates <u>Advances in research and practice in self-directed learning.</u> Norman, Oklahoma: Oklahoma Research Center for Continuing Professional and Higher Education, The University of Oklahoma, 145-156.

Thorndike, R.M., & Cunningham, G.K., & Thorndike, R.L., & Hagen, E.P. (1991). <u>Measurement and evaluation in psychology and education</u> (5th ed.). New York: Macmillan.

Tough, A. (1966). The assistance obtained by adult self-teachers. <u>Adult Education</u> (USA), <u>17</u>, 30-37.

West, R. and Bentley, E. Jr. (1989, February). Structural analysis of the self-directed learning readiness scale: A confirmatory factor analysis using LISREL modeling. In H. B. Long and Associates, <u>Advances in research and practice in self-directed learning</u>. Norman, Oklahoma: Oklahoma Research Center for Continuing Professional and Higher Education, The University of Oklahoma.

CHAPTER THIRTEEN

SELF-DIRECTED LEARNING IN THE FEDERAL REPUBLIC OF GERMANY

Gerald A. Straka & Joerg Will

In recent times the concept "self-directed learning" is widely used in the Federal Republic of Germany. However, different meanings are attached to it depending on the areas in which it is discussed. The educational discussion about self-directed learning started in the mid of the seventies and the beginning of the eighties on a larger extent. At that time the focus was mainly on school learning (Weinert 1982). Two approaches can be differentiated.

SELF-DIRECTION AS AN EXTERNAL CONDITION FOR INSTRUCTION

One aim of education and instruction in school is the "mature citizen" and the "self-determining and self-responsible individual". However, in strictly pre-structured and -determined classes self-determination and -responsibility can't be learned or at least trained. To realize "self-directed learning" as the goal of instruction it is necessary that instruction offers possibilities for pupils to influence the learning-teaching process ("open classroom", "open education"). These possibilities include the definition of and decision about learning-objectives, time and methods of learning, and implementation of individual standards to evaluate ones own learning-outcomes. The "open classroom"-design also determines the instructional approach. Pupils' ability for self-directed learning is supposed to be augmented in and through classes by a stepwise transfer of control of the learning-teaching process from teachers to the pupils. In this sense, Neber (1978) considers learning to be self-directed, if the regulatory components of the learning-teaching process are generated by the learner himself or - in terms of possibilities - are not determined totally by the learning environment. Immanent in this definition is the notion that learning in an absolute self-directed form does not exist in school.

Weinert (1982) sets up different criteria for the term "self-directed" which enclose situational/environmental as well as personal dimensions:

- The learning situation must have degrees of freedom which allows learners to set up learning objectives and to decide when and how to learn ("openness").

- Learners have to make use of these possibilities and to translate their decisions about learning into (not necessarily cognitive reflected) learning activities (self-determination, includes ability and readiness to learn in a self-directed way).

- Learning activities and -outcomes have to be (self-) attributed to made decisions. The learner must see himself as responsible for his own learning - at least to some extent.

SELF-DIRECTION AS INTERNAL CONDITION OF LEARNING

Neber (1982) made a distinction between two internal perspectives: first he distinguished "self-directed learning as a phenomenon of behavior" (p. 93). Based on "mechanistic models of association theory" this field of discussion is concerned with behavioral repertoires relevant to self-directed learning. The second aspect refers to self-directed learning "as a phenomenon of understanding/recognition and knowledge" (p. 99), with emphasis on the information processing activities of learners. Using the term "self-regulated learning" this research area is concerned with the strategies learner use for information processing (e.g. analyzing and structuring of information) and for the regulation of their learning process (e.g. monitoring and evaluation) (Friedrich & Mandl 1986). Therefor, results of research on cognition and meta-cognition are highly relevant (Mandl & Fischer 1982). Research on metacognition and self-regulated learning can be seen as "basic research" for self-directed learning (Neber 1982).

Presumably because practice in school is highly structured and limited (inclusive teachers) the discussion about self-directed learning shifted from school to other fields, e.g adult education.

Self-directed learning here is discussed on one hand as "autonomous learning" (Weltner 1978). Autonomous learning - or independent learning, autodidactic learning, self-study to give some synonymously used terms - takes place outside schools and courses. It is (or at least should be) independent from teachers or trainers and/or institutions (Weltner, Hoffmann & Kanig 1981). Autonomous learning consists of two components: self-determination of learning objectives and self-determination of learning activities (Weltner 1978). Autonomous learning corresponds to "learning projects" as discussed by A. Tough (1967). On the other hand there are different approaches in adult education which do not limit self-direction on isolated autonomous learning.

SELF-DIRECTED LEARNING IN ADULT EDUCATION

The conceptions about "self-directed learning" in adult and general education both reflect a humanistic and emancipatory view of man with its basic idea of individual autonomy and self-responsibility. Each process of learning and education therefore focus on the development and actualization of personal freedom and self-determination. In this context the thesis is, that the learning potential of adults will be only fully developed if learners themselves can decide what, where, how and with whom they learn (Breloer, Dauber & Tietgens 1980). A consequence of this notion is that adult learners are held to be responsible to possess the relevant abilities and skills necessary for their learning or at least to be motivated to acquire these prerequisites i.e. in learning-to-learn classes.

These theoretical considerations are more often discussed under the label of participant-orientation (Teilnehmerorientierung) rather than under the label self-directed learning. Participant-orientation is realized when the learners are taking part in goal setting, realization and the evaluation of the learning-teaching process. There are three variations of participant-orientation: learner-oriented planning, learners participation in setting up learning objectives and self-directed learning of the individual learner or a group of learners.

Participant-orientation is to be supported with the "open instructional design". Its characteristics are openness in the learning-teaching process, openness in contextual, instrumental and philosophical orientation, variability in the instructional methods, and openness of the learning outcomes (Breloer, Dauber & Tietgens 1980).

Similar to participant-orientation is the approach of "individual continuing learning". Objectives, content, methods, location, time and conditions of learning are not fixed by a superior institution. They have to be determined by the individual learners according to their learning needs and interests (Dohmen 1979). Dohmen sees individual continuing learning as equivalent to "open continuous learning", which can be realized under the assistance of experts and educational institutions.

"Open learning" is focussing on learners' disposal of the conditions of their learning which are both ecological and individual: offered possibilities for learners to organize and manage learning and the learning situation and the individual readiness, ability, and attitude of learners (willingness to take risks, self-reliance, and personal freedom) to recognize and to use such possibilities (Reischmann 1988). Therefore "openness" is a gradual variable, depending on ecological and individual characteristics interacting in the learning situation.

Open learning has to be distinguished from participant-orientation, which implies to a larger degree an instructional design and a teacher/trainer. It also should not be used as a synonym for "self-directed learning". Self-directed learning represents only one and - according to Reischmann - the extreme form of open learning.

SELF-DIRECTED LEARNING IN VOCATIONAL ADULT EDUCATION

The Federal Republic of Germany is - like other developed countries - in transition from an industrial to an information society. A consequence of this development is that more abstract and complex qualifications are and will be required (Straka 1990c). For instance, the profile of a new-type skilled worker employed in industrial production is outlined as following: Sound system-related knowledge of electronic data processing, including programming qualifications, flexibility and employability in different fields of activity, more polyvalent professional knowledge and in altogether better background knowledge of function and order of complex systems, ability to be in full control of a situation, diagnostic knowledge, readiness to accept responsibility for high quality installation systems, and the capability to cooperate at work (Kern & Schumann 1986).

In offices and administrations, integrated work organizations models that combine unqualified, formerly independent tasks with qualified tasks will become the general standard. An example for this development is the integration of a typist's work into specialized tasks, data input and control, typing and accounting, combined with advisory, service and information activities. The result is an integrated treatment of different and complex cases (Baethge & Overbeck 1986).

As these examples show, the information society will lead to the end of Taylorism and a renaissance of the skilled worker and expert. In reaction to this beginning development, the concept of "key qualifications" (Schluesselqualifikationen) introduced by Mertens (1974) is increasingly discussed in primary and continuing vocational training in the Federal Republic of Germany. These qualifications comprise three dimensions: professional competence, methodical competence and social competence. Professional competence means skills and the knowledge that the skilled worker needs to cope with the concrete tasks relating to his job. Methodical competence comprises a) the ability to use existing skills and knowledge in complex working processes, b) the ability to obtain and use information, and c) the ability to evaluate completed actions and their results and to derive consequences for future actions. Social competence is the ability to cooperate effectively with superiors and colleagues, to make allowances for different interests, and to deal openly and fairly with factual and personal conflicts (Rottluff 1988). The dimensions are interrelated to each other and built up and used in an autonomous way.

The key qualifications thereby outline the aims or goal qualifications of vocational training, and can be placed as element in a learning-training-model, Figure 13.1 (Straka 1986, 1990b). Further elements of this model are the entry qualifications, the learning process and the external conditions.

Figure 13.1
Learning-Training Model

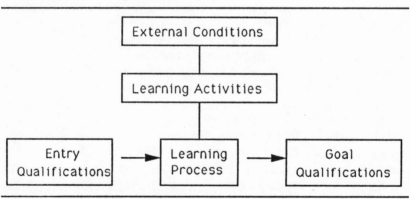

Regarding the entry-qualifications, considerable individual plasticity and reserves of capacity even in old age can be assumed (Baltes 1987), and also the existence of substantial individual differences (Lehr & Thomae 1987).

According to the theses discussed in adult education adults are motivated to learn after having experienced a need in their life situation. They enter a training activity with a life-centered, task-centered, or problem-centered orientation to learn (Friedrich & Meier 1984, Knowles 1984). The desire to participate and learn may be masked by fear of failure or the fear of not being able to compete with younger, better-educated trainees (Friedrich & Meier 1984, Sterns 1986). The learning process as an individual and active interaction with the external conditions then comprise the task, the media, social interaction forms and the trainer's behavior (Straka 1986, 1990b).

In vocational education the learning process often is divided into several phases: Preparation and demonstration by the trainer, repeating and practicing by the trainee, and control by the trainer ("four-steps-method"). In the discussion about key qualifications it became apparent that this instructional design is not appropriate for building up the required qualifications. Here, a self-directed learning process seems to be better suited, consisting of building up a cognitive structure via problem-solving, the constructive reflection of this structure, its practice and its repetition for the purpose of consolidation and its application in new problem situations (Aebli 1987).

One instructional method to facilitate this process is the "guiding-text method" (Leittext-Methode). Guiding texts are learning materials which intentionally and systematically facilitate self-directed problem-solving oriented learning and make it easier for trainers to support and help each trainee individually. Guiding-texts normally describe a complex and practical task as a whole, and also the subtasks which are part of it. They indicate the qualifications to be acquired, structure the gathering and processing of information by the trainees (in most cases by questions), and support the trainees to plan the steps of their learning and practicing, thereby preparing them for their "real" work. Furthermore they systematically enable the self-control of the learner (Rottluff 1988, Straka 1990a).

Learning with guiding-texts ideally comprises six phases: information, planning, decision, execution, control and evaluation. In the information phase the task itself is presented or pre-structuring questions are used to describe what is to be done. In the planning phases, a work plan outlines the various steps. Then this plan is discussed with the trainer and laid down in a final version (phase of decision). A work plan is drafted, which is carried out in the next phase. The execution is checked and - as the next step - evaluated in a discussion with the instructor.

The concept of guiding-texts shows great resemblance to the discovery method and activity learning (Belbin & Belbin 1972, Bruner 1966). Instruction becomes less important while the organization of the framework of external learning conditions facilitating self-directed problem-solving oriented learning gains importance. If the trainer is asked for concrete advice by the trainee he or she should give process-orientated learning aid, and result-orientated aid only if it cannot be avoided (Eigler & Straka 1977).

THE PRACTICE OF SELF-DIRECTED LEARNING

In the Federal Republic of Germany self-directed learning and open learning were realized in different settings. Four examples are reported below:

Elementary School

Wagner (1978) describes an experiment with open learning in the third grade of elementary education. Every week two hours of elementary maths' lessons were arranged according to the concept of open learning. Four "learning corners" with different tasks and learning materials were established in the classroom. It was up to the pupils to chose one of these arrangements. Different forms of the evaluation of the learning outcomes (i.e. learning contracts, informal tests) were applied. Only to a certain degree the pupils participated in planning the instructional process. According to Wagner's experiences pupils and teachers positively appraised open learning, although the teachers needed a little more time to get acquainted with. Open learning lead to positive effects in the social behavior, and, to a certain amount to better problem solving and complex thinking. However, self-direction in the organization of learning and task selection by the pupils themselves could only be realized to a certain degree.

Adult Education

Reischmann (1988) realized open learning with a "newspaper-college" (courses by newspapers). Several series of articles, each one of a different topic, were published in about a quarter of the daily newspapers of the Federal Republic of Germany. The readers could order additional learning materials and study guides to obtain detailed knowledge of the subject. In addition institutions of adult education offered classes corresponding to the topics of the "newspaper-college". The users of the "newspaper-college" were completely independent in deciding in which way to use it. A telephone survey and a mail questionnaire found out that about five percent of all the newspaper readers regularly read the articles. One of five hundred households ordered the additional learning materials. but only a small number of classes were held. Considering that five percent of the millions of newspaper readers is still a large number the "newspaper-college" was and is a potential trigger for open learning.

Training Older Workers

Guiding-texts and other instructional methods for building up key qualifications have been tested so far mostly in primary vocational training. With a research and development project on self-directed and individualized learning of older employees using personal computers - FESILI-2000 (Straka 1990a)- the guiding-text method will be tested in the further vocational training. Older employees of a big shipyard are introduced to the application program MS-

EXCEL for calculation and cost accounting. In this project individualization comprises several dimension. First, learning takes place in the individual's work place. Second, the problems to be solved with MS-EXCEL are chosen according to the learning prerequisites of each trainee. Third, the tasks and their now computerized procession are "real" tasks each trainee has to perform at work. They procession requires problem-solving and self-directed learning from the employees. Here, specially developed guiding-texts will support and facilitate this process. Furthermore, the trainers are instructed to consider individual differences in previous knowledge, learning ability, the type and pace of learning, and individual ability and motivation for self-directed and self-evaluated learning when interfering the learning process (e.g. on demand of the trainee). The main point of research will be the question of how much such a treatment can contribute to building up key qualifications, and the motivation for self-directed learning.

Educating Older Adults

In a research project on the relation between elderly and cable television a conception of activating media work based on open and self-directed learning was developed. The intention was to support elderly in producing a video film in self-determined and self-directed manner. The participants determined the topic of the video and the steps and way of production. Also it was up to them to evaluate the final product. Assistance was provided by people who were trained to support them according to the idea of the facilitator concept. Used to receptive institutional learning during the life span the participants had difficulties in practicing open learning at the beginning of the experiment. Getting more acquainted to the idea and possibilities of self-directed video production the elderly became increasingly independent of the facilitators (Fabian, Straka & Will 1989, Straka, Will & Fabian 1990).

OUTLOOK

A major problem up till now is the only slight empirical evidence concerning the effectiveness of the guiding-text method, partly because the notion that self-directed learning and self-evaluation seem to exclude external empirical control. Another factor is, that no instruments like the Self-Directed Learning Readiness Scale (Guglielmino 1977, Guglielmino, Guglielmino & Long 1987) or the Oddi Continuing Learning Inventory (Oddi 1986) are available in the Federal Republic of Germany up till now. FESILI-2000 will make a tentative step towards an empirical evaluation of self-directed learning of adults.

With the discussion about key qualifications and guiding-texts, the general opinion has come to be the fore that theory and practice of vocational training must be seen as an integrated whole. Vocational training also will become a form of general education. The continuous and continuing rapid technological changes do not only occur at work. People increasingly will be confronted with new tasks in everyday life. To manage these tasks with old fashioned solution patterns will have no further chance. In an information society key qualifications therefore become the "survival kit" for successfully coping with new tasks in work and daily life.

REFERENCES

Aebli, H.(1987). Zwoelf Grundformen des Lehrens. Stuttgart: Klett-Cotta.

Baltes, P.B. (1987). Theoretical propositions of lifespan developmental psychology: on the dynamics between growth and decline. Developmental Psychology, 23, 611-626.

Baethge, M. and Overbeck, H. (1986). Zukunft der Angestellten. Frankfurt/New York: Campus.

Belbin, E. and Belbin, R.I. (1972). Problems in adult retraining. London: Heineman.

Breloer, G.; Dauber, H. and Tietgens, H. (1980). Teilnehmer-orientierung und Selbststeuerung in der Erwachsenenbildung. Braunschweig: Westermann.

Brookfield, S.D. (1988). Conceptual, Methodological and Practical Ambiguities in Self-Directed Learning. In Long, H.B. and Associates. Self-Directed Learning: Application & Theory. Athens, Georgia: Dep. of Adult Education, University of Georgia, 11-37.

Bruner, J.S. (1966). Toward a theory of instruction. Cambridge: Harvard University Press.

Dohmen, G. (1979). Individuelles Weiterlernen in der Erwachsenenbildung. In V. Otto u.a.. Offenes Weiterlernen - Erwachsenenbildung im Selbstlernzentrum. Braunschweig: Westermann, 17-29.

Eigler, G. and Straka, G.A. (1977). Mastery learning - Lernerfolg für jeden? Muenchen/Wien/ Baltimore: Urban & Schwarzenberg.

Fabian, T.; Straka, G.A. and Will, J. (1990). Mediennutzung und Lebensbewältigung im Alter. In D. Kleiber and D. Filsinger (eds.) (1990). Altern - bewältigen und helfen. Heidelberg: Asanger, 35-56.

Friedrich, H.F. and Mandl, H. (1986). Self-Regulation in Knowledge Acquisition: A selection of German speaking research. Tübingen: Deutsches Inst. für Fernstudien a.d. Univ. Tuebingen, Forschungsbericht 38.

Friedrich, W. and Meier, R. (1984). Bedingungen erfolgreicher beruflicher Qualifizierung aelterer Arbeitnehmer im Betrieb. Karlsruhe: Fachinformationszentrum.

Guglielmino, L.M. (1977). Development of the self-directed learning readiness scale (Doctoral dissertation, University of Georgia). Dissertational Abstracts International, 38, 6467A.

Guglielmino, P.J.; Guglielmino, L.M. and Long, H.B. (1987). Self-directed readiness and performance in the workplace: Implications for business, industry, and higher education. Higher Education 16, 303-317.

Kern, H. and Schumann, M. (1986). Das Ende der Arbeitsteilung? Muenchen: Beck.

Knowles, M. S. and Associates (1984). Andragogy in action. San Francisco: Jossey-Bass.

Lehr, U. and Thomae, H. (eds.) (1987). Formen des seelischen Alterns. Stuttgart: Enke.

Mandl, H. and Fischer, P.M. (1982). Wissenschaftliche Ansätze zum Aufbau und zur Förderung selbstgesteuerten Lernens. Unterrichtswissenschaft 2, 111-128.

Mertens, D. (1974). Schluesselqualifikationen. Thesen zur Schulung für eine moderne Gesellschaft. Mitteilungen aus der Arbeitsmarkt- und Berufsforschung 7, 36-43.

Neber, H. (1978). Selbstgesteuertes Lernen (lern und handlungspsychologische Aspekte). In H. Neber; A. Wagner and W. Einsiedler (eds.). Selbstgesteuertes Lernen. Weinheim: Beltz, 33-44.

Neber, H. (1982). Selbstgesteuertes Lernen. In B. Treiber and F.E. Weinert (eds.). Lehr-Lern-Forschung. München: Schwarzenberg, 89-112.

Oddi, L.F. (1986). Development and Validation of an Instrument to Identify Self-Directed Continuing Learners. Adult Education Quarterly 2, 97-101.

Pampus, K. (1987). Ansätze zur Weiterentwicklung betrieblicher Ausbildungsmethoden. Berufsbildung in Wissenschaft und Praxis 2, 43-51.

Reischmann, J. (1988). Offenes Lernen von Erwachsenen: Grundlagen und Erprobung im Zeitungskolleg. Bad Heilbrunn/Obb.: Klinkhardt.

Rottluff, J. (1988). Neue Wege der betrieblichen Ausbildung. In C.K. Friede (ed.). Neue Wege der betrieblichen Ausbildung. Heidelberg: Sauer, 149-163.

Sterns, H. (1986). Training and retraining adult and older adult workers. In J.E. Birren; P.K. Robinson and J.E. Livingstone (eds.). Age, health, and employment. Englewood Cliffs: Prentice Hall, 93-113.

Straka, G.A. (1986). Features of a form of didactics based upon teaching-learning-theory. Education 28, 56-68.

Straka, G.A. (1990a). Technisch-organisatorischer Wandel und alternde Belegschaft. In P. Strittmatter (ed.). Zur Lernforschung: Befunde - Analysen - Perspektiven. Weinheim: Deutscher Studien Verlag, 99-112.

Straka, G.A. (1990b). Training older workers for and in the years after 2000. Journal of Educational Gerontology 5, 2, 68-78.

Straka, G.A. (1990c). The impact of Technological Change on Employment for Older Persons from a West German Perspective. In J. Habib and C. Nusberg (eds.). Rethinking Worklife Options for Older Persons. Jerusalem: JDC-Brookdale Institute of Gerontology and Adult Human Development in Israel ,149-164.

Straka, G.A.; Will, J. and Fabian, T. (1990). Aktivierende Medienarbeit mit älteren Menschen - Ein Leitfaden zur Videoarbeit. Mensch und Technik, Sozialverträgliche Technikgestaltung. Werkstattbericht 76. Düsseldorf: Ministerium für Arbeit, Gesundheit und Soziales des Landes Nordrhein - Westfalen.

Tough, A.M. (1967). Learning without a teacher. Toronto: The Ontario Institute for Studies in Education.

Wagner, A.C. (1978). Selbstgesteuertes Lernen im offenen Unterricht - Erfahrungen in einem Unterrichtsversuch in der Grundschule. In H. Neber; A.C. Wagner and W. Einsiedler (eds.). Selbstgesteuertes Lernen. Weinheim: Beltz, 49-67.

Weinert, F.E. (1982). Selbstgesteuertes Lernen als Voraussetzung, Methode und Ziel des Unterrichts. Unterrichtswissenschaft 2, 99-110.

Weltner, K. (1976). Förderung des autonomen Lernens. Konzept, Realisierung und Evaluation von Studienunterstützungen. Unterrichtswissenschaft (2), 114-127.

Weltner, K. (1978). Autonomes Lernen. Stuttgart: Klett-Cotta.

Weltner, K.; Hoffmann, K. and Kanig, G. (1981). Diagnose der Lernkompetenzen, Unterstützung des Lernverhaltens und Kompensation von defizitäten Lernstrategien. In H. Mandl (ed.). Zur Psychologie der Textverarbeitung. Ansätze, Befunde, Probleme. München: Urban & Schwarzenberg, 478-508.

CHAPTER FOURTEEN

ADULT LEARNERS IN ACADEMIC SETTINGS: SELF-DIRECTED LEARNING WITHIN THE FORMAL LEARNING CONTEXT*

Carol E. Kasworm

The adult self-directed learner was conceptualized in the early literature, as a unique individual. This individual had specialized characteristics and behaviors identified through autonomous pursuits of non-institutional and nonformal learning. Recent discussions have raised issue with this perspective and have suggested a more complex and multi-dimensional set of perspectives of self-directed learning in both formal and informal contexts. This chapter builds upon the notion of adult self-directed learning as developmental, dynamic, and learner-controlled. In particular, this discussion will continue the exploration of adult self-directed action through the role of "master planner" within the traditional classroom environment. Research on adult self-directed learners in undergraduate degree programs will be presented. In this case study research, four key patterns of adult learner interaction will be presented. Each of these patterns suggests that adult self-directed learners have highly varied internal meanings concerning their involvement within formal classroom contexts and their actions as master planners.

---

* This research was funded in part by the Department of Technological and Adult Education of the Bureau of Educational Research and Service, College of Education, University of Tennessee-Knoxville.

PAST PERSPECTIVES ON SELF-DIRECTED LEARNING

Past theory and research have painted a dualistic picture of the adult self-directed learner within an instructional context. Either the classroom was focused upon giving the adult learner full-control and autonomy over the learning process, or the classroom environment denied individual self-directed learning expression and therefore denied adults the opportunity to learn. Implicit in these discussions were the issues of external forms of control versus individual learner control within the learning experience. It was assumed that the formal classroom was antithetical in format, philosophy, and opportunity to self-directed learning. The formal classroom setting not only denied the opportunity for expression of self-directed learning, this environment created powerlessness and passivity in the learner. It was believed that the "schooling" phenomena, its pedagogical structures and authoritarian processes, forcibly obstructed adult self-direction in the learning process (Kasworm, 1988b).

These early perspectives of the unidimensional nature of adult self-direction in learning seemed shallow and somewhat superficial. Early research defined self-directed learning as an phenomena in opposition to formal classroom instruction. However, as I and many other researchers suggested, self-directed learning was not "context-specific". Rather, self-directed learning should be considered as an interactive set of knowledge, attitudes, values and behaviors of the individual in pursuit of purposeful self learning experiences within any environmental context. In the First International Symposium of Adult Self-direction in Learning, I reexamined the early assumptions of self-directed learning through past literature and an exploratory case study. From this examination, supportive evidence suggested that self-directed learning can and does occur within a formal classroom settings (Kasworm, 1988a, 1988b). I suggested that self-directed learning should not be defined by the learner's total authority and control over learning structures and processes. From the exploratory case study, adults in formal classroom settings reported acting on

224

self-directed learning activities and noted their conscious choices over their own learning related to the classroom experience. They spoke to their own sense of choice through planning and utilizing the form, the structure, and the resources of a higher education course in their own journey of learning. In particular, they spoke to active cognitive control over the acceptance and internalization of the classroom-related learning experience.

Through these discussions and further examination of Tough's research on adult learning projects (1979), it was evident that the classroom experience should be reframed as a "learning episode" within the learner's broader learning project activity. Of greater significance, the adult, as a self-directed learner, should be viewed in a role of <u>master planner or architect</u> within the formal education context. This role of master planner redirects the dynamic process of self-directed learning away from the external structures of curriculum and the power relationship between faculty and student. Rather this role suggests adult self-directed learners use "internal judgements, perspectives, and meaning-defined actions" as they chose to act or not act in the classroom setting and the broader self-defined learning environment.

Concept of the Master Planner Role

In considering the broader perspective of adult self-direction, this central focus upon the "master planner role" is important. The concept is premised on Tough's original designation of the planner role in adult learning projects. Tough's research thoughtfully articulated the varied strategies of adult learners who used both self and others as planners in their learning projects. Although the formal classroom has an "expert" (faculty instructor), the adult learner may use that individual as one of many resources and as one of my experts in the planning process of a broader learning project. Thus, the concept of master planner presumes that each adult can create processes, as well as participate in pre-defined processes of learning. This master planner role assumes that the learner in a formal education context draws upon formal and nonformal learning experiences as "learning episodes". The outcomes of these episodes are partially defined and measured through the formal classroom evaluation structures. However, the self-directed learner also conducts an internal examination, through acceptance, rejection, or modification of elements of the formal learning experiences. The adult self-directed learner actively considers the meaningfulness, relevance and application in these metacognitive actions. For example when an adult reads a text, the word-for-word text does not reflect the actual memory of the learner. Rather, the learner's metacognitive actions selectively identifies and retains learner-selected information, as well as creates and strengthens individual meanings of the text. As Bruner eloquently suggests, we engage in a learning process which is "beyond the information given" (Bruner, 1973).

This concept of a Master Planner SDL role suggests that adults have highly significant individual decision-making involvements within formal classroom and institutional contexts. Adult learners engage in complex interactive judgements and behaviors. These actions meet both the expectations for personal learning goals, as well as comply with external institutional and cultural expectations and involvement. Although we should be cognizant of the external structures and behaviors of the formal authorities in a teaching-learning process, the master planner role refocuses our concerns. This concept suggests that research should concentrate upon the adult's own sense of meaning and choice of actions in relation to the learning activities and in relation to those formal authorities. Thus, a formal classroom experience may be highly appropriate and meaningful for one adult self-directed learner, and may be highly detrimental for another learner. Based on this conceptual background, the current chapter examines case studies exploring the master planner role of the adult learner and the highly diverse interactions between the adult self-directed learner and the university classroom environment.

Four Patterns of Adult Undergraduate Interaction

How do adult self-directed learners interact with a formal instructional setting? This study examined rich narrative case studies of adult self-directed learners as undergraduate degree-seeking students. Grounded in the phenomenological tradition, the narratives of each case study were examined in order to delineate key themes. These themes reflected categories of undergraduate adult learners' beliefs and actions in their pursuits of undergraduate course learning and of learning related to other life roles.

The interviewees for these case studies were selected from a sampling pool of adult undergraduates from each of three institutional sites. The development of a sampling pool was based upon several key criteria of adult undergraduates, to include individuals: 1) who were 30 years of age or older, 2) who had completed at least 60 credit hours of undergraduate coursework (potentially involved in upper-division coursework) and were currently enrolled, and 3) who reflected diverse academic disciplines and course load enrollment patterns. Selection of initial contacts for the interview sample was based on the above criteria, as well as the desire to interview equivalent numbers of men and women. In addition, this research desired diverse case studies based on the selection of individuals with dissimilar academic majors.

This current discussion represents a cross comparative analysis of a total of 35 case studies from two of the three institutional sites (Glaser & Strauss, 1967). These two sites include an initial first round site of an urban adult-oriented university with a commuter population; while the second round site is an urban-rural university of both residential and commuter population. This second round site is unique in its service to adults through an evening school structure, which recruits and serves adult students across the university in evening classes.

In the Glaser and Strauss tradition, initial themes, categories and patterns were induced from the first round which examined the first institution case studies. This current discussion reflects an inductive analysis of the second round case studies and cross comparative analysis between the two rounds of themes, categories, and patterns. (Complete background of nature of research inquiry, protocol procedures, research consent procedures and findings are noted in Kasworm, 1991).

Each case study used an audio-taped semi-structured interview. Each interview of up to 90 minutes in length followed a protocol format with facilitated spontaneous discussion and probing, as well as clarifying questions of adult learner perspectives. For the interview, each adult student was asked probes regarding descriptive characterization and personal meanings for involvement as an undergraduate adult learner, as a learner in a formal classroom setting, and as a learner who reported self-directed learning activities outside the classroom experience. Four major patterns were identified in the inductive analysis of these case studies of adult undergraduate interaction. The four patterns (Kasworm, 1988, 1991) were identified as:

* **Conflict,**
* **Transformative,**
* **Accommodation, and**
* **Withdrawal.**

Each of these patterns suggested highly differing dynamics between the adult as self-directed learner, the adult as undergraduate student, and the adult learner in a broader life context. Each pattern elaborated unique ways in which learners acted as a master planners, and unique ways in which the learners acknowledged the formal classroom experience vis a vis their own preferred learning paths and learning agendas. These patterns also suggested learner differences in the design, control and execution of learning experiences, in concepts of efficacy of learning, and in the relationship of formal classroom learning to personal learning agendas.

Each of these patterns represents a differing action meaning for the master planner role. In the first pattern (Conflict pattern), the learner as master planner operates both beyond and within the institutional parameters to maximize one's own learning experiences and outcomes. Inside the academic enterprise, this individual speaks to manipulation and negotiation with administrators and instructors to pursue one's desired learning path. The adult learner views important learning as often beyond the current institutional structures and perceives the master planner role as the major resource to direct and evaluate learning activities in relation to other "collegial experts" of instructors, practitioners, and the written knowledge resources. As master planner, these learners identify a set of ideas and processes to pursue and personally evaluate through the course of the undergraduate experience. In the second pattern (Transformative pattern), the master planner values the collegiate instructional experiences, favors the formal classroom experience, and presents an interactive participation in the classroom experiences and in varied self-defined and self-directed learning experiences beyond the classroom context. In this pattern, the master planner utilizes both the classroom context, but also move beyond the classroom boundaries in complex self-defined learning episodes. These learners often speak to constructing new knowledge and making active applications of new knowledge and skill across the varied life roles and environments of classroom, work and community. They see value in both the faculty expertise and evaluation system, as well as their own personal actions of self-directed learning (within and outside the classroom) and in self evaluation (of both class and self-directed learning experiences).

In the third pattern (Accommodation pattern), the adult student designates the master planner activities solely within the boundaries of the classroom and the undergraduate learning environment. These individuals are focused upon learning how to be successful in the content expertise and in the student learner role. In addition, the master planner role in this pattern is focused upon developing foundational knowledge (for learners entering new fields of study) or upon developing "conceptual" or "enhanced" knowledge (for learners who work in jobs reflecting the course content).

229

Thus, self-directed learning is embedded within learning how to be a "student" and a "knower of specific content, conceptual frameworks, and learning processes". The formal classroom interactions provide these adults with a valuable framework and resource for efficient learning. In particular, they desire the validation by experts and an expertise system (undergraduate academic faculty and courses) for their personal or professional roles. In the final pattern (Withdrawal pattern), the master planner is anxious and threatened and therefore acts as a protector of the learner's self-concept. The learner is focused more narrowly on the acts of learning than the above Accommodation pattern. These individuals view student learning without a clear sense of personal meaning or application of the learning. For them, learning is an act of external compliance towards an outcome desired by an employer, family, significant others, or their future life goal requirements. This perspective of the master planner requires them to provide external acts of learner compliance in the classroom. However the master planner role is also devoting major internal emotions and actions dealing with the incongruence between self expectations for high academic performance and environmental messages of the adult's inadequate academic performance. It is evident that this pattern may not reflect either traditional notions of self-directed learning or of any effective learning process. However, this pattern does suggest that a master planner role acts to facilitate the learner in the learning context through developing meaning and learner actions to handle difficulties with the learning context. In this pattern, the master planner role separates the learner's self-concept from the evaluation impact of the environment. Given this overview of the four patterns, the following discussion presents a more indepth presentation of each of the patterns of adult self-directed learner interaction within the undergraduate classroom context from case study analysis.

Conflict Pattern

The Conflict pattern reflected a unique group of individuals who spoke forcefully and eloquently to their own self-directed learning desires and needs. These individuals presented a most vivid portrayal of their private, autonomous pursuits of learning within an undergraduate context. They spoke to a determined sense of self-investment, a strong ego drive and a highly defined personal notion of a preferred knowledge base. Their pursuits of learning were often cast as negotiated and often conflicting interactions between the learner and the institution. Across the diverse case studies, this pattern represented approximately 10% of the cases.

Unlike the other patterns of adult learner interaction, these individuals had extremely focused expectations of themselves and their interactions in higher education. This focus incorporated three aspects. First, they had specific goals for their future life, often including a specialized work goal and/or pursuit of a graduate degree. (This definition of goal pursuits sometimes occurred early in their undergraduate work through their negotiated involvement in the university). Secondly, they spoke to a defined area of desired expertise. However, these individuals reported that this desired knowledge expertise was not "available" through traditional curricula of their higher education institutions. Lastly, they discussed their personal efforts to negotiate their learning agenda in the bureaucratic undergraduate system. These efforts usually focused upon identifying a faculty member, a program, or a strategy which gave them support, opportunities, and a formal sanction to pursue their learning agendas through the institution. At times, they spoke to their manipulation of a perceived archaic (incompetent) institution by their interventions with a supportive faculty instructor or academic administrator. This negotiation process was sometimes also discussed in relation to conflict in their work environment as they pursued their learning agenda.

These individuals viewed themselves, their perceived learning goals, and their life world as the valid system for defining relevant learning within the institution. Although they did not deny their status as student learners, these individuals knew that their frame of reference did not fit the "novice student role." Thus, they often reported the undergraduate education environment as insensitive and uncooperative as they attempted to pursue their own learning agendas. These students did respect and value the faculty for their expertise; but they also viewed themselves, other individuals, activities and resources as also offering expertise.

Most students in the Conflict Pattern reported a key resolution to this "conflict between self pursuits and institutional structures" by engaging in an interdisciplinary involvement. This interdisciplinary involvement reflected either 1) general coursework with special focused papers or projects on interdisciplinary topics (often with negotiated activities with a faculty instructor); 2) individualized studies (courses focused on individualized topics, such as independent studies or research projects utilizing interdisciplinary learning activities); or 3) interdisciplinary or individualized curricular programs of study (degree programs which were designed for student-developed degree pursuits). This interdisciplinary involvement provided them the opportunity to implicitly frame or reframe their desired learning agendas. Thus, these individuals described a basic operational mode which expected faculty support and flexible institutional structures to support their learning agenda or their active manipulation of the instructional system to develop their expertise. Their academic pursuits were usually portrayed through securing external (faculty and other experts) recognition of their competence, developing a support structure of knowledgeable others for their learning pursuits and pursuing higher-order knowledge and skills for a more influential and preferred future existence.

The master planner role in this pattern was clearly evident in visible external activities, as well as rich introspective discussions of their own internal paths of learning. These individuals created their own unique path within the structured undergraduate curriculum and courses. In particular, they presented four characteristics to their roles as master planners. These characteristics included: (1) Creating a personally relevant place within the instructional system; (2) Defining one's relationship with faculty; (3) Acting on one's own learning processes and procedural reasoning; and (4) Conducting one's own personal evaluation and monitoring. In this pattern, the master planner role was highly autonomous and active in creating learning boundaries which had a limited relationship to current undergraduate structures. Thus, for this pattern, these individuals created a dominant self-defined learning path reflecting unique and negotiated or collaborated actions which would be viable in a credit-oriented degree-seeking program.

Transformative Pattern

The Transformative Pattern reflected the most integrated and complex of patterns in the case studies. This pattern represents approximately 30% of the adult undergraduates case studies.   In particular, adult learners in the Transformative Pattern reflected self-directed learners with broad, encompassing learning relationships across both the undergraduate classroom, as well as other life involvements and roles.

Individuals in this pattern were uniquely oriented to world views concerning the nature of higher education and the undergraduate learning process. Each of these adults was involved in undergraduate coursework for a "society-recognized credential"; however, they spoke to a prominent, definitive perspective of their own internal value of learning, their involvement across their life work in learning, and their commitment to undergraduate work as a broadening of values, perspectives, and beliefs. In the interviews, these individuals identified activities of learning and knowledge development across a variety of settings: the classroom, the worksite, their family or their community. In addition, these individuals cogently spoke to their own cognitive transferring of knowledge, understanding, and application between these settings.

This pattern of interaction reflected the concept of "transformative learners".   The adult undergraduates'

233

cognitive activity was often linked to the reframing of knowledge beyond the classroom setting and of constructing new connections, usage or understanding beyond the original content. These undergraduate adult students were engaged in an ongoing activity of transforming their learning experiences between the classroom and other parts of their lives in a continuous cycle of action and reflection. [This pattern was also reflected the majority of the graduate student case studies in the First Symposium (Kasworm, 1988b)].

There were three subcategories of engagement which characterized the role of master planner in this pattern. As master planners, these transformative learners saw their involvement by (1) connecting personal knowledge with academic knowledge, (2) viewing learning through perspectives reflecting andragogical assumptions, and (3) emphasizing their learning as an interactive process and as the construction of viable personal knowledge. These individuals spoke to their awareness of their own internalized notions of learning and of their own learning goals, as well as the externalized expectations of the professor and the class. They clearly redefined the notions of learning beyond the traditional expert-novice construct of a teacher-student relationship, viewing the professor as one of many experts and the classroom as one of many sources of expert information. These individuals defined their learning boundaries based upon their personal learning goals, evolving interests or resources to support their learning, and the opportunity structures of the formal undergraduate setting. Within these learning boundaries they spoke to many strands of learning engagement and activity. One of those strands was focused upon the instructor, the course content, and the course evaluation. They viewed the classroom as a resource. However, they also noted other strands representing their current life agendas and learning projects. Thus, they saw their learning as acts of meaning and understanding partially grounded in the classroom experience, but also enhanced or created through their own cognitive activities.

Accommodation Pattern

The Accommodation Pattern reflected the most predominant interaction framework for the adult undergraduates, with over 52% of the case studies. The pattern represented adult undergraduates who framed their learning involvement within the traditional higher education instructional environment. These students spoke to their acceptance and the congruence of their expectations within this educational setting. These students valued the curriculum, the course-defined content, and the traditional format of undergraduate teaching-learning. They spoke to the importance of the expertise of the professor. This expertise was described as providing guidance to their learning and to substantiate that they had met the expert-defined outcomes for the course and the curriculum. Although there were subtle variations, these individuals framed the undergraduate experience as an expert-novice interaction. They saw the professor as an expert, higher education as the appropriate place to gain expertise, and themselves as novices within the content or projected outcomes of the course.

In this master planner role, the explicit framework of undergraduate curriculum and instruction was also the accepted framework for these students. Thus, these adults suggested that the key values and perspectives of their role as master planner also reflected the current undergraduate student role. These learners perceived their sense of involvement, expectations, and outcomes premised within the formal classroom and directed by the expert instructor. They believed that the teacher was an expert of the necessary knowledge and of the real-world expectations for a graduating student. Thus, these individuals assumed that the teacher was handing down the "holy Grail" of information and skill for their future success in a real-world context. Most of these students noted their focus upon developing skills and knowledge to succeed as students (learning how to be good students) and developing strong base of knowledge and skill (learning how to be expert in the content). These individuals gave great credence to the expertise of the professor in the design, instruction, and evaluation of the course. When asked about independent studies or self-directed learning, most spoke to the necessity of the structured class to gain the requisite foundations of the subject. They often related a judgement against self-defined learning experiences, such as: "How could a student know what was important to know?"

These adults perceived that viable, necessary knowledge came through this undergraduate structure, from the expert faculty and from an evaluation process which demonstrated that they were "certified by the experts". Thus, they did not stand apart from the class experience or the professor to judge self goals and outcomes. Rather, these individuals often spoke to their internal assessment of judging the capable professor as an expert of knowledge and as a capable instructor. They also noted their judgements of the appropriateness of evaluation for feedback and for assessment of gained knowledge and competence. Although they did report specific aspects of criticism and questioning with regards to lack of quality or commitment by the faculty or certain course activities, they believed that valuable learning outcomes could only occur through this structured process.

In examining these cases, three major subcategories of interaction through accommodation were induced from the interviews. These subcategory patterns included: **Validated Expertise, Measured Expertise, and Exploration beyond Expertise**. Each of these subcategories reflected a screen of judgement on the nature of the accommodation process.

The first subcategory of Validated Expertise in the accommodation pattern reflected a particular **screen of judgement** regarding the accommodation pattern. This subcategory of students were particularly focused upon seeking a credential in relation to entry into a new career, promotion to a new job, or in maintaining job security. These students strongly believed that an outcome of the undergraduate experience was a **validation of their "gained" expertise**. They assumed that most of the curriculum and courses were purposefully designed to provide appropriate and relevant knowledge for their future career activities. In describing this assumption, they usually assumed that the professor or program reflected this expertise and understanding of the "real world", with the student as a receiver of this transmitted knowledge and expertise. Some of these students noted a two-layered perspective, with a predominant in-class knowledge transmission orientation, and a secondary emphasis focused on learning application activities in the "real world". This secondary notion of application was inferred by those who also desired or valued internships, projects, or real-world interactions to "apply" the knowledge gained in the classroom. This subcategory of Validated Expertise reflected five themes of the master planner role: 1) defining undergraduate education as a ticket to a better future; (2) valuing the formal classroom structure, (3) judging the capable professor and instruction process, (4) screening for utility or pragmatic application of information, and (5) learning to adjust (to accommodate) to the structure and to the expectations of formal classroom learning.

The individuals in the subcategory of Measured Expertise considered learning through a **screen of judgement** of **time and energy commitments**. These adult students spoke to highly complex lives with significant overload in their involvements. Although most individuals in each of the four patterns revealed highly complex lives and multiple role demands, the individuals in this subcategory more clearly and strong articulated their student role through some form of "measured involvement". This notion of measured involvement was suggested in their discussion of the student role either 1) through psychological compartmentalization of each of their life roles, 2) as an ancillary activity built onto their major roles through discretionary time, or 3) as an overload involvement while they maintained full-time work roles, family roles, and community roles. These students viewed the student learning role as part of an intricate balancing act. They noted insufficient time and resources to meet all the commitments and expectations of each role demand. Thus, the student role was carefully "measured" by time allocation, schedule, and energy load. They did view the student role as important, but it was not primary in their time or identity investment.

Because these students in the Measured Expertise subcategory saw their learning activities from a time frame referent and/or energy allocation, they preferred the discipline and structure of a formal class. As with the subcategory of validated expertise, they rarely conducted learning activities beyond the required coursework. Although they saw value in the interaction between students, faculty, and the campus, they spoke to significant personal time constraints. These individuals enjoyed their learner role, but often spoke to their dislike of wasted time in the class, or to specific requirements which were perceived to be childish proof of homework completion. They often suggested ways to lessen time commitments, such as an accelerated curriculum and elimination of non-essential information in the classroom. They spoke to valuing the expert-novice relationship, particularly in the professor's structuring of the learning as an efficient, quality-based experience. However, they also saw themselves as a co-expert in judging the importance of specific course activities for its time and energy expenditures in relation to course outcomes. This psychological balancing process was dynamic and often suggested a conflict between competing values, tasks, and relationships in the adults' lives. Thus, the two major unique themes of the master planner role to this subcategory were 1) balancing time and energy commitments and 2) equating the good class and the good grade through this time and energy allotment process.

The third subcategory of Exploration beyond expertise represented adult students who accommodated themselves to the undergraduate experience, but also established their operational **screen of judgement** on the **personal value of learning for self growth**. These adult students viewed their learning world as deeply embedded within the traditional class structure and defined by meeting the instructor's stated expectations and evaluation for the course. However, these students presented a unique operational framework, that of exploration of self in the knowledge world. For many of these individuals, these pursuits of self growth often related to involvement in a particular major and development of a future career identity. For others, it was an involvement in coursework which provided opportunities for self exploration and validation. There were also others who noted the value of exploration in the self through a recognition of a specific "fit" and validation within the student learning role and within higher education.

In this subcategory, the exploration process was not premeditated. Rather, most students reported that this discovery of self and enhancement of self esteem was an unplanned fortuitous outcome. They entered or reentered the undergraduate program to develop and validate academic expertise. This expertise often translated into a stronger sense of self, a greater sense of internal control over their lives, or a greater opportunity to explore and develop themselves. They often suggested an introspective and changing awareness of themselves in relation to the undergraduate learning process. These individuals often reported that the involvement and subsequent success in the student role changed their sense of efficacy and identity. For the adult students in this subcategory, current learning was viewed either as an activity for exploration of new worlds and new ideas, or an activity of refining the meaning and understanding of themselves in relationship to course content and learning inquiry. The key themes in this group represented 1) developing self-confidence and self-esteem, 2) believing in the improvement and growth of self, 3) valuing the class structure and the grading process, and 4) valuing positive interactions with faculty.

Withdrawal Pattern

This fourth pattern identified a small grouping of adult students (approximately 8%) who outwardly conformed to the external boundaries and expectations of the formal classroom. However, these adult undergraduates did not state any self-defined involvement or internal engagement in the classroom learning process. Nor did they suggest any broad intrinsic goals or desires for their undergraduate pursuits. Rather they were pursuing undergraduate work for future external life goals, a credential for work promotion or job change, or perceived status and related social pressure from job colleagues or family members with undergraduate degrees.

For these students, learning was focused upon getting "good" grades and passing the tests. These students not only defined their learning by the boundaries of the class, their notions of learning were more narrowly focused towards passing the test or submitting the appropriate answers on an essay. Underneath the appearance of accommodation to the undergraduate learning context, these students shared an inner conflict. These students were caught in a serious dilemma between their perceptions of personal competence and the judgement by their professors of their lesser abilities to academically perform. A key theme for these students was their significant feelings of incongruence and frustration due to receipt of lower grades (C,D,F) in courses. They could not visualize any other cause for this dilemma, other than taking issue with the grading system.

These adult students viewed themselves as competent adults and students. They did not perceive themselves as having learning or studying difficulties. Rather these students often focused blame for lower-than-expected grades upon a particular method of academic evaluation (essay or multiple choice tests); they perceived a particular evaluation method to be unfair in reflecting their true knowledge base. Some of the students focused blame upon faculty and the higher education environment for their "unfairness"; these students blamed "the system" for a lack of recognition of the complex and demanding lives of adult students. They believed that adult students, given their life circumstances, should be graded differently from younger students. Unlike young students who supposedly had limited pressures and infinite time to study, these adult students felt that they should be judged by an "opportunity standard". This notion of an "opportunity standard" would provide a differential adjustment in grading due to their complex lives and more limited energies. These adults perceived the grading system to be unfair, because it focused upon an "outcome standard".

They believed that this standard only considered the tested evidence, and due to its format and time constraints did not adequately reflect their capabilities and competencies.

These individuals portrayed a perspective of "approach-avoidance" in the undergraduate classroom. This perspective was most evident by examples of passive resistance to the classroom experience. These students did not vocalize this resistance, but did describe the nature of their involvement and interaction in the classroom by nonresponsive, noncommunicative, and passive behaviors. For these learners, their sense of self and learner role was caught up in a more dominant arena of loss of esteem, of feelings of vulnerability, and of a lack of connection between themselves and the learning environment. These students did not explicitly cite any negative, antagonistic, or hostile learning experiences; nor did they suggest any overt negative interactions with the faculty. But their sense of futility with receiving "bad grades" clouded their perceptions of the classroom experience and of themselves as learners in a student role.

In this pattern, it was evident that these individuals were experiencing a contradiction which impacted their self-concept and their role as master planner. The two unique characteristics of the master planner role included: 1) Compliant non-involvement, and 2) Coping with the tyranny of the judging structure. As master planners, they dealt with the formal learning experience through guarded behaviors and judgements of perceived self protection. Although these individuals did report self-directed learning projects in other parts of their life, in the undergraduate classroom environment they were not cognitively involved in the learning beyond external expectations and demands.

CONCLUSION

This study presented adult self-directed learners who make personal choices regarding their level of involvement, interaction, and desired learning in relation to a formal undergraduate classroom context. All of these adults were self-reported self-directed learners in fairly similar classroom environments. From these patterns of interaction and the identified actions in the master planner role, it is obvious that different learners perceived and acted upon similar institutional learning structures in very differing ways. These differences reflected the variability between adult learners in their framing and acting upon a learning experience, rather than the structure and process of the external learning experience.

As suggested in the beginning of this chapter, adult self-direction in learning does occur within formal classroom contexts. However, the nature of self-direction is embedded within the adult and may be manifest in highly varied ways. For many adults, the formal classroom is a valuable source of expertise and guidance. As master planners, these adults make a decision that the classroom becomes the framework for structuring their learning experiences, and the instructor becomes the major resource for planning and executing learning activities. On the other hand, there are adults who view the classroom as an archaic structure which impedes the individual's personal learning goals; thus, these individuals focus their master planning strategies on creating the best path which maximizing their goals and minimizes the institutional directed control in their learning. Given the institutional context and concomitant demands, these individuals manipulate the environment in attempting to meet those individual learning needs and goals. For some adults, the formal classroom represents a structure for external acts of compliance, with subsequent difficulties in meeting external expectations for performance. This inability to perform, according to external standards of faculty or academic program, create negative experiences for the learner. Thus the learner as master planner, continues to comply with external demands of the classroom, while also shielding the learner's sense of self worth. Lastly, there are also adults who view their formal classroom experiences as not only a content to be learned, but also as a leavening structure for learner self growth and self identity. Their role as master planner places a value emphasis on introspection, acquired competence, and validation of self identity.

This study suggests that the theory of adult self-direction should be anchored within the learner's internal acts of reference, action and meaning-making. Effective adult self-direction occurs both within, as well as, outside of institutional structures. External control by the learner over classroom format, instructional strategies and content is not the key issue for adult self-directed learning. The complexity of these case studies reflects the adult's sense of development as a learner, of the significance of their perceptions as a novice or an expert in relation to their undergraduate studies, their judging structure based on past and current educational experiences, and their sense of cognitive orientation towards the nature of the learning process. Adult self-direction should be reframed to consider the centrality of the master planner role within the adult learner. As a master planner, the learner makes many cognitive and affective decisions which influence the sense of self as learner, the use of learning resources (faculty, students, tests, and readings), and the assessment of short-term as well as longer-term learning outcomes. The more significant sense of self-direction is reflected in the internal acts of making meaning, of involvement, and of interaction within and beyond the classroom experience.

REFERENCES

Bruner, J.S. (1973). Beyond the information given. New York: Norton.

Glaser, B.G. & Strauss, A. L. (1967). The discovery of grounded theory: strategies for qualitative research. Chicago: Aldine Publishing.

Kasworm, C. E. (1988a). Part-time credit learners as full-time workers: The role of self-directed learning in their lives. An exploratory examination. Paper presentation at the American Association of Adult and Continuing Education, Tulsa, Oklahoma.

Kasworm, C. (1988b). Self-directed learning in   institutional contexts. An exploratory study of adult self-directed learners in higher education.   In H.B. Long and Associates. Self-directed learning: Application and theory.   Athens, Ga.: University of Georgia, Department of Adult Education.

Kasworm, C.E. (1991). <u>Self-directed learning in formal learning settings: A paradox.</u> Paper presentation at the Fifth International Symposium on Adult Self-Directed Learning. Norman, Oklahoma.

Tough, A. (1979). <u>The adult's learning projects</u> (Second Edition), Austin, TX.: Learning Concepts.

CHAPTER FIFTEEN

A COMPARATIVE STUDY OF SELECTED STUDENT DATA TO DETERMINE RELATIVE SUCCESS OF STUDENTS ENROLLED IN TELECOURSES VERSUS THOSE ENROLLED IN LIVE CLASSES AT ROGERS STATE COLLEGE

**Tobie R. Titsworth, James D. Hess &
Lois Hawkins**

You may have heard of Will Rogers, Claremore, Oklahoma's favorite son and the best known American in the world during the 20's and 30's. He was the top box office draw in Hollywood in 1934, was paid $500 per minute for his radio time and $10,000 per month to write his newspaper columns. Will was not fond of formal schooling and was quoted in 1917 as saying, "...I guess I bogged down in that fourth grade for at least six years. I had education pretty well figured out--I could have a good time and still not learn anything" (Collins, 1978).

"It's all so pointless.... I could be spending all this time learning to fly. There's so much to learn!" , thought Jonathan Livingston Seagull (Bach, 1970, p. 14-15). He was an extra-ordinary seagull that worked so hard on his flying that he was finally able to move from one place to the other as fast as "thought". Impossible? Already a single fiber-optic strand the size of a human hair can carry 90,000 calls simultaneously (Kiplinger Washington Letter Staff, 1986). WilTel, a Tulsa based firm has recently installed over 11,000 miles of fiber-optic cable in unused pipelines all across the United States (Hartnett, 1988). Satellites bounce signals all over the world at the speed of light.

Angie, a Rogers State College student working on a degree in psychology, admits she sometimes feels silly trying to replace leg movements with arm movements. Why? What on earth is she talking about? It might make more sense to you if you knew that she had been confined to a wheel chair since the age of five and she's talking about taking aerobics by telecourse (The Claremore Progress, 1990).

What do Angie, Jonathan and Will have in common? They are all perfect examples of highly motivated self-directed learners. It's too late for telecourse instruction to help Will. Just think what he would have done with the medium. Of course, Jonathan is a fictitious character. But what about the Angie? She's both alive and real!

Anthropologist Margaret Mead must have just read Jonathan Livingston Seagull when she said, "We are now at the point where we must educate people in what nobody knew yesterday and prepare in our schools for what no one knows yet, but what some people must know tomorrow" (Dallas Telecom 90, 1990). Her statement seems even more important if one agrees with Kiplinger when he talks about education in his book The New American Boom:

> In 1925 Calvin Coolidge said, "the business of America is business." Today, I say "the business of America is EDUCATION." Education constructs the foundation of technology, and technology in turn provides the track for industry and commerce to advance into the 21st century....Evidence is mounting that the U. S. economy, in the 1990's and extending into the 21st century.(Kiplinger Washington
> Letter Staff, 1986, p. 5).

Dale Parnell, president of the American Association of Community and Junior Colleges, sounds the alarm in his book Dateline 2000:

> Two converging forces, a skilled worker shortage and the development of a permanent underclass, are bearing down upon the United States. Demographers tell us that by the year 2000 there will be a significant shortage of qualified people to fill the available jobs, and many of the individuals who should fill these jobs will be unmotivated, undereducated, underhoused--a permanent underclass (Parnell, 1990, p. 103)

The key word here is undereducated. What a paradox! At the same time it seems that Jonathan's dreams could come true, educators like Dale Parnell are making those statements. He's not by himself, of course, as you well know. At the height of record breaking enrollments in our nation's community colleges, the president of Dalton Junior College in Georgia, is quoted in Shared Vision (Rouech, Baker & Rose, 1989) as being concerned about the addition of barriers to education just when we (as a country) need education most. A good example of the type barrier is illustrated by the airline industry. The U. S. airline industry is one of the most advanced in the world, but the Federal Aviation Association (FAA) still requires exactly X hours of "seat time" in the class room and lab before a license to work on aircraft will be issued. These requirements, by the way, still include fabric and wood work for aircraft common to the early 20th century flown today only by the hobbyist.

In order to provide avenues for self-directed individuals to make even greater use of the system of higher education, we must move to break down barriers that have been erected to satisfy our need for stability and turf control. Our goal must be to develop ways that will let us educate all of the citizens of the world to their greatest capacity.

Greenberg (1990), points out that many barriers remain in place for minorities, women and older students, the very groups we are going to have to rely on to fill those positions in the United States' shrinking workforce.

Another factor that will make it even more difficult to break down these and other barriers is the faculty shortage that is predicted to continue to worsen into the 90's (Parnell, 1990).

As educational needs multiply exponentially and as faculty numbers decline, telecommunications must be developed to its fullest to expand the capabilities of the teaching profession.

REVIEW OF SELECTED STUDIES:
DO STUDENTS REALLY LEARN BY TELEVISED METHODS?

Educational television had its beginnings in the 1950's. According to Ediger (1990), and others, distance learning provides: (1) quality programs for students at different locations than the instructor, (2) quality learning activities for specified subjects previously unavailable to certain students, and (3) staff development and inservice education programs for teachers at a lower cost than traditional programs.

Why, then, has it taken us so long to incorporate televised instruction into our educational systems? Of course, cost has been a major factor. Aside from that, resistance to change continues to be a major player in the slow-down of significant use of technologies of all kinds in education. The first urge was to argue that television would take the place of teachers altogether. You thought that theory died out in the fifties? As late as 1987, in a faculty meeting at the Rogers State College campus, one faculty member, who will remain anonymous, stated, "you'll get me on tape, fire me and use the video for free from now on."

But even more basic is what Bruder (1989) alludes to in her article about distance learning published in <u>Electronic Learning</u> when she says, "...concepts fade without practical applications and, as can be expected, the application of this relatively new educational delivery system incorporates countless concerns, possibilities, and some confusion." (p.30) It seems that a combination of high cost, resistance to change and lack of practicability has kept us from really using telecommunications as a meaningful educational tool.

Telecourses seem to be one answer to change the first concern mentioned--high cost. With consortia arrangements such as the Oklahoma Higher Education Telecommunication Association, courses can be leased and/or purchased cooperatively at a much lower cost than going it alone. But, still the question is, do the students really learn anything?

Several specific studies have addressed the issue for target students. For example, Larry Adams from John Tyler Community College reported that telecourse students received better grades than independent study students.

In a recent study of continuing education for teachers located on the Minnesota-North Dakota border, several methods of distance education were compared. The data indicated that the different instructional formats had little effect on student achievement or course evaluation (Beane, 1989). A similar study compared nursing students at Weber State College using interactive television versus traditional campus lecture methods. The "live teacher" was the preferred method; however, the finding of no significant differences in the examinations scores between the classes is consistent with other researchers in this field (Parkinson and Parkinson, 1989).

Some recent studies on broader groups of students have established that telecourses are an effective means of providing education to time and place bound students. A study entitled "Video Telecommunications in Washington Community Colleges" (1990) asked this question, "do telecourses provide quality instruction?" The students responses to all questions in the study show evidence that students perceive telecourses to be of equal quality with other courses.

Dillon, in two studies for the Oklahoma State Regents for Higher Education reported positive results. In an evaluation of the Summer 1988 College by Television program she determined: (1) in general, the telecourse faculty believed the telecourse to be equal or greater in difficulty for the students as the equivalent on-campus course, (2) a comparable percentage believed that the telecourse students performed as well or better than the on-campus student (Dillon, 1988). The second study showed: "that the Oklahoma Televised Instruction System provides for effective reintegration of the teaching-learning acts as measured by the distance students attitudes toward the system, confidence in course performance and actual performance." This was further seen by the fact that distance students actually made better grades than did the on campus students (Dillon, 1990).

ROGERS STATE COLLEGE INVOLVED IN OUTREACH

Rogers State College's conscious effort to serve a broader spectrum of the population in its service area began with its name change in 1982. It was previously known as Claremore College, officially Claremore Junior College. A concentrated effort was made to involve the community in selection of course offerings primarily located in the public schools. That small beginning in 1982 led to 3,781 students during the 1989 Summer Term, 1989 Fall Semester and the 1990 Spring Semester, enrolling in over 11,000 semester credit hours. Presently classes are offered at permanent off-campus sites located in Bartlesville and Pryor. The Bartlesville site increased its enrollment from 17 students in the 1985 Spring Semester to almost 600 the 1990 Fall Semester.

This concept of "taking the education to the people" soon permeated the institution and led to the question, "what other ways can we get this done?" Rogers State College was a charter member of the Oklahoma Higher Education Telecommunications Association and is one of the leaders in enrollments through OETA. During the school year 1989-90 RSC enrolled over 1,000 students and provided 3,216 semester credit hours.

Not satisfied that all its citizens had access, the College also applied for a license to operate a full power television station, KXON TV-35 to complement KNGX FM-91.3 that had been on the air since 1980. On July 1, 1987, the station came on the air operating 11 hours a day, 7 days a week. KXON offers over 25% local programming and has won several awards for its community education efforts. The station does not duplicate the offerings of Oklahoma Education Television Authority (OETA), but expands upon the telecourses that the college is able to offer to its students.

In addition to non-duplicated telecourses that are pulled down from The Learning Channel, the faculty have developed several courses of their own, copyrighted in 1987 by President Richard H. Mosier, as Multiple Learning Opportunities. (MLO's) The concept basically provides a student-centered, print-based, video-taped/live format that is totally designed and taught by individual faculty members. The concept is described by Emily Dial-Driver, RSC faculty member, in an article entitled, "Multiple Learning Opportunities: Inception of Innovation" in Community College Review (1989) and Tobie R. Titsworth, RSC Vice President for Academics, in "Innovative Instructional Techniques Offer Students Multiple Learning Opportunities", in the ATEA Journal. (1990) Limited studies have shown that the 11 courses offered in this mode are preferred by the students to the telecourses produced by other colleges and marketed nation-wide (Titsworth, 1989).

The station recently received a substantial grant that will increase its broadcast power from approximately a 20 to 75 mile radius, allowing the entire service area, including Bartlesville, access to a full power educational station.

METHODOLOGY - ASSUMPTIONS - LIMITATIONS

The purpose of this study was to determine the relative success of students enrolled in telecourses compared to those enrolled in the on-campus equivalent courses and to identify any differences in the level of success as measured by completion rate and GPA. The study was not intended to determine what characteristics if any contributed to the presence of or lack of a relative difference between the groups studied. While it is assumed that students enrolling in telecourses may have a different academic motivation, it was not the intent of this study to identify those motivations. Rather, the scope of this study was limited to the measurement and comparison of completion rate and GPA to determine if any notable differences existed between the groups.

The courses selected for the study may be categorized in two separate and distinct categories. The category of telecourses represents the total number of telecourses offered during the academic year studied. A total of 32 telecourses were studied in this category. The category of on-campus courses represents the equivalent courses offered on campus during the same period of time. A total of 80 courses were reported in this category. The academic year utilized for each period included the summer, fall and spring semesters. No courses falling into either of these categories were excluded from the study.

Completion rates were determined for both groups by subtracting the number of withdrawals from the total enrollment after the census date and dividing that number by the total enrollment at the census date. Students who dropped prior to the census date (the first three weeks of the semester) were not included for either group.

Grade point average was determined by dividing the total number of grade points awarded by the total credit hours attempted by the student. The standard grade point system was used to determine the number of grade points awarded (A=4, B=3, C=2, D=1, F=0).

COMPARATIVE STUDY TELECOURSE STUDENTS VERSUS TRADITIONAL STUDENTS

The profile of a telecourse student at Rogers State College is very similar to the typical community college student both at Rogers State College and nation-wide.

Profile of a Rogers State College Telecourse Student

The typical telecourse student is a Caucasian woman between the ages of 22 and 39. Sixty percent are married or have been married and have from one to four children. The average student is taking between 13 and 18 credit hours combining on-campus and distance education. Most have some previous college experience and take telecourses due to a conflict with their work or home schedules. Students report the telecourses were selected because of the broadcast schedule and the on-campus instructor. Thirty-nine percent are seeking an associate degree at Rogers State College.

Profile of an Average Rogers State College Student

The average Rogers State College student is a 30 year old Caucasian woman. She is a part time student taking less than 12 hours, living in Rogers County, slightly more likely to be married than not (Hess, 1990).

Profile of an Average Community College Student

The average community college student is a 28 year old Caucasian woman taking classes part time (National Center for Higher Education, 1989).

Demographic Trends

The following tables compare several semesters of telecourse students for various demographic characteristics. Each one will be reviewed and then compared to the 1990 Fall Semester Demographics to see if any significant differences exist. (17)

Tables 15.1A and 15.1B and others reported at the end of the chapter, show that the White student dominates enrollment in approximately the same percentages in both the telecourse student and total student body (Hess, 1986, 1988, 1990). The slightly larger percentage of Native American students taking telecourses may be significant. A potential untapped market exists in this category.

CONCLUSIONS

David M. Grossman, expressed his concerns about using television for instruction in this conclusion:

> In short, instruction will be of high quality to the extent that distance-learning programs and technologically delivered instruction allow the faculty to profess, to achieve the full realization of their professional responsibilities. To the extent that technology and distance learning compromises that professionalism and subverts the role of faculty, then no standard measure of quality will have any meaning (Grossman, 1987).

This involvement of the faculty is key to the success of any distance education program. Another crucial element is the provision for adequate student support. To accomplish the first element we use only full time teachers or by special exception of the President, highly qualified part time teachers. Their role is to coordinate the telecourses and develop, produce and instruct the MLO's at Rogers State College. A new phone system has been installed on campus so that each faculty member has an answering service, allowing the telecourse student to call and leave a message 24 hours a day. The second element is coordinated by the Director of Education Programming at KXON with the help of college support staff. For example, viewing sites are established at Bartlesville, Pryor and on campus so that students may watch a tape over or catch one they might have missed over the air.

The students enrolling now and in the foreseeable future years will have been taught by other-directed methods so long that most will continue to prefer the face-to-face instruction that a classroom environment provides. However, this study shows that there is no significant difference in performance by most students taking telecourses versus the ones taking on-campus courses.

Telecourses provide a great opportunity for self-directed learners (who are not interested in grades or credits) to gain knowledge and information. This instruction takes place outside the formal setting of the institution, but through courses developed in an academic setting by professionals in the various fields.

As more telecourses and other self-directed types of courses become more available, the self selection process that we see now in telecourse enrollments will decline. This may lower the retention rates and grade point averages of telecourse students.

RECOMMENDATIONS

1. Continue to offer telecourses at a greater rate and variety as soon as they can be produced in a quality manner using full time faculty coordinators whenever possible.

2. Market the telecourses available to the self-directed learner market not presently interested in earning credit.

3. Carefully consider setting up open-entry, open-exit courses using a check out system for home study.

4. Telecourses, in combination with a schedule of week-end and evening classes should be marketed as stand-alone degree programs to working adults.

5. More attention should be given by faculty and administration to the concepts of psychological self-directedness as described by Long , Staged Self-Directed Learning as presented by Grow and the Teaching Learning Cycle portrayed by Baker, Roueche and Gillett-Karam. These concepts have a great deal to say about the methods we use, the way materials should be developed and the outcomes we should consequently expect.

6. Live, on-air question and answer tutoring sessions with interactive audio capability should be developed to assist those students that need more help in getting started and continuing in the process of self-directedness in their learning processes.

7. Sessions should be incorporated into the faculty development plan to instruct in ways to help the instructors include techniques of helping the students become more self-directed.

8. A special class should be designed to assist learners that need to become more self-directed because of their need for more education, complicated by a hectic life-style.

9. A special effort should be concentrated on the faculty of our colleges and universities to inform them of the great need to radically change the way we are teaching our students. The new era of technological advances will require the student to become more self-directed.

10. As a greater number of less self-directed students take telecourses as more are available, it may be necessary to take a different approach to the support system that we have available.

REFERENCES

Adams, Larry (1987, April). Comparisons of Grade Distributions for Telecourses and Print Bases Course. John Tyler Community College: Chester, VA.

Bach, Richard (1970). Jonathan Livingston Seagull. New York: Avon Books.

Beane, Paul L. (1989). The comparative effectiveness of videotape, audiotape, and telelecture in delivering continuing teacher education. The American Journal of Distance Education, 3, 57-66.

Bruder, Isabelle. (1989). Distance learning: What's holding back this boundless delivery system? Electronic Learning, April, 30-35.

Center for Telecommunications. (1990). Dallas Telecom 90. Dallas: Dallas County Community College District.

Collins, Reba (1978, Winter). Will Rogers Part I. Oklahoma Today, pp. 6-9.

Dial-Driver, Emily. (1989). Multiple learning opportunities: Inception of innovation. Community College Review, 16, 38-40.

Dillon, Connie (1988, Dec). Evaluation of the Summer 1988 College by Television Program. A Report for the Oklahoma Higher Education Telecommunications Association. Oklahoma City.

Dillon, Connie and Charlotte Gunawardena (1990, Jan). Learner support as the critical link in distance education: A Study of the Oklahoma Televised Instruction System. Oklahoma State Regents for Higher Education. Oklahoma.

Ediger, Marlow (1990). "Distance learning and the curriculum." ATEA Journal, 18:1, 10-11, 30.

Greenberg, Elinor M. (1990, July). Meeting workforce needs - How is higher education responding? Network News, pp. 1-4.

Grossman, David M. (1987). "Hidden perils: Instructional media and higher education." Occasional Paper 5, National University Continuing Education Association.

Hartnett, Dwayne (1988, April). "WilTel success more than pipe dream." Tulsa World. Sec. G, p. 1.

Hess, James D. (1986). Telecourse demographics, (Report to the Administrative Council), Rogers State College, Claremore, OK.

Hess, James D. (1988). Telecourse demographics, (Report to the Administrative Council), Rogers State College, Claremore, OK.

Hess, James D. (1990). Telecourse demographics, (Report to the Administrative Council), Rogers State College, Claremore, OK.

Kiplinger Washington Letter Staff. The new American boom: Exciting changes in American life and business between now and the year 2000. Washington, D.C.: Kiplinger Washington Editors, 1986.

Kobler, Nancy (1970). Think rural means isolated? Not when distance learning reaches into schools. The School Administrator, Nov., 16-24.

National Center for Higher Education. A summary of selected national data pertaining to community, technical and junior colleges. Washington, D.C.: AACJC. 1989.

Staff (1990, Nov. 11). Paralyzed RSC student takes full credit load - Even aerobics class. The Claremore Progress, p. 1.

Parkinson, C. F. & Parkinson, S. B. (1989). A comparative study between interactive television and traditional lecture course offerings for nursing students. Nursing & Health Care, 10:9, 499-502.

Parnell, Dale (1990). Dateline 2000. Washington, D.C.: The Community College Press.

Roueche, J. E., Baker, G. A. III, & Rose, R. R. (1989). Shared Vision. Washington, D.C.: The Community College Press.

The State Board for Community College Education. (1990, June). Video Telecommunications in Washington Community Colleges. Olympia, WA.

A Comparative Study

Titsworth, Tobie R. (1989). Innovative Instructional Techniques Offer Students Multiple Learning Opportunities. ATEA Journal, 16, 22-23.

Table 15.1A
DEMOGRAPHIC TRENDS - ETHNICITY ROGERS STATE COLLEGE
TELECOURSE STUDENTS

	Fall, 86 (N=186)	Spr, 88 (N=436)	Spr, 90 (N=666)	Fall, 90 (N=621)
International	03.2%	01.1%	02.5%	02.3%
Black	01.1%	02.3%	01.2%	01.8%
Native American	14.0%	10.6%	09.4%	12.6%
Asian	00.5%	00.2%	00.5%	00.8%
Hispanic	00.5%	00.9%	00.7%	01.0%
White-Non Hisp	80.6%	84.9%	85.8%	81.6%

Table 15.1B
DEMOGRAPHIC DATA RSC FALL 1990 (ETHNIC OVERVIEW)

International	3.2%
Black	1.2%
Native American	12.7%
Asian	0.7%
Hispanic	0.7%
White-Non Hisp	81.4%

Table 15.2A - DEMOGRAPHIC TRENDS - CLASS LEVEL
ROGERS STATE COLLEGE TELECOURSE STUDENTS

	Fall, 86 (N=186)	Spr, 88 (N=436)	Spr, 89 (N=666)	Fall, 90 (N=621)
Freshman	57.0%	62.8%	58.6%	60.2%
Sophomore	30.1%	27.1%	27.6%	31.1%
Special	12.9%	10.1%	13.9%	08.7%

Table 15.2B
DEMOGRAPHIC DATA RSC FALL 1990 (CLASS LEVEL)

Freshman	53.1%
Sophomore	26.3%
Special	20.7%

Tables 15.2A and 15.2B, Class Level, seem to show an increase in degree seeking students taking telecourses and at a higher percentage than the student body as a whole (Hess, 1990).

Tables 15.3A and 15.3B, Sex, show a trend toward females taking telecourses at a rate of 6% greater than the total student body (Hess, 1986, 1988, 1990). This would sound reasonable and implies that a place-bound need is being met here.

Table 15.3A - DEMOGRAPHIC TRENDS - SEX
ROGERS STATE COLLEGE TELECOURSE STUDENTS

	Fall, 86 (N=186)	Spr, 88 (N=436)	Spr, 89 (N=666)	Fall, 90 (N=621)
Male	34.9%	31.7%	28.6%	28.3%
Female	65.1%	68.3%	71.5%	71.7%

Table 15.3B
DEMOGRAPHIC DATA RSC FALL 1990 (SEX OVERVIEW)

Male	34.5%
Female	65.5%

Tables 15.4A and 15.4B, Marital Status, do not indicate a trend nor any significant difference between the two groups (Hess, 1986, 1988, 1990).

Table 15.4A - DEMOGRAPHIC TRENDS - MARITAL STATUS
ROGERS STATE COLLEGE TELECOURSE STUDENTS

	Fall, 86 (N=186)	Spr, 88 (N=436)	Spr, 89 (N=666)	Fall, 90 (N=621)
Married	56.5%	47.2%	51.0%	53.3%
Single	43.5%	52.8%	49.0%	46.7%

Table 15.4B
DEMOGRAPHIC DATA RSC FALL 1990 (MARITAL STATUS)

Married	56.8%
Single	43.2%

Tables 15.5A and 15.5B, Entry Status, imply that more returning students tend to take telecourses than do first time students. No trend is noticeable (Hess, 1986, 1988, 1990).

Table 15.5A - DEMOGRAPHIC TRENDS - ENTRY STATUS
ROGERS STATE COLLEGE TELECOURSE STUDENTS

	Fall, 86 (N=186)	Spr, 88 (N=436)	Spr, 89 (N=666)	Fall, 90 (N=621)
First Time	19.4%	23.6%	26.1%	22.1%
Returning	80.6%	76.4%	73.8%	77.8%

Table 15.5B
DEMOGRAPHIC DATA RSC FALL 1990 (ENTRY STATUS)

First Time	27.9%
Returning	72.1%

Tables 15.6A and 15.6B, Credit Hour Load, indicate that a significantly higher percentage of telecourse students are taking over 12 hours (Hess, 1986, 1988, 1990). This does not seem to be increasing, but implies that many students are using telecourses to increase their total load.

260

Table 15.6A - DEMOGRAPHIC TRENDS - CREDIT HOUR LOAD
ROGERS STATE COLLEGE TELECOURSE STUDENTS

	Fall, 86 (N=186)	Spr, 88 (N=436)	Spr, 89 (N=666)	Fall, 90 (N=621)
1 to 3 hours	12.4%	14.9%	14.2%	13.2%
4 to 6 hours	16.1%	16.1%	18.7%	18.8%
7 to 11 hours	17.2%	17.2%	20.5%	16.6%
12 or more hours	54.3%	53.4%	46.7%	51.4%

Table 15.6B
DEMOGRAPHIC DATA RSC FALL 1990 (CREDIT HOUR LOAD)

1 to 11	60.2%
12 or more hours	39.9%

Tables 15.7A and 15.7B, Age Group, show that over 61% of the telecourse students are between the ages of 17 and 30 which indicates a lower average age than the 30 years of the typical RSC student (Hess, 1986, 1988, 1990). This agrees with the higher percentage taking over 12 hours and taking telecourses.

Table 15.7A
DEMOGRAPHIC TRENDS - AGE GROUP
ROGERS STATE COLLEGE TELECOURSE STUDENTS

	Fall, 86 (N=186)	Spr, 88 (N=436)	Spr, 89 (N=666)	Fall, 90 (N=621)
17 to 20	--	19.7%	15.2%	23.4%
21 to 30	--	38.5%	41.6%	37.7%
31 to 40	--	29.4%	27.6%	27.4%
41 to 50	--	10.8%	13.5%	09.5%
51 to 60	--	01.4%	01.7%	01.8%
61 and over	--	00.2%	00.5%	00.0%

Table 15.7B
DEMOGRAPHIC DATA RSC FALL 1990 (AGE OVERVIEW)

17 to 24	41.7%
25 to 34	30.1%
35 to 44	18.9%
45 to 54	7.2%
55 to 64	1.3%
65 and Over	0.8%
Average Age	29

Table 15.8, Selected Majors, indicates that students are taking telecourses in all areas (Hess, 1986, 1988, 1990). This distribution of majors is approximately the same distribution rate as the total student population. No significant differences were noted.

Table 15.8- DEMOGRAPHIC TRENDS - SELECTED MAJORS
ROGERS STATE COLLEGE TELECOURSE STUDENTS

	Fall, 86 (N=186)	Spr, 88 (N=436)	Spr, 89 (N=666)	Fall, 90 (N=621)
Accounting	06.5%	07.6%	06.6%	07.6%
Bus Ad (trans)	21.5%	18.1%	15.8%	11.9%
Business Mgt	06.5%	08.0%	18.3%	14.8%
Education	09.7%	12.9%	08.6%	09.8%
Computer Sci	08.1%	07.1%	03.5%	04.0%
Liberal Arts	14.0%	08.0%	03.1%	05.3%
Pre-Nursing	05.9%	06.9%	08.3%	10.6%

Tables 15.9A and 15.9B, Selected Counties, are probably the most significant tables shown (Hess, 1986, 1988, 1990). The percentage increase of students taking telecourses has more than doubled in Washington County while total enrollment in traditional classes at that site has continued to grow at a fast pace. Another factor is that the total student body is only represented by 16.3% from Washington County while over 24% of those taking telecourses are from that county. This indicates a greater desire for higher education offered in any format.

262

Table 15.9A - DEMOGRAPHIC TRENDS - SELECTED COUNTIES
ROGERS STATE COLLEGE TELECOURSE STUDENTS

	Fall, 86 (N=186)	Spr, 88 (N=436)	Spr, 89 (N=666)	Fall, 90 (N=621)
Rogers	35.5%	40.6%	30.2%	26.9%
Mayes	14.5%	13.1%	14.9%	15.3%
Tulsa	14.0%	15.6%	13.0%	15.3%
Washington	11.8%	12.8%	24.3%	24.6%

Table 15.9B
DEMOGRAPHIC DATA RSC FALL 1990 (COUNTY OVERVIEW)

Rogers	37.6%
Mayes	17.0%
Tulsa	12.6%
Washington	17.1%

In Table 15.10, Completion Rates, we see that completion rates for the telecourse students are approximately the same as those for our on campus courses (Hess, 1988, 1990). The downward trend may be accounted for because of the larger number of students enrolled in telecourses, thus becoming less self-selected in nature. Telecourse totals for each year were compared to all on-campus equivalents by department and course number. For example, the Accounting I telecourse was compared to the totals for all on-campus Accounting I courses.

Table 15.10 - COMPLETION RATES
TELECOURSE STUDENTS VERSUS ON-CAMPUS STUDENTS

YEAR	CATEGORY		COMPLETION RATE
88-89	TELECOURSES	N=32	76%
88-89	ON-CAMPUS COURSES	N=80	71%
89-90	TELECOURSES		77%
89-90	ON-CAMPUS COURSES		76%
90-91	TELECOURSES		71%
90-91	ON-CAMPUS COURSES		72%

A Comparative Study

Table 15.11, Grade Point Averages, shows that the grade point averages for telecourse students approximates those of on-campus students in the same courses (Hess, 1988, 1990). For example, in 88-89, the GPA for telecourse students was 3.02 compared to 3.06 on campus. In 89-90 it was slightly higher with 3.12 for the telecourse students compared to 2.97 for on-campus students. The 1990-91 year again shows an increase for both types of students, slightly favoring the telecourse students. Telecourse totals for each year were compared to all on-campus equivalents by department and course number. For example, the Accounting I telecourse was compared to the totals for all on-campus Accounting I courses.

Table 15.11 - GRADE POINT AVERAGES
TELECOURSE STUDENTS VERSUS ON-CAMPUS STUDENTS

YEAR	CATEGORY	GPA
88-89	TELECOURSES	3.02
88-89	ON-CAMPUS COURSES	3.06
89-90	TELECOURSES	3.12
89-90	ON-CAMPUS COURSES	2.97
90-91	TELECOURSES	3.30
90-91	ON-CAMPUS COURSES	3.12

CHAPTER SIXTEEN

EDUCATIONAL CONTEXT, MOTIVATIONAL ORIENTATION AND COGNITIVE FLEXIBILITY IN UNDERGRADUATE NURSING EDUCATION

Gary L. Loving

Teaching students to think freely about alternative solutions to problems and to independently identify the information necessary for problem solution is a tremendous educational challenge. In fact, whether these thinking skills can be explicitly taught is questionable. According to Frederickson (1984), the knowledge required to solve most ill-structured problems may be so broad as to be unteachable. Simon (1980) contends that generalizable problem- solving methods do exist and that they can be taught. Other authors have argued that practitioners do, with practice, develop powerful problem-solving tools that are specific to the area of expertise obtained in their practice (Chase & Chi, 1980; Elstein, Shulman, Holmes, Ravitch, Rovner, Holzman, & Rothert, 1983).

Regardless of whether problem-solving skills can be taught, educators are challenged to create an educational environment in which they can be learned. To create such an environment requires that educators be willing to support students' intrinsically-motivated efforts to learn from their experiences. The data upon which this paper is based suggest that students' perceptions of formal and informal evaluation contingencies in the educational program impact their abilities to develop an intrinsic motivational orientation. Students' motivational orientation, in turn, affects their developing abilities to flexibly identify and process appropriate information for problem solution.

The purpose of this paper is to describe selected concepts from a theoretical model built upon a grounded theory (Strauss & Corbin, 1990) investigation in nursing education (Loving, 1991). It is important to note that the unit of analysis for the investigation was students' perceptions. Thus, the resulting theoretical framework is based on research that is interpretive in nature in that the framework is grounded in data describing students' perceptions. Concepts from the model described in this paper include competence validation, cognitive flexibility, motivational orientation, and educational context.

COMPETENCE VALIDATION

Competence validation is identified as the core category of the theoretical model. Competence validation is the process by which the student's identity as a competent nurse is established. The process of competence validation varies with students' perceptions of educational context. Two educational contexts are described in the model, an evaluation context and a learning context.

Motivational orientation is identified in the model as a dimension of competence validation. The process of competence validation may be extrinsically motivated in an evaluation context or intrinsically motivated in a learning context.

In a perceived evaluation context, students are motivated to achieve an external validation of their competence in the form of a grade or the approval of faculty. Student strategies in the educational program are directed towards this end. Cognitive evaluation theory (Deci & Ryan, 1985; Deci & Ryan, 1987; Ryan, 1982) cites evaluation as one of many events that are viewed as controlling rather than autonomy-supportive. Cognitive evaluation theory is based on extensive research in social psychology (e. g. Benware & Deci, 1984; Enzle & Ross, 1978; Grolnick & Ryan, 1987; Harackiewicz, Abrahams, & Wageman, 1987). As a controlling event, evaluation decreases intrinsic motivation and changes the locus of causality to external. So, according to cognitive evaluation theory, events that individuals view as controlling decrease intrinsic motivation.

In a perceived learning context, students are motivated to acquire skills and knowledge necessary to provide competent, patient-centered nursing care. When students experience success in patient-centered nursing care, they develop an identity as a competent nurse and are intrinsically motivated to continue learning from their experiences. In a learning context, interactions are what Deci and Ryan (1987) refer to as autonomy-supportive. That is, interactions are directed towards assisting students to acquire the knowledge and judgment required to independently perform competent, patient-centered nursing care.

COGNITIVE FLEXIBILITY

Cognitive flexibility is identified as a consequence of competence validation in a learning context. Cognitive flexibility is the ability to identify information appropriate to problem solution and the ability to synthesize that information in a way appropriate for patient problem solution. Controlling events, such as evaluation, appear to decrease the student's cognitive flexibility.

> "It appears that when cognitive activity is controlled, it is more rigid and less conceptual perhaps with a more narrow focus than when it is self-determined." (Deci & Ryan, 1987, p. 1027).

The construct of cognitive flexibility represents a continuum. The opposite of cognitive flexibility, cognitive rigidity is identified as a consequence of competence validation in an evaluation context. It is important to emphasize that students do not always perceive an evaluation or a learning context. Descriptions of conditions that comprise an evaluation context and a learning context are about interactions, how these interactions cumulatively affect students' motivational orientation, and how motivational orientation cumulatively affects students' development of self-directedness and cognitive flexibility. Figure 16.1 illustrates the theoretical model.

EVALUATION CONTEXT

The description of an evaluation context includes a discussion of interactional and curricular conditions that comprise an evaluation context, strategies students employ to validate competence in an evaluation context, and cognitive rigidity as a consequence of strategies and interactions in an evaluation context.

Figure 16.1
Competence Validation, Intrinsic Motivation (IM),
Extrinsic Motivation (EM), Cognitive Flexibility (CF), and
Cognitive Rigidity (CR), in Two Educational Contexts.

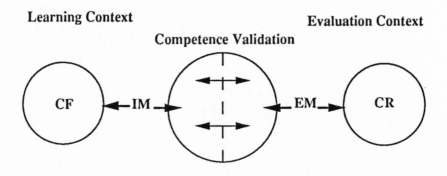

Conditions

Conditions that contribute to students' perceptions of an evaluation context are curriculum structural conditions and evaluation-centered interactions with faculty or staff nurses. Potential evaluation contingencies associated with the above conditions often force the student to focus on achieving the evaluation standard, rather than focusing on the patient. A senior nursing student states:

> D: I just get by...and that's terrible, but I just have the attitude that I need to pass. And I feel like I don't have the time to explore the things that I want to. I feel like if I waste time on this I'm not gonna have the time to learn the things that I need to learn for the tests or for the objectives.

Curricular conditions that contribute to an evaluation contextual perception include emphasis on formal written tests and the academic care plan, as well as explicit policy emphasis on evaluation. Informants report that on nursing tests, questions often have more than one right answer, and that students must determine which is the most right. Nursing faculty often report that formal tests should be constructed to measure students' ability to apply, analyze, or synthesize knowledge. When discussing tests, however, student informants report not on strategies directed towards learning knowledge application, analysis, or synthesis, but on strategies for learning how to take the test based on test construction cues provided in the question, as is evidenced by this excerpt from the interview with T. M., a senior student.

> G: Are those kind of tests playing a role in your ability to think through patient care problems?
>
> T: Yeah, I don't know if they meant it that way. But you go back and you look at the question, and try to figure out if they want something specific, or something more general, or, but at least for me, you're doing the same kind of thing. You're learning how to think.
>
> G: And what would be some of the things you'd think through in a situation on the test?
>
> T: Well, leave out the always and nevers. You know, there's some little test-taking things that kinda help you out a little

bit. But, whenever I come to a situation where two answers could be right, I usually end up picking the one that's most specific. The more specific answer was usually the right one. And I've just kind of figured that out on my own.

Trying to figure out the answers to test questions often becomes an exercise in finding out what the teacher thinks is the right answer. Feeling the need to employ such strategies contributes to an evaluation contextual perception. Another nursing student states:

S. E: That's a lot of what school is, finding out what they want and giving it to them. And I don't like to do that. I've gotten a lot of lower grades because of that. I'm a very creative person and in some ways (School One) kind of kaboshes creativity... Give them what they want. It's kind of a guessing game sometimes.

The relationship of emphasis on formal tests, students' perceptions of context, and students' perceptions of self-competence is supported by Sarason and Stoops (1984), who discuss a phenomenon they termed cognitive interference. They found that students' performances on tests were decreased by a preoccupation with the lack of personal competence and self-oriented negative thoughts.

Another curricular condition that sometimes contributes to students' evaluation-context perceptions is the academic care plan, a written case study assignment. A senior nursing student describes her feelings regarding the academic care plan.

S: ... And I'm still wondering how applicable (academic) care plans are to the real world. I mean we do them on our unit, but nothing compared to what I'm used to doing in clinicals (for school). Are they putting our efforts and energies into something that's not gonna be that useful? ... I definitely think that we have to focus so much energy on getting the right wording. And I'd like to just write it the way it really is, but sometimes you just can't write it that way.

M. L., a new graduate nurse states that academic care plans are done "for the teacher's benefit, so they'll have something to grade you on (in clinical laboratory)". When students hold this perception of the academic care plan, strategies for making the grade take priority over strategies for using the care plan as an exercise in knowledge application. A., a new graduate, discusses the role of the academic care plan in official competence validation.

> A: I would do a care plan.   It would take me 20 hours altogether...and at first, it was because you just really didn't know what you were doing.   You know, you were just spinning...to me it was just all too overwhelming...   And then the more you were in nursing school, the shorter your care plans got.   I think it was individualized because the teacher knew you knew what you were doing.

Students' care plans are graded using specific evaluation criteria that focus heavily on the form of the care plan rather than the content.   Students must therefore place information in the appropriate form and sequence to meet evaluation criteria.   To place information in the appropriate form and sequence requires theoretical knowledge and the ability to apply that knowledge to a complex clinical situation, or the ability to apply the complex clinical situation to their limited theoretical knowledge.   This application of limited knowledge often proves to be a difficult fit.   Students, therefore, develop strategies to reconcile ambiguities between clinical reality and theoretical knowledge. Some of these strategies are discussed later in the paper.

Formal policy emphasis on evaluation is evidenced in a review of selected course materials from the nursing schools used in the study.   The following quote is from course requirements outlined in the syllabus of a first-semester clinical nursing course in one of the nursing schools:

> If a student is in danger of missing or has missed 20% of
> clinical practicum, the individual instructor must counsel the
> student of a probability of a deficiency due to inadequate
> observational time for clinical evaluation.

The requirement that 80% of the clinical practicum be
attended seems reasonable, particularly since most of the
students voice a concern for the limited amount of time spent
in patient care practicum activities. The emphasis in the
policy statement, however, is on the evaluation component of
the clinical practicum rather than the learning component of
the practicum.

In addition to curricular conditions, interactions between
students and faculty or between students and staff nurses
appear to play an important role in students developing their
perceptions of educational context. Interactional conditions
that contribute to students' developing an evaluation-context
perception include faculty's affective attitude communicated
during interactions with students and types of questions that
faculty use when interacting with students.

Faculty affect refers to the way in which faculty present
themselves in their interactions with students. Students
perceive some faculty to be primarily evaluative in their
interactions and others to be primarily learning-centered in
their interactions. S. C., a new graduate nurse states, "Some
faculty make it feel like evaluation. Others make it feel like
learning".

Another nursing student describes her perceptions of the
affective component of interactions with a faculty whom she
perceived to be evaluative.

> P: She is the one that would be aloof, nonresponsive
> emotionally. You don't know where she is or what she's
> thinking...You don't know if you're saying what she wants or
> if it's the right answer..."

The way questions are asked appears to affect students'
perceptions of faculty/student interactions. Many students
report that questions that appear to have a right-or-wrong

answer contribute to their evaluation-context perceptions. If one thinks of nursing's practice base as a complex network of knowledge that expert practitioners use with facility, novices perhaps cannot be expected to use that complex network with the same facility. When questions are asked that relate to what Benner (1984) terms paradigm cases, that is questions that have a right-or-wrong answer, either theoretically or for the particular patient situation, an expert practitioner could perhaps readily enter the knowledge network at the appropriate point to determine the answer. The student, however, not having the benefit of experience, would not necessarily know which part of the knowledge network is relevant to answering the faculty's question. If the student is unable to answer the question correctly, the student perceives that he or she has failed the evaluation.

Learning the Tricks

Students learn certain strategies or "tricks" for trying to make the grade. There are strategies that are used as tricks on written work, and there are strategies that are used to deal with faculty/student interactions.

Examples of tricks that students use to make the grade on academic care plans include copying standard care plans, copying previously-developed plans for particular disease processes, and making up data to fit the theoretical picture of the patient's problems. This "fairy-tale planning" is directed towards filling in the boxes in the academic care plan. In the following excerpt, P., a senior student, describes the use of standardized care plans.

P: ...but the care plans are, for the most part, prefabricated.

G: What do you mean by prefabricated?

P: Typewritten, already presented. You have a person over here, and he's got pulmonary edema. OK, here's your care for pulmonary edema...

> G: Do you think that most of your classmates use those standardized care plans?

> P: The teacher says that you have to individualize, so we'll change this, this, and this.   ...go to a care plan book, and these are examples of what a care plan is supposed to look like...I looked at a couple, and I've got a diagnosis of this, and I reworded it so that it sounded pretty good.

"The teacher says that you have to individualize.." The motivational orientation for learning tricks is extrinsic. The student is seeking to achieve competence validation through an external stamp of approval.

Another strategy for getting by in an evaluation environment is "maintaining a low profile". This strategy, among others, is in response to one or both of two factors, fear of making a mistake, thus harming the patient, and fear of receiving an unfavorable evaluation. D. P. describes the strategy in this way.

> D.P: When I feel that way I try to stay in the woodwork and I'm usually a real outgoing person.   But when I'm afraid of looking like a fool, I try to play it cool, and not draw attention to myself.   When it's really necessary to discuss something with a nurse or a doctor, I do.   But it's like, let the nurses figure it out, you know?

The phenomenon of "learning the tricks" to survive in the academic system is not a newly-discovered phenomenon. Other authors have noted the phenomenon, particularly as occurring in curricula involving a practicum component such as nursing (Oleson & Whitaker, 1968; Reilly, 1974). Each of the above authors describe tricks in terms of students' gamesmanship, and list numerous other exemplars of the phenomenon.

Cognitive Rigidity

Cognitive rigidity is the negative extreme of cognitive flexibility, and was identified as a potential consequence of practice in an evaluation context. "My brain just locks up", "My mind goes completely blank", and "My brain shuts down" are illustrations from the data of the perceived consequences of evaluative questions. T. C. further differentiates an evaluative questioning approach and a learning- centered questioning approach, as reported in the following excerpt.

> T: I feel that everybody needs to have a background, but you know there are some nit-picky things that not everybody needs to know about the patient's disease, especially starting out...
>
> G: So, you're saying ask me about diseases, but help me relate it to...
>
> T: what I'm supposed to be doing as a nurse. Like ...the type of medication that they take, "what exactly does that help them do?" and there's a difference than just saying, "What is this medication?" And it just comes across a lot differently. And I think you learn, instead of just having a definition of what this is, but how it affects the patient.

Attention to details whose relevance to the patient is unclear to the student contributes to cognitive rigidity and to students' subsequent feelings of incompetence. D., a new graduate nurse, discusses her feelings regarding the consequences of evaluative questions.

> D: ...when you're in clinical you want to know what you're doing. And part of it is just the stress of knowing the teacher is evaluating you. And I guess there's just something about being a student, anyway, that made me think sometimes I don't know anything.

With continued practice in a perceived evaluation context, cognitive rigidity may become a permanent part of the nurse's practice. Reliance primarily on the judgment of others is an indicator of such cognitive rigidity and is consistent with an extrinsic motivational orientation. Prescott, Dennis, and Jacox (1987), in their study of 267 nurses from a wide geographic distribution, found that nurses do rely heavily on the judgment of the physician rather than their independent judgment.

LEARNING CONTEXT

Description of a learning context includes learning-centered interactions of students with faculty, connecting strategies that faculty and students use in a learning context, and cognitive flexibility as a consequence of the strategies and interactions employed in a learning context.

Since many of the curricular conditions support an evaluation context, the major conditions identified to support a learning context are learning-centered interactions of students with faculty or with other nurse role models. These interactions are conceptualized as "sticking with the student."

D. T., a new graduate nurse, describes interactions with a teacher that exemplify "sticking with the student".

> G: What would be some characteristics of teachers that would help you learn judgment?

> D: Well, you know, the professor I was talking about earlier, I don't know how she did it, but she just seemed to know when we needed to be pushed and when we needed to be helped. And I couldn't even begin to know how she knew that. But I think part of it was just the fact that she was so involved with us. She wasn't just interested in our learning. She was interested in each of us as a person. Like when we were overwhelmed, she was in tune with that. She wanted to talk about it.

276

In the perception of most informants in the study, an important condition related to "sticking with the student" is a faculty's relating to students as people. Faculty-student relations are manifest not only by formal interactions, but by informal interactions. Students perceive that faculty who are able and willing to engage in social talk with students are more accessible to them for formal educational interactions that impact their learning experiences.

Data from previous research indicates that time faculty spend one-on-one with students is limited. Wang and Blumberg (1983) observed 44 faculty in 20 different clinical settings. These authors concluded that there is not much involvement of students with faculty in actual decision making. One-third of interactions with faculty were less than one minute, and two-thirds of the interactions were less than five minutes in duration. The most frequently observed techniques were either leading questions or information giving. Demonstrations and using hypothetical situations were the least frequently observed interaction techniques.

Sparking

"Sparking" is one of many strategies identified that help the student gain access to resources and knowledge necessary to learn clinical judgment. Sparking is a set of strategies employed by nursing faculty that appears to support cognitive flexibility. Sparking is designed to facilitate students' thinking about patient care alternatives or patient problem identification.

The discussion of evaluation context included a description of specific questions with a right-or-wrong answer that often contribute to cognitive rigidity and to students' perceptions of being evaluated. Faculty use of open-ended questions appears to have different consequences. "What are your thoughts about this patient?" is an example of an open-ended question. Such a question does not imply a right or wrong answer and, therefore, affords the student flexibility for communicating what is known about the patient. It also helps to focus the student on the patient rather than specific pathophysiologic or psychopathologic details. Open-ended questions that elicit students' knowledge of the patient situation can then be followed by more specific questions that help the student zero in on problem solution.

Whereas evaluative interactions with faculty often lead to students' feelings of incompetence, being able to communicate what is known about the patient provides the student with positive competence validation. Competence validation in a learning context provides the student with confidence that independent practice is possible. This confidence impacts students' abilities to practice decision-making. "Indeed, people who believe strongly in their problem-solving capabilities remain highly efficient in their analytic thinking in complex decision-making situations" (Bandura, 1990, p. 321). The following excerpt from T. M., a senior student, illustrates how the nursing faculty assisted the student to connect with the patient's problems.

> T: ...and he had so much anger...and he never would bring it up. He was just trying to let me know how intelligent he was, where his injury was and things like that. And my instructor knew his situation. And she wanted to know if I had gotten him to open up, because I had spent most of the morning just sitting there at the bedside with him. And we weren't really getting anywhere. And I had not identified at that point that he was just intellectualizing.
>
> G: Uh-huh, not dealing with his emotions.
>
> T: Oh, yeah. And she helped me by pointing out, "Do you think he's trying to hide his feelings a little bit...She was really good about talking me through it, and it was a psychological thing and we hadn't dealt much with that. And I don't remember the specific conversation, but she did help me through the way she questioned me. I came to the conclusion that he was intellectualizing and it gave me a little better feeling when I went back into the room. Then I could see it so clearly and I knew how to route the conversation.

G: She didn't really come out and tell you that this person was intellectualizing?

T: And they do that a lot. And I know, especially with her, it was...uh, she's real good about that. She doesn't want to tell you the answers. She wants you to figure it out for yourself.

In the following excerpt, a junior student discusses a staff nurse whom she perceived adept at sparking.

Student: She's great!

Researcher: In what way?

Student: She asks questions.   She gets my brain started. Sometimes when S. (clinical faculty) asks me questions about drugs or something, my brain just shuts down.

"Sparking", as a teaching strategy, is a way to initiate what some authors have termed reflection (Schon, 1983; Tanner, 1990). Reflection is a method for learning from experience.   Each patient encounter is characterized by conflict, uniqueness, and ambiguity (Fox, 1991). By viewing individual patient care as having inherent conflict, uniqueness, and ambiguity, one is able to learn from his or her experience through experimentation.   In a perceived learning context, the student has both a role model for reflective thought and the intrinsic motivation to engage in reflective thought.   In an evaluation context, experimentation through reflection is often thwarted by the threat of evaluation if the student perceives that experimentation resulting in failure will result in an unfavorable evaluation, thus decreasing his or her self-competence perception.   "Those who are plagued by self- doubts are erratic in their analytic thinking" (Bandura, 1990, p. 321).   According to Tanner (1990), reflection gives practitioners the fuel to learn from their practice.

COGNITIVE FLEXIBILITY

As a consequence of practice in a learning context the student develops some degree of cognitive flexibility. Cognitive flexibility is an important skill one uses to apply knowledge.

If one thinks of the driving force for problem-solving as cognitive energy, then maximizing cognitive energy would allow the problem-solver greater power for judgment. It is postulated that focusing exclusively on the potential evaluation consequences of actions decreases one's cognitive energy for independent problem-solving. The greater the level of cognitive energy, the more one is able to gain judgment practice in specific clinical contexts. This practice builds the network of practical knowledge available for clinical judgment. Fredericksen (1984) describes numerous strategies from cognitive psychology reported to be effective in teaching problem-solving. All of these techniques, however, are dependent upon practice with feedback.

Two dimensions of cognitive flexibility were identified, habituation and patient-centeredness. Knowledge is identified as a condition for cognitive flexibility.

> "...theory and principles allow the practitioner safe and efficient access to clinical learning, provide the background knowledge that enables the clinician to ask the right questions and look for the correct problems. The person with limited background knowledge will lack the tools needed to learn from experience." (Benner, 1984; p. 184).

Informants who were seniors or new graduates, when asked, "What is the most important difference in where you are now and where you were as a first-semester junior in your judgment ability?", stated that knowledge was the primary difference.

The amount of knowledge one possesses is obviously not a static condition. Knowledge acquisition is an example of shifting conditions that impact the context within which the student operates.

Habituation is the first of two dimensions of cognitive flexibility. Habituation may be defined as routinization of the cognitive and/or psychomotor processes required for specific skills. The more one has developed required skills into habits, the more cognitive flexibility one possesses. Without some degree of habituation, the individual's short-term memory is constantly crowded with details.

> P (Last semester senior): ...I will be glad when those things get to be habits, when it's a habit to know how to hang an IV or start an IV, because what I'm having to do with that stuff is make it a habit. It's nothing more than learning how to do something. You have to do a certain amount of thinking about it, but it's not analytical thinking. What you do with the patient is analytical thinking, and that's a different kind of habit than just going in and knowing how to hang a medication...but practicing the skills increases confidence. Confidence relates to how you feel about yourself as a person and a nurse. If you don't feel that you are capable, you're gonna be insecure.

One condition for habituation is work experience, as this senior nursing student who had worked as a nurse extern reports:

> D: I think it helped give me a lot more confidence before I started my senior year, just because I got used to working with patients on a daily basis, just doing basic nursing tasks, just got used to being in the atmosphere and watching what the nurses did, dealing with the hospital routine, checking orders, talking with doctors. I kind of got accustomed to it.

Students place a great deal of importance on technical proficiency. A part of the student's identity as a competent nurse is dependent upon a self-perception of technical competence. This self-perception of technical competence is validated when others, especially nursing faculty, communicate their perceptions of the student's technical competence.

281

Students' perceptions of technical competence enhance their confidence to practice judgment. Cohen and Jordet (1988) studied the relationship between faculty's and students' role identities in baccalaureate nursing programs. Twenty-three faculty and 324 students from different levels were included. Many of the students reported that their nurse aide experiences provided them more confidence, particularly in psychomotor skills, allowing them to "develop their cognitive skills during faculty-guided clinical experiences" (p. 40). As the student's repertoire of technical skills becomes habituated, this technical habituation also contributes to the amount of cognitive energy available for performing problem solving, since performance of habituated skills no longer requires acute attention to each and every detail of the skill.

Patient-centeredness is the other dimension of cognitive flexibility. If clinical judgment is defined ultimately as knowing what to do for the patient, then a sensitivity to the patient and his concerns seems integral to the nurse's ability to make clinical judgments. Students' concentrating exclusively on activities to meet evaluation contingencies can be viewed as the negative extreme of patient centeredness. That is, if students expend their cognitive energy deliberating about how they will make the grade, limited energy is available for contemplating alternatives for patient care during the clinical practicum. In an evaluation context the patient is not the basis for decisions that the student makes regarding patient care and educational activities. Potential evaluation consequences are the primary bases for these decisions.

There are also data indicating that the student's self-evaluation of technical competence impact the student's ability to be centered on the patient, as indicated by the following excerpt from the interview with A. B., a new graduate nurse.

> A.B.: We really didn't do anything. The first semester, we couldn't give meds. So what you learned was how to make a bed, how to give a bath, psychosocial, how to talk with the patient, how to ask open-ended questions, more stuff like that. We really didn't do anything technical.

Ryan (1982) in a study involving 128 college students enrolled in introductory psychology, found that controlling feedback, such as evaluation, may be intrapersonal as well as interpersonal. Controlling intrapersonal feedback involves the individual's view of what she or he <u>should</u> be able to do.

T. C., in her second interview of the current study, reports the following information regarding nursing students' perceptions of intrapersonal performance expectations.

> T: You do your best, or your worst, however you feel you're doing or what level you're at. And it's like people who feel they're on a C level, it seems like that's as hard as they work, is just to get that grade, as a C, as opposed to those who expect an A. And they put in that little extra. And it's all grade-oriented. From kindergarten on up, we've all been focused on that, I guess.

The student may be focused on self and what the student feels she or he should be doing to maintain a self-identify as a competent nurse through "making the grade", or the student may be focused on the patient and what he or she needs to do to learn patient-centered nursing care. Patient-centeredness may be conceptualized as a continuum. The more the student is focused on the patient, the greater the degree of cognitive flexibility the student possesses, and the greater the degree of cognitive energy is available for practicing patient problem solution.

SUMMARY

The theoretical model proposed herein is tentative and awaits further investigation. Since relationships among the concepts are based on students' perceptions, however, the model is potentially applicable to a variety of educational situations, given further testing and refinement.

It is proposed that current models of student evaluation have potentially negative consequences on students' abilities to learn self-direction and problem-solving skills. When students focus their energies exclusively on meeting evaluation contingencies, limited cognitive energy is available for practicing problem-solving and learning to apply theoretical knowledge.

It appears that, even given current models of evaluation, learning-centered interactions of faculty or other role models with students can support students' intrinsically-motivated efforts to learn from their experiences. These learning-centered interactions are based on an understanding of the way students perceive the context of education. Through reflective interactions with trusted role models, students can learn to independently identify the information necessary to solve problems, and thus to be self-directed in learning from their experiences.

REFERENCES

Bandura, A. (1990). Conclusion: Reflections on nonability determinants of competence. In R. J. Sternberg & J. Kolligian, Jr. (Eds.), Competence considered (pp. 315-362). New Haven, Conn: Yale University Press.

Benner, P. (1984). From novice to expert: Excellence and power in clinical nursing practice. Menlo Park, CA: Addison Wesley Publishing Co.

Benware, C. A. & Deci, E. L. (1984). Quality of learning with an active versus passive motivational set. American Educational Research Journal, 21, 755-765.

Chase, W. G. & Chi, M. T. (1980). Cognitive skill: Implications for spatial skill in large-scale environments. In J. Harvey (Ed.), Cognition, social behavior, and the environment. Potomac, MD: Erlbaum.

Cohen, B. J. & Jordet, C. P. (1988). Nursing schools: Students' beacon to professionalism. Nursing and Health Care, 7, 149-154.

Deci, E. L. & Ryan, R.M. (1985). Intrinsic motivation and self-determination in human behavior. New York: Plenum Press.

Deci, E. L. & Ryan, R. M. (1987). The support of autonomy and the control of behavior. Journal of Personality and Social Psychology, 53, 1024-1037.

Elstein, A. S., Shulman, L. S., Ravitch, M. M., Rovner, D. R., Holzman, G. B., & Rothert, M. L. (1983). Medical decisions in perspective: Applied research in cognitive psychology. Perspectives in Biology and Medicine, 26, 486-500.

Enzle, M. A. & Ross, J. M. (1978). Increasing and decreasing intrinsic interest with contingent rewards: A test of cognitive evaluation theory. Journal of Experimental Social Psychology, 14, 588-597.

Fox, R. (1991, January). Teaching and learning in the clinical setting. Paper presented to the Oklahoma Geriatric Education Center, Oklahoma City: University of Oklahoma Health Sciences Center.

Fredericksen, N. (1984). Implications of cognitive theory for instruction in problem solving. Review of Educational Research, 54, 363-407.

Grolnick, W. S. & Ryan, R. M. (1987). Autonomy in children's learning: An experimental and individual difference investigation. Journal of Personality and Social Psychology, 52, 890-898.

Harckiewicz, J. M., Abrahams, S., & Wageman, R. (1987). Performance evaluation and intrinsic motivation: The effects of evaluative focus, rewards, and achievement orientation. Journal of Personality and Social Psychology, 53, 1015-1023.

Loving, G. L. (1991). Nursing students' perceptions of learning clinical judgment in undergraduate nursing education. Unpublished doctoral dissertation, Austin: The University of Texas at Austin.

Oleson, V. L. & Whitaker, E. W. (1968). The silent dialogue: A study in the social psychology of professional socialization. San Francisco: Jossey-Bass.

Prescott, P. A., Dennis, K. E., & Jacox, A. K. (1987). Clinical decision making of staff nurses. Image: The Journal of Nursing Scholarship, 19(2), 56-62.

Reilly, D. E. (1974, April) Evaluation and grading: Are they compatible? Paper presented at the meeting of the EACT Section of the Oklahoma Nurses Association, Tulsa, April, 1974.

Ryan, R. M. (1982). Control and information in the intrapersonal sphere: An extension of cognitive evaluation theory. Journal of Personality and Social Psychology, 43, 450-461.

Sarason, I. G. & Stoops, R. (1984). Stress, anxiety and cognitive interference: Reactions to tests. Journal of Personality and Social Psychology, 46, 929-938.

Schon, D. (1983). The reflective practitioner. New York: Basic Books, Inc.

Simon, H. (1980). Problem-solving and education. In D. T. Tuma and F. Reif (Eds.), <u>Problem solving and education: Issues in teaching and research</u>. Hillsdale, NJ: Erlbaum.

Strauss, A. & Corbin, J. (1990). <u>Basics of qualitative research: Grounded theory procedures and techniques</u>. Newbury Park, CA: Sage.

Tanner, C. A. (1990, July). Clinical nursing judgment. Laverne Gallman Lecture, Austin, TX: The University of Texas at Austin School of Nursing, Austin, Texas.

Wang, A. M. & Blumberg, P. (1983). A study on the interaction techniques of nursing faculty in the clinical area. <u>Journal of Nursing Education</u>, 22, 144-151.

CHAPTER SEVENTEEN

EVALUATION AND SELF-DIRECTED LEARNING

Sara M. Steele

There is a growing interest among adult educators in forms of education that empower people and help them to continue to learn on their own. The ability to evaluate appears to be an essential skill both in being able to learn through self-direction and in being able to cope with the world around them. How can an independent learner evaluate learning? I started thinking about evaluation as a tool for learners after attending the Fourth international Self-Directed Learning Symposium in 1990. I'm an evaluation specialist who has focused on program evaluation for more than twenty years, but I have only recently begun to look seriously at self-directed learning. Within self-directed learning, my interest lies with the autonomous learner who takes complete control both of content and of sources of learning. (Steele, 1991)

In developing this chapter, I found that I had to look at both evaluation and learning in new ways. The evaluation literature I had studied or scanned over the years had very little to contribute. The first leg of my journey in exploring the kind of evaluation that would fit autonomous independent learners involved critically examining current concepts in terms of their value to the independent learner. This chapter presents the results of that analysis.

1. **Most of the current literature on evaluation is written to meet the needs of institutions, program funders, or teachers, rather than learners.**

Think about the last five things you've read about evaluation. Millions of words have been written about the nature of evaluation and how it should be done. Little of it considers the learner's perspective. The literature is designed either to help a teacher seeking information useful in grading or revising teaching strategies, to help administrators seeking to account for funds and develop institutional image, or to help major funders interested in policy formation and validation. The questions addressed by most evaluation and the methods of conducting evaluations are the questions and methods most useful to the professionals involved. The professional's perspective controls how we think about evaluation. It is very hard for us as educators or administrators to step away from our past training and view it from an individual learner's perspective. If you wipe out the agency's needs (carrying out mission, attaining objectives, meeting accreditation standards) you wipe out most of the content of evaluation.

2. **Criteria for what constitutes "successful/good" learning is set by agencies and professionals, not by the learner.**

Success is usually defined in terms of what the professional or agency believes is "good" and what professionals believe should result. Teachers set goals that learners are to attain. Success/good is judged in relation to the teacher/leader and the agency's mission and goals. Learners, on the other hand, may be concerned about how what they learn fits their life situations as well as what they have gained. Learners may use criteria such as relevant, stimulating, applicable, practical, and satisfying, as they examine learning experiences. The autonomous learner is free from the criteria and judgments fostered by agencies, and has to establish his or her own concept of what constitutes good learning and what constitutes success. Unless we have been able to "decondition" learners from our criteria and to help them formulate their own, the highly schooled individual may be like a person using a video game without any idea of the how the game is played. The action is fast, but incomprehensible.

3. In much of the literature and our professional preparation, evaluation is viewed as formal studies.

A Phi Delta Kappa evaluation committee once defined evaluation as a process of collecting and organizing information for decision makers (PDK, 1971). Most of us read tests, surveys, and statistical analysis into that description. Adult learners, however, can't conduct a survey every time they want to evaluate their own learning. They must rely on their own judgment. For them, evaluation is primarily an internal thinking process. Informal, reflective evaluation is seldom discussed in evaluation literature. In fact, the role of thinking in evaluation is ignored even in literature designed for professionals (Steele, in press).

This internal process of evaluation of one's own learning requires awareness, discernment, and judgment. It requires both critical thinking and the creative thinking that is visionary to see how the learning can be used in the future. It comes about through reflecting, perceiving, summarizing and challenging. In other words, a process designed to help individuals evaluate learning has to help them understand and use a variety of mental skills.

4. The prevailing concept focuses on one specific learning opportunity and what is learned at one time.

Most evaluation focuses on a program or what is learned from a specific unit of instruction over a specified period of time. The unit of instruction could be a non-credit seminar, educational media production, or a class. From the standpoint of the agency and teacher, programs start at a certain time, have a certain focus, and end at a certain time.

Learners, on the other hand, accumulate knowledge, skills, and attitudes about a subject from a variety of learning opportunities over a period of years. Understanding, attitudes, abilities, and skills develop over time, rather than being absorbed within the time boundaries of one experience. It may be hard for learners to separate the effects of one experience (for example, class) from other experiences (books, television, discussions). A learner-centered concept of evaluation has to let (help) a specific opportunity take its place among other sources from which the learner accumulates learning. Program evaluation often assumes that learners are empty jugs when they enter the program and, that by the time they leave the program, they have enough in their jugs to last a lifetime.

Learning involves going from awareness to use. Sometimes this occurs almost instantaneous when the light dawns and you use the insight to frame a new question. Sometimes it takes months or years for the "picture" to come together. For example, I first became aware of the potential difference between positivistic approaches and phenomenological approaches eight years ago, but the terms lacked relevance for me. I sluffed them off. I became more interested when I found that qualitative research accepted different perceptions of reality. Last year I was fascinated by exploring literature that outlined the history of different approaches to knowledge. As an autonomous learner my movement from awareness to use in thinking (and in class) was slow.

5. The prevailing literature concentrates on results or program quality. Little attention is given to examining the value of the program.

Only Scriven (Shadish et. al, 1991), Guba and Lincoln (1989) and a few other authors are willing to put a valuing component in evaluation. Administrators and policy makers, for whom much of program evaluation is done, want proof of accomplishment. Professional evaluators who are trained as researchers have been conditioned to avoid value judgments. Thus, there is little in the literature which helps us deal with the process of valuing. It is probable, however, that learners are more interested in securing value in learning than they are expectant of specific results. They do not begin or they rapidly abandon a learning situation where they cannot detect value. The TV program is turned off. The book is put down. The discussion with the expert is switched to a different subject.

6. Learners may conceive of learning differently than do teachers.

Learning has both an external and an internal component. For learners who work with a teacher, the external component might be called the **"receiving"** phase. However, for self-directed learners the external component might best be called the **"securing"** phase. It is the activity through which a person absorbs information, ideas, directions, from an outside source (teacher, book), and takes them into the mind. During the receiving/securing process, the learner functions as a recorder, simply making a record of what is seen or heard.

I call the internal component the **"knowing"** or **integrating** phase. It includes the thinking processes through which the person deals with what has been taken in, sorting it for value, and integrating it into what he or she already believes.

The third phase is the **"using"** phase which may have an internal and/or external application. The new material can be used internally in thinking or externally in communication or action. Often, learning is increased as the individual uses what is already known.

Some adult education experts seem to assign the term "learning" primarily to the "receiving/securing" part of the process. They want to be sure what they are teaching enters the mind of the learner. Some de-emphasize the thinking component because it is almost impossible to know what is going on in the minds of the learners. On the other hand, many learners are most interested in the "knowing" stage or the extent to which that which is received helps them think. For many, learning isn't recognized until they have processed it and feel in control of what they know.

7. Learners may be aware of a broader range of valuable results than are teachers.

Results are the specific gains and losses that accrue from taking part in programs or other learning experiences. Teachers see results in terms of what they want to help occur. Some years ago, the scope of educational evaluation was so narrow that it was defined as measuring the extent to which objectives were attained. Certainly, that is too narrow a definition of the evaluation that is useful to learners. On the other hand, participants may see those outcomes in terms of what all of the participation has contributed, including contacts made and what they have learned from other participants.

As one builds a framework from a learner's perspective, it is tempting to transfer the professional's view of evaluation into the learner framework. If that is done, the focus of results would be on whether the participant met his or her own objectives. Certainly whether the purpose for taking part in the program or using the media resource was met is a part of what should be examined by learners. But, if you remember Houle's (1961) exploration of major reasons why people take part in educational programs, you will recall that not all participants have specific goals in mind. Some come with only a general interest. Some come for social reasons, rather than the content of the program. It is possible that those who have no goals or no expectations can still gain a lot from learning opportunities which they select either on general interest, social, or professional reasons. As we examine our own experiences, we probably find that some of the most valuable learnings have been those we didn't expect or seek. For example, I had no clear expectations or goals, either in attending the 1990 annual conference of the American Association for Adult and Continuing Education at Salt Lake City or in attending a specific session, and, yet, the accumulation of ideas from various presentations is very valuable in relation to this paper.

A learner can gain much more from a program than from the teacher's intent. He or she may gain from the other participants. Huey Long (1990) uses a framework that asks students to look at results from a class in three categories: 1) results specific to the objectives of the course 2) auxiliary results, things coming up in the class situation that are in addition to the intent of the class, and 3) what one has learned about oneself or others through participating. It seems much more logical to consider a broad spectrum of areas where learners may secure gains and/or experience losses than to look only at the intent of the program. I found Long's approach very useful and will append an example of my work in adapting it as a tool to help the students to become more independent in evaluating their own learning.

8.   Learners may be aware of losses as well as gains.

Learners may have losses in relation to a learning experience which teachers are not likely to be aware of or may ignore in program evaluation as carried out by teachers or professional evaluators.   I am so conditioned to education as having positive outcomes that I find it difficult to imagine what the losses or negative outcomes may be.   Misinformation is certainly one kind of loss.

Cluttering one's mind with irrelevant details might be another. Many of the examples of losses that come to mind deal with feelings about self and emotional reaction to that which is being learned. The experience might cause a person to loose confidence in what he or she already knows or in his or her ability. The experience might arouse strong negative emotions. For example, one may learn math, but hate to do math. Or, one may learn to use a big city library, but see it as an untouchable resource because of fear of getting lost in it.

9. Learners may recognize other results than those recognized by teachers and evaluators.

In order to determine what results have occurred, the learner has to have a meaningful framework. Professional educators and evaluators use a variety of frameworks. One that is often used in my field is a hierarchy which includes specific learning or KASA, practice adoption, and end results. Within specific learning, we look for gains in **Knowledge, Attitudes, Skills, and Aspirations.** Beyond specific learning, we look for changes in use **of practices** and **overall performance.** This framework was developed by Claude Bennett (1975) for the Cooperative Extension Service. It was based originally on the work of Don Kirkpatrick in training in business and industry. Some years ago, college experts made the distinction between **cognitive learning (ability to secure and use information) and affective learning (learning dealing with the emotions, values, interests, attitudes).** (Bloom, 1956) Some adult educators are concerned with broad areas of **physical, mental, and social development,** but, in general, adult educators seem to focus more on specific learning than such development. However, we may be moving into a new era. Employers today say that they are looking for broad abilities I would class as development -- abilities such as, leadership ability, the ability to solve problems, and the ability to get along with others even under trying circumstances. Learners need to be concerned about broad areas of development to which specific learning makes contributions.

What kinds of outcomes and relationship among outcomes do learners see? Often, when program people evaluate, they assume that learning is acquiring something new and do not consider other kinds of results. For the learner, however, results and value may occur even if the content is not new. The first time that one hears something which is very new, **awareness** may occur. Then, the learner begins to collect "pieces" and to put them together until full **understanding** occurs. Thus, in addition to receiving new information, the learner supplements what he or she already knows through taking part in a learning experience. He or she can **correct errors** by comparing what he or she already knows to what is presented by the expert, gain **greater understanding (comprehension of how things fit together)** or **greater insight (deeper penetration)**.

In relation to the affective area, the learner can become **more tolerant** of a different attitude, or can come to **understand** better why he or she **values** what he does. Perhaps, in all three areas (cognitive, affective, and practice usage), the layers of learning may start with awareness; move on to constructing an adequate picture; trying out the new knowledge, attitude or practice; and, then **improving** that knowledge, attitude or practice, as time goes along.

In some instances, the greatest contribution from a learning experience may be that of catapulting the learner into new use of what he or she already knows. When a particular attitude or skill is difficult, value can come from a learning experience which **reinforces one's commitment**. Such a gain may not show any change in practice, but it prevents an erosion of performance. In other instances, the learning experience may trigger a greater understanding which results in a transformative experience.

There is evidence to show that even learners in teacher-guided programs recognize gains in addition to new knowledge. For example, seventy-two participants in a program on parenting teens were asked to indicate gains they had received from a list provided in the questionnaire. The numbers and choices indicated are as follows: 48, better understanding; 44, new ideas; 42, reinforcement and reassurance that we are on right course; 41, feeling of support from meeting with other parents; 34, desire to change or try something suggested; 29, more awareness of local resources; 23, new questions; 26, awareness of symptoms of problems; 4, help with a specific problem. (Steele, 1991a)

In another attempt to see gains and results from the participants' standpoint, 75 farmers responded to a check list related to a dairy feeding program. The responses and items were as follows: 44, a challenge to think about some aspect of my feeding program; 43, reinforcement for what I already knew; 36, better understanding of something I already knew or was doing; 17, new information about feeding; 19, new ideas that I will try; 3, an answer to a question or solution to a problem; and 2, nothing much that seemed valuable to me. Neither survey asked respondents to indicate which of the kinds of gains were most valuable to them. (Steele, 1991b)

Some learners are not able to articulate the kinds of results and value they see from learning. Some think only in terms of the frameworks to which teachers have conditioned them. As teachers, we can help students to establish broader frameworks for assessing the value of what they learn.

10. Learners may define quality in results differently than do program personnel.

Examining results requires much more than determining what results have occurred.

There are other decisions. For example, was what the learner abstracted from the experience **accurate?** One of the most worrisome areas for teachers, with regard to encouraging people to learn on their own, is the question of whether they retain accurate information.

Did the learner go far enough in exploring the topic and in what he or she abstracted from the experience? In other words, were the results **sufficient?**. Sufficiency may have two dimensions: sufficient for this point in time and sufficient in the long run. Evaluation from the teacher's standpoint usually focuses on sufficient for the time spent in this program. From the learner's standpoint, it is more likely to be "sufficient for what I need to know."

A third question, which professional educators sometimes ignore, is, "Were the results **appropriate** for this learner in this life situation?" A learner is more likely to judge appropriateness than is the teacher. Learners often are more aware of changing times. Teachers often teach what their teachers taught them. Sometimes, this content and emphasis was developed under the guidance of experts who wrote or taught for a society fifty years previously. For example, now that the writing of John Dewey is fitting the needs of the

1990's, I am aware that, although I never studied his teaching, many of my undergraduate professors in the early 1950s carried out his principles. As a result, I carried a good deal of the Dewey approach to teaching with me through the Tylerian era.

Perhaps the greatest difference between evaluating learning from a traditional standpoint and from a self-directed learning standpoint, is **how** one defines that <u>enough</u>, <u>appropriate</u>, <u>accurate</u> learning has occurred. In traditional forms of evaluation, the teacher, agency, or professional evaluator does that defining. The amount, kind, and accuracy of learning is compared with what was actually taught or with the teacher's objectives. In autonomous learning, there isn't the "solidness" of an expert's set of objectives or teaching plan to evaluate against.

When learners take control and pull together information from a variety of sources without relying on one expert source, they have to find their own way of checking the quality of the learning. Autonomous learners are faced with choices: "swallow the content whole," relying on the source to be accurate and appropriate, or make their own decisions about the quality of their learning. Some function as sponges, not trying to decide what to keep or what to let go, but soaking up what they can from "expert" sources. If their minds can only hold part of the content, the part that stays is by chance rather than by choice. Some are "knowledge misers" who accumulate just as many pieces of information as they can about the topic without considering what is most important. Some forms of K-12 and college teaching lead people to accept docilely and try to retain anything said/written/demonstrated by an "expert." Traditional forms of testing, which randomly sample learning rather than focusing on the most important points, tend to reinforce this approach.

It is likely that the most alert of autonomous learners (even those who employ self-direction even within teacher dominated activities) use **validation** rather than evaluation. They test the accuracy and sufficiency of what they already know against an expert source. They may use a variety of means of validation. Some listen to or read an expert in order to validate what they already know. In part, that explains why we often find that many of the people who come to non-credit courses already know a lot about the subject. They are seeking validation of what they have previously pulled together rather than seeking new information. Some use informal **triangulation** to see if they understand the same thing when they use two or more sources. Some use **discussion** to compare their understandings with those of another non-expert whom they trust.

These forms of validation help the self-directed learner to deal with questions of accuracy, sufficiency, and appropriateness of understanding. For example, have you ever turned to someone you consider well versed in a field and asked, "What out of all of this stuff do I really need to know?" to check that you have indeed been able to prioritize and decide what is most important?

When you listen to informal discussions on the part of program participants, you may find a learner who sets forth his or her interpretation of a particular point in a tentative way with the hope that others will either validate or challenge the statement. (Perhaps that is the real purpose of discussion sections. Unfortunately, teacher's sometimes turn such sessions into question and answer periods rather than using them as a time for students to validate their interpretations).

11. The Value of learning may take many forms for the learner.

A program's value is the worth of the participation and results to: 1) the participant; 2) others, employer, coworkers, family, friends, affected by the participant; and/or 3) the community and the broader society. When results affect others the overall value from the specific learning can increase. The response to the question, "What good did it do?" is a way of approaching value. For example, because a learner learned about nutrition and became more committed to planning family food intake based upon the dietary_guidelines for Americans, the health of family members was protected. Or, as another example, adults who learn about recycling and diligently recycle, not only show a specific behavior change, but are doing something valuable for society.

We are aware that learning can be used to achieve value in a variety of spheres of our lives. For example, learning can provide **economic value** through increasing the salary we earn or through helping us invest it wisely. Learning can provide **political value** when we can use it in power struggles. It can provide **social value** when it helps us as we relate to other people. It can provide **aesthetic value** when we take pleasure from what we have learned.

There is **personal value and social value** from most learning. Often, learners are most conscious of the personal value; the social value is serendipitous. However, for those who take "causes" seriously, learning is more often directed to social value rather than personal value. For example, a person committed to peace is involved, in part, for self protection, but is more likely to be involved in peace for society. If one is only interested in personal peace, the content explored would be much more limited than are the areas explored by "peace for society" advocates.

Personal value has the dimensions of **"value in external use"** and **"value in internal use"**. Value in external use comes about when the person can fit what is taken in into conversation or action. Value in internal use comes from the satisfaction of knowing. Value in internal use also occurs with "taking out" a bit of knowledge and thinking about it. For example, few people who read poems use them in conversation. Many simply store them away and savor the beauty of the words or ideas that are expressed. The words are like a bright bauble we keep on our desk to rest and refresh us. Or, as another example, some sports fans know the highest scoring batters of each year since 1930. Sports broadcasters use this information externally in their work. Sports fans, who are in contact with other fans, may use it in one-upsmanship games. But most sports fans do not live with other sports fans. Spouses become bored with this kind of information, so the value becomes internal.

"Enough" and "appropriateness" of results are intertwined with value for those learners who take control and are self-directed.

12. Self-directedness is dependent upon being willing to take responsibility for determining what is valuable learning.

In traditional methods, the expert determines what is valuable and what results should be secured. When learners subject themselves to a teacher, the formal decisions about selecting the "most" valuable content rests with the teacher and the question of value is seldom raised by the teacher or agency during evaluation. Learners on the other hand, sometimes will say, "That sure was a waste of time."

Contract learning and other teaching strategies, which permit some degree of student choice, can open up value for negotiation between the student and teacher. Often, self-directed learning, as it applies within college courses, permits the student to spend more time on some topics than others if the learner feels they will be more valuable, recognizes a greater personal need, or is more interested. The teacher-student negotiation may or may not continue as far as a negotiation of what within the topic is most important to be retained. For example, an English Literature teacher might permit students to choose the poet, but expect the student to make the same interpretation as the teacher.

In autonomous learning (the learner in complete control of both content and method), the learner has to define what is valuable and take the consequences of misjudging value. The ability to take responsibility for identifying what is valuable probably is a deciding factor in the extent to which a person is able to be a deliberate self-directed learner.

Some identify the amount and content of learning in a very rational manner. They are able to translate needs and cues from their environment into specific questions, problems, a desired skill, or a topical outline, and are then able to decide whether they have answered the questions, solved the problems, mastered the skill or covered the gaps in their mental outline. When they are satisfied that they have answered the questions, solved the problem, or filled in the outline, they are satisfied that they have "learned what I need right now." They are able to define, start, and stop out of learning.

Some succeed in doing so intuitively. "I feel that I should explore this topic further." "There is something missing, I haven't learned enough." "It's strange, I have a hunch that by reading more about X, I will better understand Y." "I've had all I can deal with. I'm putting it aside." Some use a trial and error method.

Some may be so sure that there is one right answer to be found that they don't trust their own judgment. It may be very difficult for a narrow positivist (one who believes in research based information and that there is always one perspective that is more correct than another) ever to be good at self-directed teaching or to be a confident self-directed learner. Such a teacher is uneasy that the "right" and the "best" will be lost sight of as the learner pursues his or her own interests. A narrow positiviticaly trained learner will be uneasy that he or she is choosing the right material.

On the other hand, when free of charisma or social force, we tend to try to retain and use that which we feel will be most useful to us or that which internally will give us the most satisfaction and pleasure. Sometimes, we consciously sort through what we hear and make an effort to retain certain things. ("Oh, I must remember that.") Sometimes, our minds do it for us without our being conscious of deliberately trying to remember or act upon certain things we learn.

It is possible that "appropriate results" and "value" are more closely related in self-directed learning than in teacher-controlled learning. The learner who is really self-directed will choose direction and will guide receiving and retention based upon his or her perception of what is relevant, interesting, and be useful. Sometimes, the perception of value is based upon interest or need within the current context. Sometimes, it is based on a guess of what will be of value in the future.

13. Context may be an important factor for learners.

When we look at context, as teachers, we often focus on the teaching and learning environment. Those aspects of context are important. But, there are other elements of context that affect the amount of results and value secured by the learner. Currently, I am using three categories of context--**the securing context, the knowing context**, and the **using context** -- but those categories may change.

The **securing context** deals with the reasons and conditions under which the learner took part in a learning experience. Was it purposeful or accidental? That is to say, did the learner have specific questions, problems, or objectives in using the learning experience or did he go out of general interest or for the social connections that could be made. Did the learner attempt to learn only for his own use or for the benefit of someone else? Experience with "train the trainer" has shown that those who know they are responsible for teaching others attend more closely and work harder at learning than those who are only learning for their own benefit.

The receiving context also includes the physical and mental states as a person takes part in the experience. Is she feeling good? Is he able to concentrate his full attention or is he distracted? Some of the learning style inventories seem to be primarily concerned with the learners' preference for certain ways of receiving.

The **"knowing"** context, on the oth1er hand, deals with basic orientation toward relating to an expert, preferred way of processing information, and the extent to which the individual expects to **think** in the process of coming to know. The person who is conditioned to try to absorb and to accept everything that an expert says will recognize different gains and losses and value different things than does the person who is conditioned to think for him or herself and is perfectly willing to challenge an expert. Some of the aspects of Kolb's learning styles concerning how one prefers to process information--(actively or passively), are part of this dimension of context.

The **"using"** context deals with motivation, tacit knowledge (a term for the ability to size up and adapt to a specific environment), and the ability to recognize and deal with barriers and identify and use enhancers (Lewin's force field analysis).

Although I am not going to take time to develop the idea of the effect of context on the learner's evaluation of his or her own learning, I will point out that context is extremely important both in understanding why a learner recognizes some gains or losses and fails to recognize others, and in judging the accuracy and appropriateness of the learning.

CONCLUSIONS

My attempt to see the nature of evaluation that is useful to the autonomous learner is just beginning. Much of the view from the learner's position that I have sketched is speculative. It is difficult to wipe out all the conditioning about evaluation which I've garnered over the years as a professional and try to start fresh by seeing the evaluation of learning from the perspective of the learner outside of the constraints of a teacher or agency.

I've touched briefly on several areas where there might be differences between a learner's view of the world and our professional educator views. Stepping back from those comments, there are six major ideas that come from this exploration.

1. Self-directed learners have to find their own way of validating the accuracy of what they learn.

2. Self-direction involves the ability to evaluate in the sense of making decisions about potential value of exploring (trying to learn) more about something. In other words, the self-directed person has to rely on self rather than on others to establish the appropriateness of the exploration and when enough has been learned.

3. Self-direction involves the ability to make decisions about what to retain and integrate into one's belief structure.

4. Decisions about value are an integral part of learning rather than something that is examined after the fact.

5. If we, as educators, want to help others to perfect their ability to evaluate their own learning, we will need to see learning from their perspective, rather than from the perspective of professional educators.

6. If we believe in empowering people to be continuing learners, we must be able to help them to develop the ability to evaluate their own learning, rather than making them dependent upon our judgment.

This is a small beginning at this kind of exploration. I hope you will take it further.

REFERENCES

Bennett, C., (1975). Up the hierarchy. Journal of Extension, Volume 13, 7-12.

Bloom, B.S. (1956) Taxonomy of educational objectives handbook II: Cognitive domain. New York: David McKay Company, Inc.

Guba, E. G. & Lincoln, Y. S. (1989) Fourth-generation evaluation. Newbury Park: Sage Publications.

Houle, C. E. (1961). The inquiring mind. Madison: WI: The University of Wisconsin Press.

Krathwohl D., Bloom, B. Masia, B. (1956) Taxonomy of educational objectives handbook II: Affective domain. New York: David McKay Company, Inc.

Long, H.B. (1990). A holistic tool for evaluation. Presentation at AAACE, Salt Lake City.

PDK National Study Committee on Evaluation. (1971). Educational evaluation and decision making. Itasca: F. E. Peacock Publishers, Inc.

Shadish, W R., Jr., Cook, T., and Leviton, L.. (1991). Foundations of program evaluation. Newbury Park: Sage Publications.

Steele, S.M. (1991). Reflection on a personal self-directed, independent learning activity. In H.B. Long and Associates, <u>Self-directed learning: concensus & conflict</u>. Oklahoma Research Center for Continuing Professional and Higher Education of the University of Oklahoma.

Steele, S. M. (1991a). <u>Dairy producers' reactions to dairy live</u>. Department of Continuing and Vocational Education, University of Wisconsin - Madison

Steele, S.M. (1991b). Preliminary findings from parenting teens satellite programs. Department of Continuing and Vocational Education, University of Wisconsin - Madison

Steele, S.M. (in press). <u>The roles of thinking in program evaluation</u>. The Netherlands: Kluwer Academic Publishers.

ADDENDUM

As I worked on the first draft of this paper, I also worked on a tool that might help participants in teacher-led learning experiences examine what they value. I adopted Long's tool and added questions which might help people better explore 1) the value of what they learned and 2) reasons why they valued some things and not others. The first draft was 25 pages long and, as such, was not workable.

I cut the first tool down to two sheets and included it at the end of chapters in class notes this semester. I gave students very little explanation to see what they could do with it on their own. They were expected to hand in four analyses. Ten weeks later, I asked them to indicate the usefulness of the tool. The responses were as follows: 1, not useful, 12, somewhat useful, 6, quite a bit of use, and 2, very useful. When I use it next year, I will explain its purpose and see if responses differ.

I have revised the tool slightly and reduced the tool to one page by taking out space for written responses and expecting people to use their own paper. (Preset forms are annoying to people who use a word processor and to those who want to write more than the space permits.) If you are interested in testing it, try to complete it based upon this chapter. If it has merit, feel free to adapt and experiment with it or develop other tools for helping learners to understand what they value and why they value what they do. This can be a step toward helping them improve their independent evaluations.

WHAT DID YOU GAIN?

Think about the material you have just read. On a separate sheet of paper, jot down the most important things you gained from the reading/presentation or things that negatively affected you in each of the following categories. DO NOT OUTLINE THE MATERIAL. ONLY JOT DOWN THINGS OF VALUE TO YOU

1. FOCUS OF MATERIAL List gains or losses directly from the content.

2. AUXILIARY AREAS List other ideas which were serendipitous or only loosely related learning. For example, if something triggered an valuable idea about some other related topic.

3. ABOUT YOURSELF As we learn, sometimes, we gain more understanding of what we believe or how we think.

4. QUESTIONS STILL TO BE EXPLORED OR RESOLVED. Few explorations are complete within themselves. Most have loose ends which can lead to further learning.

Understanding What You Value. Go over your responses. Can you find any patterns in what you selected as valuable? Go through and categorize the items you listed in the first three areas using the questions below. After you categorize them, look to see whether certain kinds of gains predominate.

1. Were the items you listed facts? questions? theories? concepts? practical suggestions?
2. Do they provide knowledge? attitudes? values? directions for doing something--if so, was it physical, social, or mental activities?
3. Indicate the kind of contribution each point made for you. Here are some examples of kinds of contributions.
   Examples of Gains
   - completely new information
   - new additions to what you already knew
   - greater understanding

- greater insight
- how something fits together into a greater unit
- inspiration or motivation to use what you already knew
- ideas which helped you overcome barriers to using what you already knew
- a challenge to think about something

Losses
- lack of confidence
- confusion
- overwhelmed
- angered

4. Is the value mostly for yourself? Or mostly in terms of how you could use it to help others?
5. How great was the value?

Understanding Factors Which Affect What You Value. Explore why you have selected some parts of the learning as more valuable than others. Here are a few factors which can affect learning.

1. Intensity of the experience for you. __ mild
__moderate __ heavy
2. What was your general learning stance when you took part in the activity? (open? indifferent? resistant?; tired? fresh?; concentrated? distracted?)
3. How much did you previously know about the topic?
Nothing 0   1   2   3   4   5   6 A Lot
4. To what extent did you agree with the ideas presented?
Disagreed 0   1   2   3   4   5   6 Agreed
5. Where did you learn what you already knew?
__graduate courses __reading __expert, mentor
__real world experiences __other, indicate
6. Did you view the source as someone who was expert? How influenced are you by experts? (not very, make my own judgments; somewhat; fairly; very influenced)
7. To what extent did you like to think as you were reading? (Not at all, somewhat, made me take lots of time out to think).

CHAPTER EIGHTEEN

PREPARING THE LEARNER FOR SELF-DIRECTED LEARNING

George M. Piskurich

Any paper on self-directed learning automatically begins with the handicap of having to choose among a number of definitions of the subject, many of which are conceptually different enough to make you wonder if they are defining the same topic at all. Long (1990) notes that even the four rather generalizing concepts of self-directed learning as: complete independence from a teacher; an all or nothing condition; an educational method; and (or) a personality characteristic, don't do justice to all the possible permutations.

Self-directed learning can be a research thesis, a how to do it handbook, or a single individual in a classroom whose mind suddenly takes that quantum jump beyond what the teacher is teaching. It comes in the guise of open curricula, contract learning, computer based instruction, and adult education classes at the local "Y." It has been termed independent study, self-paced instruction, student determined programming, and learner centered instruction.

PREPARATION NEED

Whatever the definition or concept, all self-directed learning has at least one thing in common, a learner. And most learners have one thing in common, they are usually not prepared to engage in self-directed learning. This isn't due, to any genetic or psychological limitation, but rather seems to be an acquired response to a society in which the learner is spoon fed and hand held during the learning experience.

Babies, by way of contrast, are great practitioners of self-directed learning. Few parents set a curriculum or develop lesson plans for their newborns, yet somehow they learn who's who, how to get food, attention, how to walk, and greatest of all miracles, how to talk. Self-directed, experiential learning is also the preferred learning methodology of childhood. "Don't touch," seldom works until the learner finds out the reality of touching, and he **will** find out for himself, when he is ready.

Then suddenly, this self-directed learner is thrust into schools, pre-schools, or pre-pre-schools. Now learning becomes structured. There is a time for blocks, a time for puzzles, and a time for reading. If you choose to do your learning at the wrong time, you are ostracized by the group (I think the newest term is given "time out") and punished by a new authority figure called a teacher. Soon it becomes a time for science, a time for math, a time for history, and no time to learn what you want to learn. The teacher tells you not only when to learn, but what to learn, and even how to learn it, and the price for failure to abide by these external controls becomes much higher than a quickly passing "time out."

I'm not making a judgement on this process. That is for another paper, one which I won't write as I passed my "teaching pigs to sing" phase back in the 60's. I'm simply presenting this learning acculturation process as justification for why most adult learners have difficulties with self-directed learning. If one spends twelve, sixteen, or more years being told what, when, and how to learn, it becomes rather disconcerting to be told "Your on your own," even if somewhere in the past it was once your natural way.

THE LEARNERS' VIEWPOINT

To better understand the learner's difficulties in dealing with self-direction, we need to look at the situation from the learner's point of view. Many have tried. Dewey (1938) states that learners <u>need</u> a "personal responsibility" for learning. Penland (1979) suggests that adults <u>prefer</u> a high degree of control over their learning. Knowles (1980) says specifically that adults have a need to be self-directed. But do most learners agree with these assessments? Or would they argue like Snow (1980), that at times they are incapable of making their own learning decisions or Reisman (1950) that they are "other directed."

To find the answer, step back from being a designer, or an instructor, or whatever it is that you have become, let the layers of experience and the knowledge of learning theory peel away, and once again, become simply a learner.

You, the adult learner, probably feel a certain sense of freedom in being able to say "I want to take charge of my own learning," or "I want to learn at my own pace and in my own style." However, when you have been externally directed, even externally motivated for years, how comfortable are you actually with becoming responsible for your own learning? How confident when you have no curriculum to follow, no time span for "getting it done," and no instructor in front of you to lead and guide you? Since kindergarten and perhaps earlier, you have always relied on someone to tell you what you "needed" to learn, what was required to reach your goal, and how long you had to do it. Someone was in charge, to check on you, reward you when you did well, or punish you when you didn't learn what was "needed." Now you find all those supports are being taken away from you. You're responsible for deciding what you want to learn, and for going out and finding it. You're responsible for setting your own timetables for completion, and for evaluating you own mastery of the material. You're on your own, you're self-directed, and you're probably more than a little insecure.

Now ask yourself, how can you, as a self-directed learning designer, help to mitigate the unease you just felt as a learner? What can you do to build the learner's self-confidence, to increase his awareness of what self-directed learning really means and how it will help him meet his goals?

One answer is to sell the learner on the advantages of self-directed learning. To do this, let's return again to the persona of a learner, and consider the advantages of self-directed learning from the learner's point of view.

ADVANTAGES

The most obvious advantage is the ability to work at your own pace. This includes the latitude to repeat any of the material as often as needed for complete comprehension, and the freedom to control the information flow by simply picking the material up or putting it down.

A second advantage is the availability of the material when the need for learning arises, or what is currently termed "just in time training." You no longer have to wait for a class to learn a new skill, or prepare for a promotion. And, you no longer have to take a class long before you have a need for it so you forget the material before you have a chance to put it to use.

A third advantage is that this is a structured learning experience in which the objectives are known to you from the beginning. Your anxiety or uncertainty about what it is that you need to know is put to rest by objectives that are stated up front, and material that follows the objectives accurately and concisely. Related to this is the fact that what you learn is what is evaluated. There are no surprises on the tests or performance evaluations. And speaking of evaluation and feedback, you can receive it at any time, because you decide when your ready, and you check your own progress. No more trying to figure out what things the teacher really wants you to remember, no more war stories, no more "Huh?" questions on the exam. Finally, the self-directed learning books can become your source for long term reinforcement and review. If you haven't done a procedure for awhile and you've forgotten some of its intricacies, you can refer right to the place and the method that you used to learn it the first time. It's almost like having an expert that you can refer to at anytime, and more importantly, you don't have to always be asking the boss.

A problem with this approach occurs when the designer looks at advantages in terms of program administration, which has little or no relation to the learner. For example, a self-directed learning package might be the most efficient way to train large numbers of employees in various locations on a new manufacturing technique, but that is not an advantage to the learner, and will hardly be useful in quelling the apprehension at being thrust back into the world of self-direction.

Yet, you can't chastise the designer too much for misreading the learner's needs. I have observed many classroom instructors who do the same thing, and the learners are sitting right in front of them. It is much harder for the designer, who will probably never see the end users of his product, to consider the advantages of self-directed learning as they relate to the learner.

DISADVANTAGES

That covers the advantages, but there are disadvantages as well. Some of these are real and some only perceptions of the learner, but as such they are just as real for both him and for the designer. Most of the perceived disadvantages are concerned with the lack of an instructor and related to the idea we discussed earlier, that learners are not comfortable with self-directed learning. They include; no one to answer questions, no one to control the learning by explaining what is and isn't important, no one to set a schedule for when to learn, or a schedule for when to exhibit material comprehension, and no one to validate the learning through verbal or non-verbal feedback. Disadvantages that relate more directly to the learner's abilities include poor reading or writing skills, and simply a lack of readiness to make learning decisions.

Now return to the role of designer, stand back, and look at the situation more dispassionately. You may note that many of the advantages of self-directed learning also seem to be disadvantages, particularly when seen from the learner's perspective. This shouldn't be too surprising. Remember, we are dealing with individuals whose natural learning style has been disturbed, perhaps in some cases destroyed, by acculturation experiences. Little wonder that they're confused by self-directed learning, wanting to take advantage of its benefits, but seeing those same benefits as creating difficulties. The designer's responsibility is to eliminate that confusion, make the advantages real, and the disadvantages, as much as possible, phantoms. In other words, "sell" the learner on self-directed learning.

I used the term "sell" earlier, just in passing, but it is the true emphasis of learner preparation. The learner must first be interested in the concept of self-directed learning, and then be convinced of its usefulness by envisioning himself using it. As the envisioning becomes comfortable, questions concerning the functions of this innovation begin to occur and must be answered. This almost classic representation of the selling process should be your goal, and to achieve it, you must develop a systematic plan based on an assessment of the advantages and disadvantages that your particular SDL system will bring **to the learner**.

Often this type of planning is simply overlooked. Even the best designers, who spend vast quantities of time developing excellent materials, forget the need to develop a plan for preparing the trainees. After all, it is self-directed learning, so when the trainees get the packages, or enter the learning center, they'll be self-directed, and learn. From our previous discussion, I hope you realize that this is not necessarily or even probably the case.

Before we look closer at the "selling" process, let me note that up until this point I have been trying to generalize this paper so it encompasses as many of the concepts and attributes of self-directed learning as possible. However, for simplicity's sake, I am going to focus most of the rest of the discussion on a singular format of self-directed learning as practiced in private industry. This particular format combines the self-directed attributes of being a specific instructional design, allowing the learner to work at his or her own pace, requiring the mastering of pre-determined material, and learning without the aid of an instructor. While this is but one aspect of self-directed learning, and includes only a few of Steinberg's (1984) learner controlled events, I'm hoping that the you will transpose my comments to your own self-directed learning situation.

THE DESIGN

The setting is a retail chain with over 1,000 locations in 10 states. Training for entry level workers must be done in each store and often, as turnover is high. The trainees are found along the entire continuum from high schoolers trying on their first job to senior citizens who for one reason or another have "unretired." The material is company specific policies and procedures, and tasks such as register operation, ordering and stocking, which are performed within the store. The design, chosen to accommodate the material and the implementation needs, is a series of self-directed learning packages, each one dealing with a particular subject that the trainee must master, and including both cognitive and psycho-motor behaviors. The packages are given to the trainee by a training facilitator who is not functioning in the role of Subject Matter Expert, but rather in an administrative capacity. After having received the package, each trainee is left alone to master the material and perform the self-evaluations. The facilitator will check progress, but is normally not available for instruction.

In this format, a systematic plan for smoothing the trainee's transition into self-directed learning is accomplished by enlisting the aid of three distinct groups, each of whom help to "sell" the trainee. They are; current trainers, direct supervisors, and package facilitators.

Current Trainers

In any industrial application, your current trainers are one of the most important and yet least considered assets in preparing trainees for self-directed learning. Often they have built strong relationships to the trainees and so represent the concept of training to them. If they do not understand and agree with the self-directed learning concept you lose a valuable support in the field, and if they see the process in the wrong light, they can become a negative force, subtlety, and often not so subtlety affecting how the trainee perceives self-directed learning, long before the first package appears.

To ensure that trainers provide a positive impact for self-directed learning, the designer must get them involved from the start. Begin with a meeting at which you explain the basic concepts of self-directed learning, and explore its advantages and disadvantages. You'll need to give them a strong definition of what you term self-directed learning, and plenty of examples that they can work through to help them individually grasp the concept. A particularly good way to provide a self-directed learning example for these individuals is to take a concept or topic that they need training in and present it to them in a self-directed learning format. For instance, since they are all trainers, a self-directed learning package on how to write objectives or perhaps test questions, will not only give them new knowledge, but will reinforce the advantages of the process.

As a follow up exercise, charge them with going back to the field and spreading the word about self-directed learning at each of their training sessions. Give them an outline of points to cover, and basically make it their responsibility to begin to sell self-directed learning to the trainees in the field.

A good job of selling your trainers will help pave the way for self-directed learning by transferring some of their credibility as instructors and leaders of learning to the packages that are to come. Ignore your trainers because you think they serve no purpose in a self-directed learning design, and you risk starting your system with a debilitating disadvantage.

This concept can be generalized to many self-directed learning formats. Substitute instructor or professor for trainer, and consider the importance of getting this group's support in a University or adult learning environment. You should find the same problems and opportunities.

316

Supervisors

The second group of "sellers" is comprised of the direct supervisors of the trainees. Though their greatest influence will be on compliance with your program as a whole, they can directly affect trainee preparation by supplying some of the external motivation and guidance that trainees perceive as otherwise missing in the self-directed learning process. External control is a very touchy concept, and I won't go into the battle of choice vs need in self-directed learning, or where motivation should come from. Research already cited and other material such as Even (1982) presents this controversy in detail. Suffice it to say that in industry a certain climate must be set that helps the trainee to take full advantage of the self-directed learning process and this climate is controlled by the supervisor.

Characteristics of this climate include providing time to do the learning, the delegated flexibility to choose which packages seem most appropriate to the trainee's current and future status, empowering of the trainee to use the material and skills gained in the learning, and the guidance to keep the trainee on a path that is personally rewarding while at the same time fulfilling the needs of the company.

To use the supervisor's acumen to help prepare the trainee for self-directed learning requires the same type of planning as was done for the trainers. An effective method, particularly when you have large numbers of supervisors in many different locations is a self-directed learning package on self-directed learning. A package of this nature can explain the basic concepts of your system to the supervisor while he is actually experiencing it. After completing the package, the supervisor will have the background necessary to discuss the process of self-directed learning with the trainees, and move them to a state of readiness for accepting the concept.

Package Facilitators

The third group that will help you prepare the trainees are the package facilitators. Their role is the formal introduction of self-directed learning to the trainees. This may sound a bit illogical, having an instructor led process to prepare for self-directed learning, but go back to earlier discussions concerning learner readiness for SDL and perceived disadvantages, and you'll see why formal trainee preparation is best handled by a live instructor.

Preparing the facilitators to prepare the trainees requires good planning and solid training. Because of their rather schizophrenic role of getting the trainee started and then getting out of the way, the facilitators need more than just a passing understanding of the precepts of self-directed learning. The best way to produce more in-depth knowledge is to combine classroom training and self-directed learning examples.

Once again a self-directed learning package on self-directed learning, this time modified for the facilitator position, is a useful tool. Follow completion of the package with a classroom or, if necessary, a one to one session, where further discussion of how to present the process to the trainees can be held.

An interesting side bar to this process is to have your trainers run these classes. This not only helps to reinforce their understanding of self-directed learning and recommits them to the process, but it allows the facilitators to discuss ideas and receive information from people who are much closer to the "reality" of the trainees than is a corporate self-directed learning "expert."

The facilitators will need solid lesson plans and tools for the indoctrination of the trainees. Checklists, summary handouts, and written exercises are useful and necessary if you expect them to do a proper job of preparing the trainees.

Facilitator preparation can be generalized into other self-directed learning formats as well. Whether they function as a member of a learning resource center staff, or in an advisor type of relationship, the facilitators must be able to expedite the transition of the learner into a self-directed mode. This requires at least the type of formal training described above, and that was for a relatively simple self-directed learning system. More general, learner choice directed systems, require even more facilitator preparation if the facilitator is going to perform the task of preparing the learner competently.

ORIENTATION

Malcolm Knowles (1980) states that while most adults are or want to be self-directed, and are capable of being so, it is not wise to "just throw them into the strange waters of self-direction and hope they swim." He suggests that they should be prepared with an orientation session, and this is the final step in selling self-directed learning.

If you've followed the plan up to this point, you now have your field trainers describing what is coming, talking about the advantages of the new system, allaying fears, and discussing how it will affect the trainees. They are transferring the credibility they have gained as instructors to the self-directed learning packages.

You have supervisors who know what self-directed learning is and how it works. At meetings they mention it, lending their authority to the process, at performance appraisals they recommend that when it arrives the individual takes advantage of it for self-development.

And you have facilitators trained and equipped with good lesson plans and tools to hold the orientation sessions that formally describe the process to the trainees, solidify that vision of doing self-directed learning, and answer the questions that arise. Their session should be divided into four parts.

In the first they need to give your overall definition of what self-directed learning is and discuss the definition as it relates to the trainees. They must point out the differences and similarities to previous training systems, and explore the things that will be more difficult and the things that will be easier due to the self-directed learning system. They must get the trainee interested.

Next they need to emphasize the advantages and discuss the disadvantages. The most important and most basic of these for your system, such as lack of an instructor should be discussed first, with both positive and negative ramifications examined. Other advantages that flow from these concepts should be discussed in as much detail as possible, complete with considerations of other disadvantages and how they can be overcome. The first envisioning by the trainees of their actually using the packages begins here, so the facilitator needs to be ready to answer questions.

Now, with the vision begun, the mechanics of the system should be gone over in detail. This will solidify the envisioning process. Start at the beginning with how to obtain and begin the process. Restress what it means to do the learning "on your own." Discuss the support that can and can't be expected. Go over areas such as self checks, performance evaluations, completion standards, record keeping, and any special aspects of the design.

The orientation program is completed by once again reinforcing the advantages of the new system (skip the disadvantages this time, they've heard them already and this is the time for a little less fairness and a little more propaganda). Be sure that all questions have been fully answered.

CONCLUSIONS

For the most part in this paper, I have dealt with a singular form of self-directed learning as practiced in a specific circumstance, that of private industry. In such an environment, because of the imperatives of skills training for mastery of a specialized set of performances, it often seems that most of the self-direction is lost from self-directed learning. Even some of the adult learning characteristics that form the theoretical basis for self-directed learning may seem to have been abandoned. This may or may not be true according to your own perceptions and definitions. However, in the final analysis all formats require the learner to have the self-directed learning characteristics of self-confidence, self-awareness, self-reflection, and task orientation (Long 1989). Well planned trainee preparation is the key to redeveloping these possibly atrophied characteristics and enhancing them.

In short, if for self-directed learning we are to as Dewey (1938) states, "replace external control with self-control," we must, in every self-directed learning situation, systematically prepare the learner for this challenge.

REFERENCES

Dewey, F. J. (1938). Experience and education. New York: Collier

Even, M. J. (1982). Adapting Cognitive Style Theory in Practice. Lifelong Learning: The Adult Years, Jan., Vol. 5, No. 5, 14-17

Knowles, M. K. (1980). The modern practice of adult education (rev. ed.). New York: Cambridge Press

Knowles, M. K. (1980) How do you get people to be self-directed learners? Training and Development Journal, May, 1980. 96-99

Long, H. (1989). Truth Unguessed and Yet to be Discovered. In H. Long and Associates. Self-directed learning: Emerging theory and practice. Norman, OK: Oklahoma Research Center for Continuing Professional and Higher Education, University of Oklahoma.

Long, H. (1990). Changing Concepts of Self-direction in learning. In H. Long and Associates. Advances in research and practice in self-directed learning. Norman, OK: Oklahoma Research Center for Continuing Professional and Higher Education, University of Oklahoma

Penland, P. (1979). Self-initiated learning. Adult Education, 29, 170-179

Reisman, D. (1950). The lonely crowd: A study of changing American culture. New Haven: Yale University Press.

Snow, R. E. (1980) Aptitude, learner control, and adaptive instruction. Educational Psychologist, 15, 151-158

Steinberg, E. R. (1984). Teaching computers to teach. Hillsdale, NJ: Lawrence Erlbaum.

CHAPTER NINETEEN

INDIVIDUALIZING THE INSTRUCTIONAL PROCESS: WHAT WE HAVE LEARNED FROM TWO DECADES OF RESEARCH ON SELF-DIRECTION IN LEARNING

Roger Hiemstra

It has been nearly two decades since Tough (1971, 1979) first published The adult's learning projects. I argue that this book, even though he had started related research earlier (Tough, 1966, 1967), really began the wide-spread interest in self-directed learning. Whether you agree with my contention or want to argue for Johnstone and Rivera's (1965) finding of considerable self-instructional involvement in learning by adults, Houle's (1961) foundational research with The inquiring mind, or some earlier genesis point, there certainly has been a sustained study of various aspects of self-directed learning in the past 20 years. Beder (1985) even suggests that self-directed learning research is one of only two relatively well developed research areas in adult education.

In that same publication, Beder wonders if such research has really done much to guide practice in important ways. Although the jury is probably still out, I believe we have learned several things that not only can and should guide our practice, but that have prompted some significant changes in the field of adult education. This chapter's purpose will be to describe some of those changes that have impacted on the instructional process, to talk about ways teachers need to view their future instructional efforts, and to suggest how future teacher training efforts should be altered.

WHAT DO WE KNOW?

Notions about self-directed learning have undergone considerable evolution over the past several years. There also has been some confusion associated with self-directed learning. Some think of it as an instructional method; others think of it in terms of personality characteristics. I and my colleague, Ralph Brockett, suggest that the term "self-direction in learning" can provide the breadth needed to more fully reflect current understanding of the concept. We believe that self-direction in learning encompasses two distinct but related dimensions (Brockett and Hiemstra, 1991). The first of these we refer to as "self-directed learning." It involves a process in which learners assume primary responsibility for planning, implementing, and evaluating their learning. An educational agent or resource often plays a facilitating role in this process as opposed to the directing role common in more traditional settings. The second dimension, which we refer to as "learner self-direction," centers on a learner's desire or preference for assuming responsibility for learning. This is associated primarily with the personality aspects mentioned above. Thus, we conclude the following:

. . . self-direction in learning refers to both the external characteristics of an instructional process and the internal characteristics of the learner, where the individual assumes primary responsibility for a learning experience. (Brockett and Hiemstra, 1991, p. 24)

What, then, do we know about these internal and external characteristics based on the past two decades of research. I will describe five conclusions that I have drawn from studying the literature since 1971. I think the first two are by far the most crucial and foundational for much of what I will say later about changing ourselves as teachers or about training future adult educators, so I will elaborate on each in some detail.

1. ALL PEOPLE ARE CAPABLE OF SELF-DIRECTED INVOLVEMENT IN, PERSONAL COMMITMENT TO, AND RESPONSIBILITY FOR LEARNING.

I draw this conclusion from the many studies of adults' learning projects that have been conducted since Tough's initial work in the late 60's. Summary information from people like Brockett and Hiemstra (1991), Caffarella and O'Donnell (1987, 1988), and Tough (1978) describe research or verification studies that have been conducted across various populations and in various settings. Consistently, this research has revealed that learning activities are self-planned nearly three-fourths of the time. Several associated findings support my notion of people being able to take personal responsibility for learning.

Thus, learning projects research has represented the first effort by adult education researchers to systematically study the concept of self-direction in learning. The learning projects approach in many ways has served a "consciousness-raising" function for the adult education field, providing data to confirm what has been known intuitively for many years. In essence, I believe the extent to which learning projects research has been replicated by so many researchers serves as testimonial for Tough's initial study to be considered as one of the most significant pieces of research in all of North American adult education.

Although the contributions of learning projects research to our understanding have been substantial, there are limitations that must be noted.

a. <u>Limitations in using the structured interview</u>. While the structured interview format has the advantage that it can be replicated, Brookfield talks about problems of bias and suggests that the methodology can "run the risk of forcing the researcher's notion of what are admissible and appropriate substantive concerns" upon subjects without taking into consideration what they believe to be relevant (1981, p. 115).

b. <u>Self-fulfilling prophesy syndrome</u>. Because self-planning was the predominant mode of learning described by the initial "Tough" interviewees, they may have had a propensity to declare a preference for this mode. However, many of the verification studies since then have found high degrees of self-planning among people of varied educational backgrounds (e.g., Baghi, 1979; Brockett, 1983, 1985; Umoren, 1978).

   c. Is it appropriate to study self-direction in learning? Brookfield also talked about appropriateness by stating the following:

. . . extended investigations into the nature of noninstitutionalized adult learning, while interesting, are inappropriate in the current economic climate. Instead of studying those adults who choose to ignore formal adult education provision and to devise their own learning schemes, we should be concentrating our efforts on retaining the loyalty and continuing participation of existing students as well as working to increase overall student numbers (1981, p. 117).

However, Brookfield negates this notion, too, by stating that if self-planning is as prevalent as the learning projects research suggests, then adult educators face challenges of identifying various ways to support such learning efforts.

   d.   The preponderance of middle-class samples. Brookfield, in his critical paradigm discussion of self-directed adult learning (Brookfield, 1984) expressed the belief that research on self-directed learning had been based up until that time almost entirely on middle-class samples. While I think he missed several important studies in coming to this conclusion (Baghi, 1979; Field, 1979; Hiemstra, 1975; Leean and Sisco, 1981; Ralston, 1979; Umoren, 1978), there had been a large number of studies where "working-class" respondents were in short supply. Some of the qualitative studies in the past decade have come to a better understanding of learning involvement by other than middle-class adults (Brookfield, 1980; Fingeret, 1983; Gibbons, et al., 1980; Henry, 1989; Hiemstra, 1982).

   e. Interpretation of learning projects research. When interpreting learning projects studies, it needs to be noted that while most researchers have used the original Tough interview schedule, there have been some variations in the questions asked, the interview process itself, and the way data are analyzed or presented. Penland (1979), for example, based his self-planning findings on the percent of respondents who completed at least one self-planned project rather than on a total percentage of all projects planned by the learners themselves. Such variations can create confusion for those interpreting or comparing results.

f. Qualitative versus quantitative focus. Another way learning projects information can be misinterpreted is when the approach is described as qualitative or quasi-qualitative. The original Tough approach is a quantitative survey approach with little latitude allowed interviewers. Some people can be confused when attempting to understand results if they believe the procedure has been qualitative because as Fingeret (1982) notes, qualitative data frequently are presented as quotations taken from interviews and not as numbers of responses. In learning projects studies, data should be treated primarily through descriptive statistics.

2. ADULT LEARNERS ARE CAPABLE OF TAKING PERSONAL RESPONSIBILITY FOR THEIR OWN LEARNING AND ASSUMING AN INCREASINGLY LARGER ROLE IN THE INSTRUCTIONAL PROCESS.

By personal responsibility I mean that individuals assume ownership for their own thoughts and actions. This is the "learner self-direction" distinction that I referred to earlier. Personal responsibility does not necessarily mean control over personal life circumstances. However, it does mean that you can control how you respond to various situation. As Elias and Merriam (1980) note, behavior "is the consequence of human choice which individuals can freely exercise" (p. 118). Thus, it is the ability and/or willingness of people to take control of their own learning that determines their potential for self-direction.

I base this notion of taking control and personal responsibility on two ideas. First, I believe that humans basically are good and that everyone possesses virtually unlimited potential for growth. Second, it has been my experience that only if we accept responsibility for our own learning is it possible to be proactive in our approach to learning. Both of these obviously imply a great deal of faith and trust in the learner.

This also is related to notions about autonomy that have appeared in the literature in the past several years. For example, Chene provides the following perspective:

Autonomy means that one can and does set one's own rules, and can choose for oneself the norms one will respect. In other words, autonomy refers to one's ability to choose what has value, that is to say, to make choices in harmony with self-realization. (1983, p. 39)

Autonomy thus is based on an assumption that adults will take personal responsibility because of being free "from all exterior regulations and constraints" (Chene, 1983, p. 39), although much of the literature on "Women's Ways of Knowing" suggests that autonomy needs to be better understood because women may value it quite differently from men (Belenky, Clinchy, Goldberger, and Tarule, 1986; Hayes, 1989; Kolodny, 1991). While I believe the assumption of personal responsibility is an important cornerstone of self-direction in learning, it is important to stress three related points.

a.   Differing degrees of assuming personal responsibility. Adults will possess different degrees of willingness to accept personal responsibility for learning. For example, you cannot assume that all adults will enter the learning setting with high levels of existing self-directed ability. You also don't need to be highly self-directed in order to be successful as a learner. However, I believe that helping people assume greater control over their own destiny is a desirable societal goal and that a corresponding role for adult educators is helping individuals become increasingly more able to assume personal responsibility for learning.

b. Social as well as individual responsibility. Accepting personal responsibility for learning does not mean that the social context in which learning takes place is ignored. A frequent criticism of personal responsibility and self-direction is the overemphasis on the individual, accompanied by a failure to consider the social context in which learning may take place. Brookfield (1984), for example, suggests that by "concentrating attention on the features of individual learner control over the planning, conduct and evaluation of learning, the importance of learning networks and informal learning exchanges has been forgotten" (p. 67). I agree that social context is vital to understanding various notions about individuality and personal responsibility, but believe Brookfield overlooks the many ways a self-directed learner can use resources like learning networks and learning exchanges. It certainly is important, however, to recognize the social milieu in which such activity transpires.

c. Responsibility for the consequences of personal thoughts and action. As Rogers (1961, p. 171) noted, being "self-directing means that one chooses--and then learns from the consequences." Day (1988) argues this same point by suggesting that adults are decision-making beings ultimately responsible for personal decisions, and the "results of our learning experiences may as likely lead to discontent as to a state of well-being" (p. 125).

3. LINKING THE INSTRUCTIONAL PROCESS WITH LEARNER INPUTS, INVOLVEMENT, AND DECISION MAKING IS CRUCIAL.

Another important variable in successful learning is for adults to become excited about a topic, want to study it, and be willing to find available resources. There is research evidence to support notions about personal involvement and decision making related to learning. Cole and Glass (1977), Pine (1980), and Verdros and Pankowski (1980) are only some of those who have studied the effect of personal involvement by adults in assessing needs, determining instructional approaches, and carrying out instructional activities. In general, researchers have found that individualized involvement usually does not increase or decrease achievement of content mastery. However, having some ownership of the process usually results in a more positive attitude about the content, process, facilitator, and desire to study the content further after any formal learning experience has ended.

There are several ways adults can maximize their self-directed skills and enhance learning based on personal involvement or control of decision making. Many adult educators have written about using needs assessment information for planning purposes (Hiemstra and Sisco, 1990) or how adults can develop meaningful learning contracts (Knowles, 1986). However, I can identify at least nine instructional activities or variables adults potentially can control in their learning efforts (Cooper, 1980; Hiemstra, 1988a, Hiemstra and Sisco, 1990): Needs identification, learning contract design or specificity of content, intended outcomes, evaluative techniques, documentation methods, appropriateness of learning experiences, variety of learning resources, adequacy of the learning environment, and the actual pace of learning.

4. THERE ARE VARIOUS LINKS BETWEEN A LEARNER'S PROPENSITY TO BE SELF-DIRECTED AND SEVERAL PERSONAL ATTRIBUTES OR CHARACTERISTICS.

While much of the scholarship related to self-direction in learning has focused on the personal control or involvement nature of the first three conclusions, there have been attempts to understand some of the characteristics of successful self-directed learners. Conceptually, notions about successful learner self-direction grow largely from ideas addressed by

Rogers (1961, 1983), Maslow (1970), and other writers from the area of humanistic psychology. Tennant (1986) suggests that Knowles' work with andragogy, for example, has been profoundly influenced from the humanist psychology framework. By inference I suggest that this influence has affected our interpretation of self-directed learning research in various ways.

The popularity of the Self-Directed Learning Readiness Scale (Guglielmino, 1977) in examining various personality characteristics for several years is another indication of this humanist influence (e.g., Brockett, 1983; Curry, 1983; Hall-Johnsen, 1986; Leeb, 1985; Sabbaghian, 1980; Skaggs, 1981). Further evidence of this personal orientation can be found in research on self-direction in relation to such variables as creativity (Torrance and Mourad, 1978), self-concept (Sabbaghian, 1980), life satisfaction (Brockett 1983; Estrin, 1986), intellectual development (Shaw, 1987), and hemisphericity (Blackwood, 1989). Thus, there appear to be positive links between self-directed propensity and several of these characteristics, but much more research is required before we know enough to use the information with confidence in our practice.

5. SELF-DIRECTION IN LEARNING CAN TAKE PLACE IN ANY LOCATION; IT FREQUENTLY IS NOT ASSOCIATED WITH FORMAL EDUCATION INSTITUTIONS.

Gibbons and Phillips (1982) talk about this notion in what they refer to as self-education:

Self-education occurs outside of formal institutions, not inside them. The skills can be taught and practiced in schools, teachers can gradually transfer the authority and responsibility for self-direction to students, and self-educational acts can be simulated, but self-education can only truly occur when people are not compelled to learn and others are not compelled to teach them--especially not to teach them a particular subject-matter curriculum. While schools can prepare students for a life of self-education, true self-education can only occur when a person chooses to learn what he can also decide not to learn. (p. 69)

While I won't go quite as far as Gibbons and Phillips, I do believe that those of us working with formal educational institutions must reexamine the way we present our courses, the way we work with learners, our use of learning resources in the community (Hiemstra, 1985), and the means we use for training future adult educators. As I note in the next section, many people have ingrained views of teaching that must be reexamined and various changes made if they are to be successful as teachers of adults.

INGRAINED VIEWS OF TEACHING

Jarvis suggests that there are three broad approaches to instruction (Hiemstra, 1988a; Jarvis, 1985): Didactic, Socratic, and facilitative. I believe the facilitative approach is the most viable one to use with self-directed learners. However, advocating for an approach, what I refer to as "individualizing instruction," is not an automatic precursor to adult educators rushing to embrace the underlying assumptions, associated techniques, and process elements. In essence, I believe many adult educators will have a traditional view of teaching ingrained as their way of dealing with learners.

Part of the problem is that if people reach a stage in life where they are called on to "teach" adults, they quickly, perhaps the word is easily, fall back on what has been modeled for them as teaching, ideas that are ingrained from years of being taught, and a fairly inadequate or perhaps no understanding of the literature associated with adults as learners or with self-direction in learning. I think most such individuals in the beginning will use, at best, a Socratic approach to involve learners, but more likely a fairly rigid teacher-directed, didactic approach until they start discovering that it does not work very well. Thus, there is a need to help promote important changes related to instructing adults. There are at least three ways of thinking about how to help stimulate such change.

One way is via "perspective transformation" notions introduced by Mezirow (1975, 1978). These ideas are based on assumptions that we "are caught up in our own history and are reliving it" (Mezirow, 1978, p. 101). Influenced by such authors as Freire (1970), Gould (1978), and Habermas (1970, 1971), Mezirow believes personal values and assumptions are changed through our learning processes. Collard and Law (1989) and Mezirow (1989) provide some useful dialogue on these notions. My point in describing this concept here is to illustrate the connections that I believe exist with teaching via what we know or what has been modeled for us. If knowledge about teaching is an accumulation of past knowledge and that accumulative collection does not include observations of a facilitative model nor an assimilation of knowledge about self-direction in learning, then how can we expect much informing of our practice from the knowledge that does exist.

A second way of thinking about change involves notions about paradigms and paradigm shifting. Our behaviors and attitudes are shaped by various paradigms we have encountered. The word "paradigm" is Greek in origin and refers to models, theories, or frames of reference. In other words, the way we see, perceive, or understand the world is through paradigms. For example, the knowledge and experience I have pertaining to self-direction in learning, a collection of paradigms, informs my view of teaching, suggests why I have embraced the facilitative model, and is foundational to the advocating I do for individualizing the instructional process.

Knowles (1989), Kuhn (1970), and Covey (1989) have all talked about episodes, insights, or paradigm shifts that can change a person's life. Covey (1989) describes an interesting technique for demonstrating how paradigms affect the way we think about or see things. By sharing with half the people in a group only pictures of an old woman and showing the other half only pictures of a young woman, a "paradigm" or model is created. Then when an optical illusion-type picture that could be seen either as a young or old woman is projected on the screen, most of those who had initially seen the older person's picture will see an old woman on the screen and vice versa.

A third way of thinking about how to help people recognize a need to change their teaching approaches is through knowledge of how personal philosophy affects ways of working with people:

1. A philosophy promotes an understanding of human relationships
2. A philosophy sensitizes one to the various needs associated with positive human interactions
3. A philosophy provides a framework for distinguishing, separating, and understanding personal values
4. A philosophy promotes flexibility and consistency in working with adult learners. (Hiemstra, 1988b p. 179)

I believe that an individual's philosophy undergirds the teaching style used, even though that philosophy may never have been formally stated. Such a philosophy impacts on personal teaching styles in various ways. I suspect that many people who are teaching adults have not thought about their personal philosophies. Thus, another task those who are involved with training adult educators is to help them think about, develop, and use their philosophies: "Philosophy contributes to professionalism. Having a philosophic orientation separates the professional continuing educator from the paraprofessional in that professionals are aware of what they are doing and why they are doing it" (Merriam, 1982, pp. 90-91). I hope those involved in helping people become better teachers of adults will assist them in thinking about one or more of these means for change.

INDIVIDUALIZING INSTRUCTION

I believe that many experienced teachers of adults are not making such changes or are not using what we have learned in two decades of research. I and my colleague, Burt Sisco, have thought much about how to make sense of all this research. We have developed what we call the "individualizing instructional" process (Hiemstra and Sisco, 1990). This process builds on the foundational work of Knowles (1970, 1980), incorporates much of the self-directed learning research described earlier in the chapter, and has evolved from many years of teaching experience and experimentation.

The individualizing process includes six steps in which the facilitator becomes involved with instructional activities before any initial contact with learners occurs and the involvement continues through the final evaluation. STEP ONE involves several activities prior to meeting with any learners, such as determining necessary competencies or requirements, acquiring learning support materials, and preparing study guides. STEP TWO involves paying attention to physical, emotional, and social environmental needs (Hiemstra, 1991). STEP THREE requires that some initial time be spent clarifying probable educational needs and focal points. STEP FOUR necessitates the identification of various ways learners can build knowledge or increase competencies through reading, writing, discussion, and design activities related to the needs they identified earlier. STEP FIVE in the process begins to parallel traditional instruction. It consists of monitoring and contributing to the progress of the initial planning efforts. STEP SIX entails facilitating learners in self, teacher, and course evaluation efforts.

The individualizing instructional process works because it helps adults take responsibility for their own learning. It does not work equally well in every teaching situation, but its foundation in the belief that all people are capable of self-directed involvement with learning makes it a process that should be studied, understood, and tried.

TRAINING OTHERS TO TEACH ADULTS

This last section contains my views regarding changes required in the way we teach others to teach so that self-direction in learning is facilitated. These changes grow out of my interpretation of what we have learned in these two decades of research. I also base much of this on what I have tried to do in my graduate teaching efforts, my own research, and the many training workshops I have conducted in the past decade.

1.   Promoting an awareness of findings like the ones reported earlier.   The literature related to self-direction in learning continues to grow.   But just having the literature available is not enough.   I think that those of us interested in and committed to this area of research must become much more proactive than we have been in ensuring a wide-spread awareness of these findings.   Besides producing literature we need to push professors in adult education to understand and use the information.   We need to sponsor debates with those who disagree with our findings so all of us can come to a better understanding and what we are discovering can be incorporated into various areas of adult education theory. Perhaps most important, we need to find ways that educators normally not inclined to read our literature can be made aware of what we know and believe about teaching.

2.   Good teaching needs to be modeled.   Obviously, I am quite biased, but I hope that an increasing number of people will incorporate the individualized instructional process, or at least those parts of the process with which they feel comfortable, into their teaching repertoire.   The more people that model giving learners personal responsibility, the more people that subsequently will use this as their main frame of reference.   In the Syracuse University graduate program, we try to ensure good modeling in our classrooms as much as possible.   For those students who plan on teaching adults as a career, we also try to give them time to practice with the individualizing instructional process and provide some critique of their efforts.

3.   Developing a personal philosophy of teaching adults. I believe it is crucial that each teacher of adults should have an opportunity to think through and develop a personal

statement of philosophy. In our graduate program at Syracuse University, we try to ensure that each student develops such a statement. I would like to see our national adult and continuing education associations take some responsibility for helping members develop and periodically update such statements or at least encourage adult education organizations and agencies to promote such activities among employees.

4. <u>Learning to assess needs and turn them into learning plans</u>. In graduate programs of adult education and the various in-service efforts to train teachers, I would like to see more attention paid to the needs assessment process. By this I mean how to do it, how to analyze the resulting information, and how to help learners turn needs information into learning plans.

5. <u>Understanding physical, emotional, and social learning environments</u>. I think we must learn much more than we already know about the learning environment. Some important questions are the following (Hiemstra, 1991): What are the best physical arrangements for adults in a learning situation? How do gender, racial, or social class differences among learners affect the learning setting? What types of emotional or psychological barriers impede learning for adults?

6. <u>Promoting expertise in using various methods, techniques, and devices</u>. Promoting self-direction in learning, using approaches like the individualizing instructional process, and helping learners take more responsibility will be more successful, from my experience, if a variety of resources and means for presenting information are used. We try to see that every graduate student in adult education at Syracuse University takes our basic teaching methods course. I hope most graduate programs already take or will adopt such a stance. This seems especially important given the increasing sophistication of technological

innovations with corresponding implications for instruction, such as computer conferencing, computer assisted instruction, and interactive video.

7. <u>Promoting critical thinking, writing, reading, and reflection</u>. I doubt that such promotion happens very well even in more traditional teaching approaches, but giving more responsibility back to learners has as one drawback the danger that not very much critical reflection will take place. I am not suggesting that the person taking a more self-directed route will purposely overlook reflective techniques, but I do think this is one aspect of the teaching and learning process where another person, usually the teacher, can be very helpful in promoting some critical thinking in various ways. I try to stress critical thinking in my own courses and workshops, but suggest that much more needs to be done throughout the profession.

8. <u>Playing a counseling or mentoring role with some learners</u>. Many adults will need some sort of counseling intervention at certain points in their learning pursuits (Brockett, 1983). Miller (1986) describes the variety of problems confronting many adults today: Career changes, family role conflicts, changing family patterns, and various social and economic trends. If left unresolved such personal or family problems can serve as a barrier to learning or training efforts.

It is my hope that these kind of changes among teachers can be promoted. The past two decades of research have given us much information to help plan future research, inform practice, and develop instructional approaches. I hope this chapter and any corresponding dialogue that is prompted will add to the growing knowledge base regarding self-direction in learning.

REFERENCES

Baghi, H. (1979). The major learning efforts of participants in adult basic education classes and learning centers. (Doctoral dissertation, Iowa State University, 1979). Dissertation Abstracts International, 40, 2410A.

Beder, H. (1985). Defining the we. Lifelong Learning: An Omnibus of Practice and Research, 8(5), 2.

Belenky, M. F., Clinchy, N., Goldberger, L, and Tarule, J. (1986). Women's ways of knowing: The development of self, voice, and mind. New York: Basic Books Incorporated.

Blackwood, C. C. (1989). Self-directedness and hemisphericity over the adult life span. (Doctoral dissertation, Montana State University, 1988). Dissertation Abstracts International, 50, 328A.

Brockett, R. G. (1983). Self-directed learning readiness and life satisfaction among older adults. (Doctoral dissertation, Syracuse University, 1982). Dissertation Abstracts International, 44, 42A.

Brockett, R. G. (1985). Methodological and substantive issues in the measurement of self-directed learning readiness. Adult Education Quarterly, 36, 15-24.

Brockett, R. G. & Hiemstra, R. (1991). Self-direction in learning: Perspectives in theory, research, and practice. London, UK: Routledge.

Brookfield, S. (1980). Independent adult learning. Unpublished doctoral dissertation, University of Leicester (England).

Brookfield, S. (1981). The adult learning iceberg: A critical review of the work of Allen Tough. Adult Education (British), 54(2), 110-118.

Brookfield, S. (1984). Self-directed learning: A critical paradigm. Adult Education Quarterly, 35, 59-71.

Caffarella, R. & O'Donnell, J. M. (1987). Self-directed adult learning: A critical paradigm revisited. Adult Education Quarterly, 37, 199-211.

Caffarella, R. & O'Donnell, J. M. (1988). Research in self-directed learning: Past, present and future trends. In H. B. Long & Associates, Self-directed learning: Application & theory (pp. 39-61). Athens, Georgia: University of Georgia, Adult Education Department.

Chene, A. (1983). The concept of autonomy in adult education: A philosophical discussion. Adult Education Quarterly, 1, 38-47.

Cole, J. W. & Glass, J. C., Jr. (1977). The effects of adult student participation in program planning on achievement, retention, and attitudes. Adult Education, 27, 75-88.

Collard, S. & Law, M. (1989). The limits of perspective transformation: A critique of Mezirow's theory. Adult Education Quarterly, 39(2), 99-107.

Cooper, S. S. (1980). Self-directed learning in nursing. Wakefield, Massachusetts: Nursing Resources.

Covey, S. R. (1989). The seven habits of highly effective people: Restoring the character ethic. New York: Simon & Schuster.

Curry, M. A. (1983). The analysis of self-directed learning readiness characteristics in older adults engaged in formal learning activities in two settings. (Doctoral dissertation, Kansas State University, 1983). Dissertation Abstracts International, 44, 1293A.

Day, M. J. (1988). Educational advising and brokering: The ethics of choice. In R. G. Brockett (Ed.), Ethical issues in adult education (pp. 118-132). New York: Teachers College Press.

Elias, J. L. & Merriam, S. (1980). Philosophical foundations of adult education. Huntington, New York: Robert K. Krieger Publishing Company.

Estrin, H. R. (1986). Life satisfaction and participation in learning activities among widows. (Doctoral dissertation, Syracuse University, 1985). Dissertation Abstracts International, 46, 3852A.

Field, J. L. (1979). The learning efforts of Jamaican adults of low literacy attainment. (Doctoral dissertation, University of Toronto, 1977). Dissertation Abstracts International, 39, 3979A.

Fingeret, A. (1982). Methodological issues and theoretical perspectives on research. In G. C. Whaples & W. M. Rivera, (Eds.), Lifelong Learning Research Conference Proceedings (88-92). College Park, MD: Department of Agricultural & Extension Education, University of Maryland.

Fingeret, A. (1983). Social network: A new perspective on independence and illiterate adults. Adult Education Quarterly, 33, 133-146.

Freire, P. (1970). Pedagogy of the oppressed. New York: Herder and Herder.

Gibbons, M., Bailey, A., Comeau, P., Schmuck, J., Seymour, S. & Wallace, D. (1980). Toward a theory of self-directed learning: A study of experts without formal training. Journal of Humanistic Psychology, 20(2), 41-45.

Gibbons, M. & Phillips, G. (1982). Self-education: The process of life-long learning. Canadian Journal of Education, 7(4), 67-86.

Gould, R. L. (1978). Transformations. New York: Simon & Schuster.

Guglielmino, L. M. (1977). Development of the self-directed learning readiness scale. (Doctoral dissertation, University of Georgia, 1977). Dissertation Abstracts International, 38, 6467A.

Habermas, J. (1970). Toward a rational society. Boston: Beacon Press.

Habermas, J. (1971). Knowledge and human interests. Boston: Beacon Press.

Hall-Johnsen, K. J. (1986). The relationship between readiness for, and involvement in, self-directed learning. (Doctoral dissertation, Iowa State University, 1985). Dissertation Abstracts International, 46, 2522A.

Hayes, E. (1989). Insights from women's experiences for teaching and learning. In E. Hayes (Ed.), Effective teaching styles (New Directions for Continuing Education, Number 43, pp. 55-66). San Francisco: Jossey-Bass.

Henry, N. J. (1989). A qualitative study about perceptions of lifestyle and life satisfaction among older adults. Unpublished doctoral dissertation, Syracuse University, Syracuse, NY.

Hiemstra, R. (1975). The older adult and learning. (ERIC Document Reproduction Service No. ED 117 371).

Hiemstra, R. (1982). The elderly learner: A naturalistic inquiry. Proceedings of the 23rd Annual Adult Education Research Conference (pp. 103-107). Adult and Continuing Education, University of Nebraska, Lincoln, Nebraska.

Hiemstra, R. (1985). The educative community: Linking the community, education, and family. Baldwinsville, NY: HiTree Press.

Hiemstra, R. (1988a). Self-directed learning: Individualizing instruction. In H.B. Long and Associates, Self-directed learning: Application & theory (pp. 99-124). Athens, Georgia: University of Georgia, Adult Education Department.

Hiemstra, R. (1988b). Translating personal values and philosophy into practical action. In R. G. Brockett (Ed.), Ethical issues in adult education (pp.178-194). New York: Teachers College Press.

Hiemstra, R. (Ed.). (1991). Environments for effective adult learning (New Directions for Adult and Continuing Education, Number 50). San Francisco: Jossey-Bass.

Hiemstra, R. & Sisco, B. (1990). Individualizing instruction for adult learners:Making learning personal, powerful, and successful. San Francisco: Jossey-Bass.

Houle, C. O. (1961). The inquiring mind. Madison, Wisconsin: The University of Wisconsin Press.

Jarvis, P. (1985). The sociology of adult & continuing education. London: Croom Helm.

Johnstone, J. & Rivera, R. (1965). Volunteers for learning, a study of the educational pursuits of American adults. National Opinion Research Center report. Chicago: Aldine Publishing Company.

Knowles, M. S. (1970). The modern practice of adult education. New York: Association Press.

Knowles, M. S. (1980). The modern practice of adult education (revised and updated). Chicago: Association Press (originally published in 1970).

Knowles, M. S. (1986). Using learning contracts. San Francisco: Jossey-Bass.

Knowles, M. S. (1989) The making of an adult educator: An autobiographical journey. San Francisco: Jossey-Bass.

Kolodny, A. (February 6, 1991). Colleges must recognize students' cognitive styles and cultural backgrounds. The Chronicle of Higher Education, A44.

Kuhn, T. S. (1970). The structure of scientific revolutions (Second Edition). Chicago: University of Chicago Press.

Leean, C. & Sisco, B. (1981). Learning projects and self-planned learning efforts among undereducated adults in rural Vermont (Final Report No. 99-1051). Washington, D.C.: National Institute of Education.

Leeb, J. G. (1985). Self-directed learning and growth toward personal responsibility: Implications for a framework for health promotion. (Doctoral dissertation, Syracuse University, 1983). Dissertation Abstracts International, 45, 724A.

Maslow, A. H. (1970). Motivation and personality (2nd ed.). New York: Harper & Row.

Merriam, S. B. (1982). Some thoughts on the relationship between theory and practice. In S. B. Merriam (Ed.), Linking philosophy and practice (New Directions for Continuing Education, Number 15, pp. 87-91). San Francisco: Jossey-Bass.

Mezirow, J. (1975). Education for perspective transformation: Women's re-entry programs in community colleges. New York: Center for Adult Development, Teachers College, Columbia University.

Mezirow, J. (1978). Perspective transformation. Adult Education, 28(2), 100-110.

Mezirow, J. (1989). Transformation theory and social action: A response to Collard and Law. Adult Education Quarterly, 39(3), 169-175.

Miller, J. V. (1986). Helping adults balance career and family roles. In J. V. Miller & M. L. Musgrove (Eds.), Issues in adult career counseling (New Directions for Continuing Education, Number 32, pp. 95-99). San Francisco: Jossey Bass.

Penland, P. (1979). Self-initiated learning. Adult Education Quarterly, 29, 170-179.

Pine, W. S. (1980). The effect of foreign adult student participation in program planning on achievement and attitude. (Doctoral dissertation, Auburn University, 1980). Dissertation Abstracts International, 41, 2405A.

Ralston, P. A. (1979). The relationship of self-perceived educational needs and activities of older adults to selected senior center programs: A community study. (Doctoral dissertation, University of Illinois at Urbana-Champaign, 1978). Dissertation Abstracts International, 39, 7196A-7197A.

Rogers, C. R. (1961). On becoming a person. Boston: Houghton Mifflin.

Rogers, C. R. (1983). Freedom to learn for the eighties. Columbus, Ohio: Charles E. Merrill.

Sabbaghian, Z. S. (1980). Adult self-directedness and self-concept: An exploration of relationships (Doctoral dissertation, Iowa State University, 1979). Dissertation Abstracts International, 40, 3701A.

Shaw, D. M. (1987). Self-directed learning and intellectual development: A correlation study. Unpublished master's thesis, Montana State University, Bozeman, MT.

343

Skaggs, B. J. (1981). The relationship between involvement of professional nurses in self-directed learning activities, loci of control, and readiness for self-directed learning measures. (Doctoral dissertation, The University of Texas, Austin, 1981). Dissertation Abstracts International, 42, 1906A.

Tennant, M. (1986). An evaluation of Knowles' theory of adult learning. International Journal of Lifelong Education, 5, 113-122.

Torrance, E. P. & Mourad, S. (1978). Some creativity and style of learning and thinking correlates of Guglielmino's Self-Directed Learning Readiness Scale. Psychological Reports, 43, 1167-1171.

Tough, A. M. (1966). The assistance obtained by adult self-teachers. Adult Education, 17(1), 30-37.

Tough, A. (1967). Learning without a teacher: A study of tasks and assistance during adult self-teaching projects. Toronto: The Ontario Institute for Studies in Education.

Tough, A. (1971). The adult's learning projects. Toronto: Ontario Institute for Studies in Education.

Tough, A. (1978). Major learning efforts: Recent research and future directions. Adult Education, 28, 250-263.

Tough, A. M. (1979). The adult's learning projects (2nd ed.). Austin, Texas: Learning Concepts.

Umoren, A. P. (1978). Learning projects: An exploratory study of learning activities of adults in a select socioeconomic group. (Doctoral dissertation, University of Nebraska, 1977). Dissertation Abstracts International, 38, 2490A.

Verdros, K. & Pankowski, M. L. (1980). Participatory planning in lifelong learning. In G. C. Whaples & D. M. Ewert (Eds.), Proceedings of the Lifelong Learning Research Conference (pp. 32-38). College Park, MD: University of Maryland, Department of Agriculture and Extension Education.

CHAPTER TWENTY

EVALUATION OF A SELF-DIRECTED LEARNING PROGRAM FOR ADULT LEARNERS

Judith K. DeJoy & Helen H. Mills

Recent work in the area of adult self-directed learning has focused on the role of educational technology in creating self-directed learning opportunities for adult learners (DeJoy and Mills, 1989; Herrmann, 1986; Mills and DeJoy, 1988; Niemi, 1987). The Personal Adult Learning Lab, at the University of Georgia Center for Continuing Education, provides an educational program which applies computer technology to adult self-directed learning activities and serves a wide variety of adult learners. In order to better understand how adult learners evaluated their learning experiences in this environment after their learning project was completed, a random sample of former adult users (conference participants, academic faculty/staff and community members) were interviewed using a telephone survey instrument designed to identify learners' perceptions of their learning, ways their experience influenced learning activities and awareness, changes in self-confidence, and the role of staff facilitation. Complex chi-square tests were applied to learners' responses by subgroup, age and sex, and the verbatim comments given to the open-ended questions were submitted to content analysis. Older users (36 yrs. and more) rated staff facilitation as very important and thought that the Lab program met their original expectations. The data suggested that those learners able to use the Lab regularly (academic faculty/staff and community members) did, indeed, acquire new information and were able to be very specific about the ways they applied their new knowledge and the ways that computer technology enhanced their learning process. The combination of hands-on experience with computer technology and staff support appeared to be critical to the success of the program.

Much has been written about the phenomenon of adult self-directed learning in the last 20 years (see these reviews: Brookfield, 1986; Caffarella and O'Donnell, 1987; Long, et al, 1988) and recent work has included discussion of the role of educational technology in creating self-directed learning opportunities for adult learners (DeJoy and Mills, 1989; Herrmann, 1986; Mills and DeJoy, 1988; Niemi, 1987).

The self-directed learning program provided by the Personal Adult Learning Lab is a practical attempt to apply computer technology to adult self-directed learning activities and to understand the "real life" learning process involved. Following the first full year of operation in new, expanded facilities, a survey of a random sample of former Learning Lab users was planned in order to extend our understanding of how adult learners evaluated their self-directed learning experience in this environment after their learning project was completed.

METHOD

Subjects

A total of 91 former Learning Lab clients were surveyed by trained staff administering a telephone interview instrument. The majority of clients surveyed were 36 years old, or older, and the majority were women. All clients had used the Learning Lab between July 1, 1989 and June 15, 1990. Each client interviewed was a member of one of three groups: conference participant, academic faculty/staff, or community member; obtained sample size for each group was 36, 20 and 35, respectively.

The Instrument

The survey instrument consisted of ten multiple-choice questions, four with open-ended (probe) components ("please give me an example of what you mean"), and one additional question about any suggestions for change, etc.

Table 20.1
Phone Interview Survey Questions

---

1. Think back on all of the learning activities in which you were involved. To what extent did you learn more about the(se) topic(s)? Would you say...

2. To what extent have you used your new knowledge in any area of your life? Would you say...

3. To what extent did using the computer-based technology enhance or improve your learning experience? Would you say...

4. In general, do you strongly agree, agree, disagree, or strongly disagree that the physical environment (furniture, lighting, noise level, and so forth) was supportive of your learning activities?

5. In general, do you strongly agree, agree, disagree, or strongly disagree that the presence of a staff person was important to your learning experience?

6. As a result of your experience(s) in the learning lab, do you strongly agree, agree, disagree, or strongly disagree that you have become more aware of different ways to learn new things?

7. Did your experience(s) make you feel more confident about your own learning abilities?

8. How interested are you in using similar computer-based technology again for future learning? Would you say...

9. How well did the things you had read or heard about the Learning Lab give you an accurate picture of the Lab's services? Would you say...

10. How well did the services offered in the Learning Lab meet your personal expectations? Would you say...

11. What suggestions do you have for improving the Learning Lab?

The questions focused on client perceptions of how much they had learned, how they had applied their knowledge, the degree to which technology supported their learning, the role of staff facilitation, any changes in awareness of learning options and/or self-confidence in learning, and the accuracy of promotional materials describing the Learning Lab. The questions are listed in Table 18.1; trained interviewers read each question, followed by a set of six or seven multiple-choice responses from which the client chose a response. Questions numbered 2, 3, 5, and 7 were followed by requests for more explanation.

Procedure

Three samples (subgroups) were randomly drawn from a sampling list of all former clients who had used the Lab between 7/1/89 and 6/15/90. Trained interviewers conducted the phone survey over a four day period at the end of June, 1990. Overall response rate was 95.8% with equivalent response rates for each of the three subgroups.

Data Analysis

Frequency and percentage of response for each question were calculated for age, sex and the overall sample; the complex chi-square test was used to evaluate the significance of the frequency of different responses to each multiple-choice question by subgroup. All open-ended responses were sorted by subgroup and question and reported verbatim.

RESULTS

Based on the overall percent of response data, the majority of Learning Lab users: 1) did learn more about their learning topic, 2) used their new knowledge to a moderate extent, 3) felt that the technology enhanced their learning, 4) strongly agreed on the importance of staff support and a comfortable physical environment, 5) agreed that they were more aware of different ways to learn and felt confident about doing so, 6) were moderately interested in using instructional technology again, and 7) felt that promotional materials represented the Learning Lab well and that the facility met their expectations.

Statistical Analyses

Complex chi-square tests were applied to the response set of each question for the variables of subgroup (conference participant, academic faculty/staff, community member), age (under 22; 22-35; 36-55; over 55), and sex. There were no sex differences found for any survey question; age differences were in evidence for certain questions. The oldest Lab users (over 55) were least likely to use their new knowledge, X^2 $(9, \underline{N} = 78) = 23.505, \underline{p} < .005$. Users 36-55 yrs. and older (over 55) most strongly agreed on the importance of a staff person being present during learning, X^2 $(9, \underline{N} = 78) = 23.310, \underline{p} < .006.$, and users 36-55 yrs. most strongly agreed that they had become aware of new ways to learn, X^2 $(6, \underline{N} = 79) = 21.504, \underline{p} < .001$. Interestingly, Lab users 36-55 yrs. old felt that the promotional information was accurate and that services met their expectations extremely well, while younger users (22-35 yrs. old) felt that promotions and services met their expectations only moderately well, X^2 $(9, \underline{N} = 66) = 17.11, \underline{p} < .047$ and X^2 $(6, \underline{N} = 80) = 12.655, \underline{p} < .049$, respectively.

Significant differences among the three subgroups were found for two of the survey questions. Academic faculty/staff and community members felt that they learned a great deal more about their learning topic, compared to the responses of conference participants, X^2 $(6, \underline{N} = 91) = 16.127, \underline{p} < .013$; however, academic faculty/staff felt they used their new knowledge only to a slight extent, relative to the two other groups, X^2 $(6, \underline{N} = 88) = 21.973, \underline{p} < .001$.

Content Analysis of Verbatim Comments

Four of the survey questions were followed by the interviewer asking the respondent to "please give an example of what you mean," "explain exactly what you mean" or to "give an explanation," depending on the wording of the specific question. These verbatim comments were recorded and a content analysis was conducted of the responses within each subgroup.

How are you using your new knowledge? Several response patterns emerged from the analysis of verbatim answers to this question, the most common of which was **very specific applications of new computer knowledge**. Individuals gave examples of using particular software programs to produce letters, resumes or standard forms, of better understanding the computer work of their employees, of learning a specific program to prepare for a job as a consultant, and of acquiring important help in deciding what type of computer to buy. The most common comment Lab users made was that now they felt comfortable and competent at their workplace computer and used their computer skills daily. A second category, **other applications of new knowledge**, involved examples of using typing skills at work, at the computer, in a business course or in preparation for a job hunt. In general, the more specific examples were given by users from the academic faculty/staff and community members subgroups. The subgroup, conference participants, provided comments in an additional two categories: **personal development** and **uninformed or negative reactions**. Answers involving using new knowledge for personal development were never specific; however, negative or uniformed comments from conference participants involved the issue of not having enough time, misunderstanding the services, or not seeing an immediate application.

How did the computer-based technology improve your learning experience? Responses to this probe question fell into two categories of reflections. One category, **heightened awareness of computer technology**, represented many users' feelings that they were now more comfortable with computers, more familiar with them, that the experience opened "a whole new door," that they had greater confidence in using computers and appreciated the capabilities. Most of these comments arose from the conference participant subgroup. The second major category, **specific features of**

computer technology, represented many users' identification of characteristics of the technology: self-paced instruction, concentration of materials, hands-on experience, chance to skip and review and appropriate feedback for learning. In addition, some users went on to comment on more substantive features: the ease of transfer of learning back to the workplace, the positive experience of independence during the learning process, and the freedom to "try new things." While conference participants tended to offer the very specific comments, it was the academic faculty/staff and community members Lab users who provided the insights about these more subtle features of the computer-based learning experience.

How was the presence of staff important to your learning experience? Two major categories emerged from user responses to this probe question; the first dealt with **specific interactions with staff**, and users described the ways staff helped solve equipment problems, helped in setting up, answered specific questions, explained the equipment and, most importantly, helped when users "got screwed up." Responders from all three subgroups contributed equally to this category. The second major category, **general staff manner**, represented users' perceptions that staff were cooperative, genuinely interested in helping users, sensitive to the need for privacy, provided good advice when asked, and established confidence in users because staff were "always on call for me." Particularly the reflections about genuine interest and always being "on call" were common to both conference participant and community member subgroups. A third, smaller, category, **criticisms of staff**, represented user perceptions that there was no one there to help, or not enough staff to provide one-on-one support, at all times.

How did your experience make you more confident of your learning abilities? Three major categories emerged from the users' responses to this question, beginning with **removal of barriers to learning**. This category represented users' feelings that they were now ready to sit down at a computer and work, that they had learned not to be afraid, that they realized computers were not mysterious and that they could "master this," that this experience helped them get over computer phobia and could help in securing jobs involving computer work. Conference participants and community members provided these comments. The second category, **enhanced self-esteem**, referred to both conference participants and community members and their new awareness about themselves as learners. These users commented on the positive reinforcement they received about what they knew and how well they could learn, on how quickly they could learn, on the fact that they realized that they had already learned correctly about computers and could utilize their knowledge, and on their sense of achievement in doing this as an individual. In addition, a set of responses within this category specifically focused on users' changed perceptions about their abilities to continue learning; several individuals commented on their feeling that "I can still learn at 36" and that "I feel I can take another course." A small set of additional responses reflected the feeling of a few learners that they were already confident of their abilities and that they would not have participated in the Learning Lab if they had not felt very confident.

Any suggestions for improvement? Responses to this final survey question did not fall into discrete categories in the same sense as those categories described above. Many users declined to offer suggestions, commenting that they did not feel qualified or familiar enough with the Lab to do so, or simply stating "no" or "I have no suggestions, things are really good." Among the suggestions offered were: additional hours of operation, such as weekends, more opportunities for one-on-one instruction by staff, more advertising of the services, and a need for additional privacy at individual workstations.

DISCUSSION

Overall, the frequency data and results of the complex chi-square analyses suggest that this computer-based learning program for adult self-directed learners serves to support the learning process. Age of the learner did not appear to be overwhelmingly important in the learning process, with the exception of the emphasis older learners placed on the need for staff presence and support.

The results of the content analysis of users' responses provide additional insight into the learning experience of Lab users using computer-based technology for their own learning. Individuals from the local community were, on the whole, clear about what they had learned and how they had applied it within their life roles (work, home, etc.), and both community people and academic faculty/staff were able to reflect, thoughtfully, on how technology had enhanced their experiences. Both groups of users also highlighted staff support as the source of both specific help and the motivation "to keep on." These reflections can only develop, it would appear, when the self-directed learner can experience the learning environment over a significant period of time, dictated by the highly individual nature of the adult learner's learning style and life.

Learning Lab users also expressed perceptions of increased confidence in their abilities to understand and use computer-based technology in work and home settings; these positive experiences appear to be directly linked to the direct exposure to these types of technologies in the non-threatening, supportive environment of the Learning Lab. Learners' recognition that "I can do this!!" would appear to flow from the combination of their hands-on experiences and their perceptions of strong encouragement from staff in a "no-lose" learning situation.

These particular characteristics of the Learning Lab program: (1) immediate and long-term access to learning resources in an individualized fashion and (2) the unique blend of staff facilitation and intensive experience with computer-based technologies would appear to be critical to the development of similar applications of educational technology to the adult self-directed learning process.

REFERENCES

Brookfield, S. (1986). Understanding and facilitating adult learning. San Francisco: Jossey-Bass.

Caffarella, R. S. & O'Donnell, J. (1987). Self-directed adult learning: a critical paradigm revisited. Adult Education Quarterly, 37, 199-211.

DeJoy, J. K. & Mills, H. H. (1989). Bridging theory and practice: applications in the development of services for self-directed learners. In H. Long & Associates (Eds.), Self-directed learning: Emerging theory and practice (pp. 99-111). Athens, Georgia: Adult Education Department of the University of Georgia.

Herrmann, B. (Ed.). (1986). Personal computers and the adult learner. New Directions for Continuing Education, no. 29. San Francisco: Jossey-Bass.

Long, H. B. & Associates (Eds.). (1988). Self-directed learning: Application and theory. Athens, Georgia: Adult Education Department of the University of Georgia.

Mills, H. H. & DeJoy, J. K. (1988). Applications of educational technology in a self-directed learning program for adults. Lifelong Learning, 12(3), 22-24.

Niemi, J. A. (1987). Contexts of using technologies for learning outside the classroom. In J. A. Niemi & D. D. Gooler (Eds.). Technologies for learning outside the classroom. New Directions for Continuing Education, no. 34 (pp. 3-8). San Francisco: Jossey-Bass.

CHAPTER TWENTY-ONE

DIMENSIONS OF SELF-DIRECTED LEARNING IN PERSONAL CHANGE: THE CASE OF WEIGHT LOSS

Sean Courtney & Sandra Rahe

Adult education researchers devote much of their efforts to the influences and motivations that lead adults to become involved in organized learning activities after they have left the school and higher education systems. This 'front-end' approach focuses considerable attention and resources on the motives and goals behind learning efforts. Excluded from study are the issues around learning and its **effects**: how knowledge is used by adults to bring about changes in their daily lives.

The purpose of this study is two-fold: 1) to focus on how adults use or fail to use knowledge in making change-related decisions, and 2) to examine women's patterns of reflection-in- action with respect to significant episodes of self-directed learning, in particular how they select information and apply it.

To explore these issues concretely the area of Weight Loss (WL) and Weight Loss Programs (WLP) was chosen. First, though much theory has been generated about the connection between motivation and WL behaviors little has been written about the connection of learning to motivation and WL. Second, studying WL and WLP means gaining access to an area of everyday life where significant personal change is at issue.

Because of the exploratory nature of this effort, a qualitative design was chosen in which thirteen adult females who have been involved in WL programs within the last five years were interviewed. An open-ended question schedule was used to elicit responses in motivation, learning and change. Results from two formal iterations of the data reveal general themes and categories.

ORIGINS OF THE STUDY

Research breakthroughs in the area of adult self-directed learning (SDL) in the United States hold much promise for efforts to break away from the equation of learning with schooling (Long, 1989). As a result, chiefly, of the work of Allen Tough, the long-held view that adult education is to be distinguished from all other forms of learning by its formality and deliberateness has given way to a renewed interest in the processes of learning within the broader social context (Jarvis, 1987).

This interest in 'alternative' ways of gaining and applying knowledge has been furthered by the influential writings of Houle, particularly Houle (1980), and his focus on the non-instructional means by which professionals keep themselves abreast of their profession. Add to this more recent formulations on the importance of informal and incidental learning in the workplace (Marsick and Watkins, 1991) and it is clear that we are on the brink of important new insights into the nature of learning as 'social process' or 'social action' embedded in the fabric of everyday life, and serving various purposes from personal change, to family relationships, community involvement and the world of work.

The particular impetus for the current study comes from the argument, elaborated in Courtney (1992), that to understand motivation-to-learn individual's orientations to action are as important to unravel as the more psychologically-grounded orientations to learning. If we take seriously the idea that adults have a strong need to apply knowledge, then we have begun to find a way into "embedded learning", the kind of activity, leading to acquisition of knowledge or rejection of it, which adults confront daily in their everyday lives. Our question becomes, when faced with the need to take various kinds of action what role does knowledge or learning play in the process? Clearly, there is difficulty in demarcating areas for analysis given the obvious pervasiveness of learning as an everyday action embedded in praxis. Our solution to this problem was to focus on the issue of **change**, on the assumption, discussed in greater detail in Courtney (1992) that behind many of the superficially dissimilar motives for learning lies a desire or need for personal change (Jarret, 1960; Aslanian and Brickell, 1980).

In studying personal change as a vehicle for the study of SDL it was important to find an area not normally associated with the field of adult education to test our various hunches there. Such an area is appetitive or addictive behaviors, particularly those which have to do with weight loss and maintenance. Despite the vigor with which this perennial obsession of late-twentieth century America has been investigated by other disciplines, it has hitherto been beyond the pale for most adult education researchers.

The logical extension of work on SDL, incidental and nonformal learning means increasingly researchers are willing to move beyond the familiar confines in which motivation and learning are investigated. This study for example benefitted from Ross's (1985)[1] dissertation on personal change and WL. Similarly, the recent paper by Strychar, Griffith, Conry and Sork (1990) underlines the growing importance of social and health- related issues to the field of adult education, and of the application of adult education concepts, e.g. Tough's 'transactional' types to the latter. It is within this growing area that the current study is situated.

---

1 Ross's dissertation was found to be most useful to the present study, particularly her connecting of SDL with the processes of Personal Change. It is important to stress here, however, that though also qualitative in nature, the present study is not an extension of Ross's work nor does it employ the same categories of analysis.

SELF-DIRECTED LEARNING: THE PROBLEM OF DEFINITION

The issue of definition is far from cut-and-dried. First there is the question of learner independence. While Tough's break with the traditional concepts of participation was dramatic, it has left the impression that in pursuing more 'independent learning projects' than they do formalized learning experiences, adults typically behave independently in all respects. Indeed, independence of choice and action has in some ways become a hallmark of the definition of SDL. This characterization has not, however, gone unchallenged (Brookfield, 1984). Being independent can mean total social isolation in which a small, eccentric(?) few pursue their own learning completely free of any commerce with their fellow citizens (Long, 1989). Can it also not mean, however, a healthy relationship with, as opposed to dependence on, others for the fulfillment of one's learning goals? Cannot self-directed learners be described as those people who know how to relate to a variety of sources and who are open to diverse learning opportunities, be they human or non-human, in the pursuit of knowledge? Raising questions such as these introduces a second major issue for definition.

The instrument developed by Guglielmino to measure readiness for SDL has been open to a number of interpretations, and in some cases criticism (Field, 1989). For some it has seemed that what is being measured is love or 'zest' (Houle, 1980) for learning as opposed to apathy or hostility towards the idea. In other words, it is the underlying orientation to learning which is at issue rather than self-directedness as such. For example, Oddi's inclusion of a dimension measuring openness to change (Oddi, 1986) seems intended to capture just such a dimension of the concept.

From orientation to learning it is but a short hop to the notion that what we may really be measuring here is personality or learning style. Thus, finding adults who are self-directed may mean finding people who have always displayed certain characteristic approaches to their environment, in terms of decision-making, problem-solving or taking action (Bonham, 1991).

A CONTEXTUAL DEFINITION OF SELF-DIRECTED LEARNING

The definition of SDL employed for this study is located somewhere between Long's "sociological" and "psychological dimensions" rather than the more familiar "pedagogical" dimension of Tough and Knowles. In other words, viewing learning within an embedded context tends to put us beyond a concern for classroom practices, e.g. setting objectives, selecting learning resources, etc. It is not that such processes are unimportant to the issue of WL--after all the women examined in this study are involved in formal programs-- rather that they may not represent how knowledge is received and applied in the learner's natural environment.

Long's depiction of the "sociological dimension" in terms of individual isolation and autonomy is not one that is accepted here. On the contrary, our view of learning-as-social-action (Courtney, 1992) tends to promote the significance of others, either directly through exhortation or indirectly through modelling (Bandura, 1964) in relation to one's own actions or decisions to act. On the other hand, the "psychological dimension", as defined by Long is a seductive one, and though not treated directly in this study, is one we are inclined to embrace, since it involves the notion of 'control', an issue at the heart of the testimonies offered by the women of this study.

In the light of this discussion, we do not feel that our decision to focus on women involved in formal weight loss programs compromises our ability to detect dimensions of SDL. First, it was not our intent to single out only those who appear to pursue learning actions in complete isolation from others. Second, and as our data reveals, individuals grapple with issues around personal change, often the same issue, over a period of years, even decades, and in such time spans it is highly unlikely that the mode of tackling the problem will remain the same through-out. In other words, it is our view, and a modest one at that, that adults will alternate between periods of self- directedness and other-directedness in their attempts to deal with personal problems and what we should be attempting to do is to capture, in precise moments of self-defined time, the interaction between such modes of action as they occur.

Third, it also seems important that individuals were selected for this study without regard for where they stood on the dimensions of SDL in that we can compare individuals who appear to be more or less self-directed with those who are not to test notions of both cause and effect. And lastly, Long's point about control is well-taken. It should be the case, as it turned out for this study, that adults demonstrate more or less ability to control or determine their own agenda in conjunction with environments which exhibit more or less structure. Thus, a woman may attempt to control her weight, on her own, without any noticeable success over a period of years. Is such a woman showing more signs of self-directedness than another who joins a program and who uses the material of this program to design her own WL 'schedule'? This is a question we take up in the closing discussion of findings.

DESIGN OF THE STUDY

The present study was designed to explore issues around motivation, learning and personal change. The central idea was to find a connection between the three dominant concepts. Though much has been written on motivation to learn and participate in formal learning activities, it was felt by the senior author that much remains unclear about the sources of individual actions, of which learning is but one specialized, if highly significant, category. Hence, our decision to approach the subject from a qualitative perspective (Ross, 1985).

Population and Selection of Subjects

Our sample consisted of thirteen adult females who had enrolled in a formal weight loss program (WLP) at some point in the previous five years. A purposive sampling approach was used to select women who represented different age groups, occupations, educational levels, and marital status. (Appendix A). (Purposive in this sense did not mean selection of subjects according to the emergence of theory as described by Strauss (1987).). Subjects were recruited by word of mouth from individuals who were aware of the research project or knew of people involved in WLPs, a form of network sampling (Merriam, 1988, p.50), at the same time attempts were made to control for a variety of demographic variables.

There was a somewhat even spread across ages, ranging from the mid-twenties to the mid-fifties, within the sample. Likewise with formal schooling, though in this case, the predominance at the 'upper-end' is not representative of the general adult population. Almost all of the women were married, though a majority did not have children at home. We estimated that most of these women would be considered of middle or upper middle socio-economic status, based on occupation, personal assessments of income and declared level of schooling. In reality, this has meant a somewhat stronger representation of subjects who are generally quite vocal and articulate about their 'problem'. Almost all of the women have lived with the 'problem' of being overweight long enough to have derived insights into their condition and to have attempted corrective actions, mostly self- directed.

Data Collection and Instrumentation

An Interview Protocol was designed consisting of questions under three conceptual headings: intentional change, learning and motivation. (Appendix B) The choice of questions and of approach was in part inspired by Tough's (1982) study of 'intentional change', and the wording of the opening question reflected his orientation to his subject. The fact that the interviewer, one of the authors, was of the same sex as the subjects, knew some of them from personal acquaintance and had worked in a program in which some of the respondents had been involved tended to give the interviews a more relaxed, conversational feel. Steps in the data collection procedure followed Lincoln and Guba's (1985) three successive phases of the qualitative inquiry: 'orientation and overview', 'focused exploration', and 'member check'.

Data Analysis

The framework for analyzing the data followed guidelines for qualitative methodologies as outlined in Patton (1980) and Strauss (1987). This may involve examining the material as a whole in addition to specific pieces to begin to develop the analytical concepts and categories. In this case, the first step consisted of each of the investigators reading and rereading the interview transcripts, meeting together a number of times and establishing a number of themes and categories consistent with the general conceptual framework concerning intentional change, motivation and learning. This process is similar to other qualitative studies in this area (for example, Ross, 1985).

The second step involved decomposing the transcripts into significant utterances. These phrases, sentences and natural paragraphs were sorted into more than thirty (30) categories of similar meaning, a number of which formed the basis for the present study.

A third step has involved focusing on all utterances in which the term "learning" or an equivalent appears in an effort to determine (1) an individual participant's 'interpretation' of the term, both within and outside of the WL context, and (2) what sorts of things utterances in response to the same questions have or have not in common across all individuals. The method used in this context was to divide the protocol into three parts: a "before" phase, meaning everything that was said before the Main Question was asked, a "main" phase capturing everything said in response to the Main Question, and an 'after' phase capturing everything said once we were 'outside' of that context and were asking other central questions. By Main Question in this context is meant one question that is intended to change the focus or direction of the interview. The question used for that purpose here was asked in the following or similar words (see Appendix B):

People learn or undertake learning projects throughout their lifetime for a variety of reasons. Learning and change sometimes overlap in a person's life. What comes to mind when you think about learning something or a learning experience?

In the following narrative the women speak in their own words as close to the original spoken word as is consistent with the need for clarity; they have been assigned fictional names to preserve confidentiality.

Analysis of Findings

How are we to make sense of individual discourse around the notion of learning? What, in other words, does learning **mean** to a woman engaged in a process of personal change? To answer these questions two levels of analysis are presented here. One, inspired by Strauss (1987) focuses on individual respondents and how they deal with the idea of learning. This represents our attempt to sift through the language of the interviews viewed as a set of 'empirical indicators' (Strauss, p.25) and begin a first articulation of grounded theory. The second level develops generalizations across individuals; the framework for emerging generalities is conditioned by one of our central questions: how is knowledge received and used by these women with respect to weight control?

According to Strauss's approach to qualitative analysis, coding of interviews involves the naming and development of categories which literally 'emerge' from the data: hence the phrase 'grounded theory.' For such coding to be effective, Strauss suggests a coding 'paradigm.' The paradigm involves the singling out of data (elements of the discourse) that throw light on the category in question by being related to it in any one of the following ways: conditions, interaction among actors, strategies and tactics, consequences and interactions among actors. How these paradigm elements--the first three in particular--function in the analysis applied to this study will be seen in what follows.

Two major categories emerged from this 'grounded' analysis:
1. Learning and its relationship to self.
2. Learning "work" and management.

Learning and its Relationship to Self. The first of these categories appears all-powerful and pervasive. It appears in three forms. According to the first, found in two of the ten respondents (minus the three subjects of the Pilot Phase), it connotes a discovery that learning isn't what they had always thought it was supposed to be: formal and independent of self as, e.g. the learning of math or poetry. We appear to have a contrast or distinction between the formal/school and the natural/personal life. The first, though no one uses the word, seems artificial, because the second represents 'true' knowledge. Thus, some respondents emphasize the means by which you achieve true learning: that a **condition** of true learning is making mistakes and experiencing negative consequences. Others, however, emphasize not conditions but **consequences**: that learning leads to personal growth or self-discovery.

Learning as True and Natural. When Jane was asked the question, her immediate response was to laugh and say: "you go away to school and you learn". Immediately however she countered with, "Probably the times I have learned the most is when I've had negative consequences and I need to do something different." For Jane then, a **condition** of learning is that she has to learn it herself: she has to be in control of the learning. Later, she reemphasizes the point when she adds: 'that's one of the things I've learned. When I say I think that's all. Not when somebody else does.' The category then appears to be one in which the individual does not count something as learning unless she decides that it is. In this passage also we are confronted with the dimension of the formal vs. the natural, the contrast or distinction between the formal/school and the natural/ one's life. Towards the end of the interview she talks about gaining self-knowledge or insight into self: the idea that a major **consequence** of learning is self-knowledge: you learn about yourself.

Learning as Personal Growth and Self-Discovery. The second form this relationship takes involves an emphasis on the **consequence** of learning as opposed to its ownership. When asked what comes to mind when she thinks about learning or a learning experience, Kate replies: 'Personal growth. I mean I just see it, I think because I came from such a low self-esteem that and the way I build myself up was from learning. Learning about me and learning about other things. Going back to school was probably the biggest thing I ever did. That really boosted my self-esteem the most. I found that I could actually go to a class and not know the answers and you know'.

While retaining the category of relationship to self Chris dwells on the idea of **strategies and tactics**: "It means getting a scheme out in your head for it. It means having in your mind a clear picture of the way you envision something whether it's a whole new concept about yourself and what your image of yourself is and what your lifestyle is."

Growth and change are at the heart of Sarah's reflection on the consequences of learning: "Change", she replied, when asked the Main Question. "You learn something good, something different. You gain more respect for yourself, you have learned. It's like a growing process."

Learning as a Feeling. The third form stresses the feelings associated with learning. Learning was an activity taking place in a different environment which, for its capacity to create opportunities for new actions, was desired in itself. Four of the ten subjects stressed: 'Something new, something different.' For Bonnie, a condition of learning is boredom or stagnation: I guess life would be pretty boring if you continued at the same level all the time. We also see evidence of **strategy/tactics** in the same context. Bonnie has a legal requirement to renew her license. 'I use this to my advantage to keep up with changes in the pharmaceutical field.' This response also throws interesting light on the way motivation to learn comes into play. Clearly, while boredom is a condition, it is not sufficient. For the action (of participation) to occur there must be some kind of external trigger; in this case provided by a legal compulsion.

Nancy explains her response this way: 'People get stuck in a rut if they don't meet new people and do new things then they learn.' Earlier respondents stressed personal growth and self- discovery, for Nancy the consequence of learning new things meant associating with different people. Before it was "railroaders", now it's "business people that come in here."

In response to the question, Why do you learn?, Sue replied: 'I guess that's my fuel that pumps me up. If I'm not learning new stuff I'm bored. I'm reading all the time and listening to what people are saying. Taking seminars.' (Referring to being at a seminar) "That's my entertainment. I entertain myself that way." (By learning?) "Yeah. I get real excited about stuff like that."

Category One: Comments. For all of these respondents, with more or less excitement, learning had become a self-defining process or experience. It defined who they were because through it they measured their ability to stay the course, put out effort for a personal goal, achieve breakthroughs in self-discovery, and so forth. It defined who they were because it involved making mistakes and learning from consequences, experiences which obviously meant personal discomfort even pain (a term, curiously enough, not used by many subjects), experiences which, however, also meant personal ownership. In these circumstances, learning was real and true because it had real and true consequences for that woman's life.

Also, it must be emphasized, learning appears to be very much a contextual variable. In our conclusions we stress the problems associated with asking general questions, questions which ask respondents to go beyond current circumstances or specific experiences. In most cases, respondents have difficulty doing so. And yet, when they do, the discourse structure and its vocabulary carry the same theme and terms as earlier discussions around the subject of WL. Thus, it appears that learning and WL involve similar realities for the individual: effort and achievement, a testing of the self, and a feeling that only when one was engaged in a new activity was there a feeling of being or coming alive.

Learning Work and Management. The second major category is less powerful and pervasive, but nevertheless it is to be found on many pages of the individual transcripts, and in responses to questions which on the surface are not asking for information under that heading. The phrase, learning work and management, is used because it connotes something, an object, property, resource or service, which must be worked on in certain ways in order to produce results. Here, though there is often a reference to self, and hence an intermingling with Category One, the stress is on the process of learning per Se. The following extract illustrates this category in action.

When asked later how she learns, Diane replied: 'I think (learning) is very hard for me. . . .I work at it.' Here we have an excellent example of Category Two, with the notion of effort or work involved as a basic dimension. We find further evidence for this Category in another context. When discussing strategies and tactics, Diane opines: 'I'm a quick learner, but I really have to want to learn what it is.'

The major question here--both in regard to pre-program and program-influenced attempts to lose weight--is, How do respondents gain the information or knowledge they need to affect change in their behavior? In other words, to what extent are these subjects self- or other-directed in their learning. The Interview question most relevant to this issue was, How do you learn? From responses to this and a number of related questions (see Appendix B), several categories, with their attendant dimensions and paradigm elements, emerged.

Receiving Knowledge or 'How Adults Learn'.   As we examined the responses of the women of this study, one dimension emerged quickly.   This had to do with the distinction between the cognitive and the experiential. For some the stress is on the cognitive side: knowledge is received easier in some "curricular" structures over others and through some modalities or senses over others. What is important here, however, is that knowledge is set down somewhere, in a book or class, or someone has it who can give it to you. Freire's notion of banking education comes vividly to mind. For others the stress is on the experiential: for some, there are things that you need to do if you want to be sure you have learned; for others, the issue is one of concreteness--some forms of learning are more concrete and palpable than others.   We shall see some interesting implications of these attributes in a moment.

1)   Learning by Instruction and Guidance
Clearly, this subcategory reflects what it is about a structured program that encourages or helps people carry out their wishes or learn the desired forms of behavior.   This is also a most interesting category because it appears to endorse the necessity of having others not simply provide you with the necessary information but also tell you, order, or command you on what to do. This gives "guidance" counseling its literal meaning. In many respects, this appears to be the antithesis of SDL, pedagogical or otherwise.

When discussing attending classes as part of the WL program, respondents tended to stress being told or being taught something rather than reading it for themselves. Said Connie: "At the program...they teach you to measure out food and stuff like that". At times, this could mean an almost illiterate approach to behavior change, as when Nancy, responding to a probe ('Some people would try to read a book and try to do it on their own') countered with: "No, I can't do that. I can't read a book, and I guess you would say follow instructions."

2)   Learning through Books, Classes
What makes this subcategory different from the first is that here the stress is on the provision of knowledge and coming to the realization that certain things are the way they are. You find things out through reading books

368

and making deductions or inferences from the knowledge they contain. On the cognitive side, this comes closest to SDL.

This category contains Houle's learning oriented type, people who have been reading a lot since childhood or who appreciate what books have to offer. In 1) above, by contrast, we have people who, though they might be in class, are suspicious of reading or will not act merely because a book says so. For the latter, in other words, the source is important: there is a teacher, doctor, who will tell you what to do and you will put yourself in his or her hands.

When asked what had prompted her to call up Smoke Enders (a smoking cessation program), Sarah said: "I just read the book. Jackie (her sister) had the book and I borrowed it. I just read the book and went from week to week for a six-week process".

How do I learn? [asked Diane, repeating the question]. I'm a visual learner. That's one way I know I learn. I can just picture something on a page, and then when I need to recall that information, I just visualize the page.

Sue told this interesting anecdote:

My mom and dad were apostles of Dell Davis, a nutritionist from way back...Dell Davis's books were in our kitchen, and my parents used those. My dad taught me how to control menstrual cramp with calcium...My dad taught me to start reading...That was outlined in our books.

The closest to a SDL ideal was Lynn, who noted, in response to the question, How do you learn overall?:

A combination of everything. I learn at work by watching, reading my manuals, listening. As far as life experiences, it is pretty much trial and error. Your parents tell you not to do something. Well, that is not going to work. You have to try it yourself to know. Mom has told us I don't know how many times different things and you don't know until you screw up.

3) Learning by Doing

The experiential side of the Receiving Knowledge category also has two subcategories: a more active, doing side and a less active or observing side. Here the focus, and many of the references, is to the experience of self in the learning process. Whereas in Category One the emphasis could be interpreted as a preoccupation with the product of learning, i.e. its impact on the ego, now we are talking about process: the self or ego as actor. The idea that you cannot say you've learned something unless you have tried it out, tested it. Diane's "I've learned that my way is better" is both an affirmation of the importance of learning in the definition of self and an assertion that learning is only true if tested on the anvil of life. Said Connie:

I have to do it myself. Everything I do. I can't just read something and understand completely how to.. I just can't sit down and do it. I have to do it myself.

To the need to experience the actuality of learning, some added the idea that you had to make mistakes or experience "negative consequences". However, this did not have to mean bad feelings or something totally negative. After mentioning mistakes, for example, Nancy added immediately, "But I get a lot of satisfaction out of when I do something right after I've learned to do it right".

4) Learning by Observing Others

Here the focus is on one's relationship to others, and the idea that you can learn by watching what other people do and following their lead. This is probably what psychologists mean by 'social learning' and 'imitation' or may reflect 'behavior modelling' (Bandura, 1964). Noted Jane, who had earlier mentioned "watching people" as a major modality,

Oh, listening to other people's experiences. I do learn a lot from hearing how other people handle situations. And then trying it, and if it works for me then I'll try it again.

Some were more specific about "watching people" as a preferred mode of learning. Noted Diane:

Like if you go to a restaurant and watch other people eat. I'll look at, what's their physique, what's their weight, and what are they eating? And so I'll think: "Oh, she's 300 lbs and look how much food she's eating; I can eat this much too. I'd better watch it." Or, if I see this skinny Minny over here and she's eating a lot of food, I think, how can she do that? She must starve herself for the rest of the day. So I try to figure out people, what they're doing.

Both of the above quotes reflect learning from a comparison group with whom one might or might not be acquainted. Particularly interesting is the idea of learning directly from a group with whom one is in regular contact. Jane, for example, stressed that "learning from a group is important". And went on to describe a group that she eats lunch with on occasion. This group, composed of "some very thin people", was also "into extremely healthy lifestyles".

Applying Knowledge. Concern for the integration of knowledge with everyday actions means connecting the receipt of information with its 'application'. People engaged in WL must confront the need to make changes in their behavior. Some feel that what is required of them demands a radical departure from current patterns of behavior. Others may feel that the ways of change are not so great. Whichever, there is a nexus within which ideas, information, attitudes, values, etc. what we might call orientations-to-action must become reality. The basic question here, then, is, What do respondents do with the information they receive? To what extent do they integrate it into everyday patterns of behavior?

To answer this question we looked at responses stemming from the opening Protocol question: the story of their attempts to lose weight. Three major categories emerged from the second iteration of data, categories which are as much logical deductions from each other as they are 'existential' in nature: 1) Following the WLP, 2)Modifying the WLP information to suit individual styles and needs, and 3) Not following or failing to follow the WLP.

1) Following the Program

This category naturally included reference to why a particular program had been chosen over its competitors. Remarked Sue:

"Optifast was ideal for me, at that point, because I didn't want to, and this was something I told them at Diet Center, I didn't want to have to plan everything that goes into my mouth all day long.

Acknowledging that what she needed was to 'learn to eat' (properly) and that is what she had obtained from Weight Watchers, Joyce said "you had to follow their instructions". Did she ever improvise, she was asked. "I pretty much followed the plan", she replied.

2) Modification of the Program

Respondents under this heading are attempting to carry out some 'program' of action, which may involve choosing between strict adherence to what they have been told or making modifications to suit their own circumstances. Typical of this approach is Bonnie who said she "took what

I agreed with in the program and threw the rest away", interestingly adding, "I guess that's the way I live my life in general, and that's not just the way I approached the program".

Jane made similar choices for a different reasons:
And that's why I'm not going to the meetings anymore. I had a choice between continuing to exercise on a daily basis or staying in Weight Watchers and I chose to continue that exercise.

Earlier, in the same interview, Jane acknowledged that the reason she was doing better in Weight Watchers than in previous programs is "mostly because I've been aware of my own learning style, and what I needed to do. I've sort of made some modifications on my own". Again a similar sentiment was expressed by Chris who said she "worked it out with the counselor that I would do mine a little differently" because there were things she disagreed with about the Diet Centers plan.

3) Not Following the WLP
This is a difficult area to analyze with certainty. Some indicated awareness of having the knowledge, knowing what they need to know and yet not being able or failing to act on that knowledge. For some the failure seemed to be gradual in nature, occurring over a period of time. They start well; it could be they have little difficulty starting or even welcome the opportunity to change current patterns or start something new.

Diane put it most poignantly: Typically, what I tend to do when I've really thought I've learned something is that I'm very optimistic that I will maintain what I've learned. I will continue to use it, that my life will be better. And what I tend to do is let it slide. I go back into old habits and old patterns. It's very hard to maintain, I think, change. Or something you've learned that is very different than what you have done for years.

For others the failure came in an apparent willfulness that is reminiscent of the Christian concept of sin. Said Sue, "I calculated it out and sat there and made this decision, 'No, you don't like those and yes they're really high in fat and yes you could stop somewhere and get a diet coke or whatever'. But I went ahead and opened that can of stuff and started in on it".

DISCUSSION OF FINDINGS

Ours is an attempt to reconstruct the relationship between motivation, learning and change from the stories of women who have been or are engaged in efforts at weight loss. It is part of a larger project aimed at explicating a general theory of practical knowledge or learning embedded in everyday life.

The study of embedded learning and its SDL components may pose problems of accessibility. We found it possible to gather a great deal of information about learning activities and change behaviors when these were associated with the discussion of WL and WLP. However, when the discussion moved to learning and change in general, the interviewer encountered resistance, silence and long pauses. Only when it could be made to turn back on the topics discussed previously could the silence be broken. This, of course, raises the question of the generalizability and transferability of findings that are central to the quantitative 'paradigm' but not to the qualitative approach (see discussion of assumptions in Lincoln and Guba, 1985). At the same time, 'general' questions may serve a purpose. For it seemed to us that among the more reflective and voluble respondents asking 'difficult' questions prodded the need to clarify earlier points about the more 'embedded' occasions of learning.

Embedded Learning and the Issue of Self-direction.

The history of these women's struggle with the issue of WL, a history partially described in the analysis of findings, reveals that over long periods of time, learning and action interpenetrate to such a degree that it is difficult to see where one begins and one ends. This makes it difficult to 'find' SDL episodes in their pure form or to know precisely where one SDL episode ends and an 'other-directed' learning effort begins (Strychar et al., 1990). For even where respondents are clearly following the dictates or guidelines of a program, as we saw above under the "Receiving Knowledge" category, there are significant examples of program modification which take into account individual circumstances and 'learning styles'. Obviously, while not SDL in the strict pedagogic sense, there are SDL 'elements' here because these modification cases clearly contrast with those in which the idea was to 'literally' follow the program in its entirety and not to deviate in case the whole effort should end in failure.

Strychar et al. (1990) note that the pregnant "women [in their study] had engaged in predominantly other-initiated learning episodes" (p. 270) in contrast to standard works by Tough and others that highlight self-initiated learning as the dominant form. In part, they argue, this may be due to the "differences in results that can be obtained by examining how individuals conceptualize their learning processes versus examining how individuals actually learned about specific subject matter" (p. 27). In the former, the self-directed form dominates the responses, in the latter, studied by Strychar et al., it is the other-initiated form which comes out on top.

This point can be broadened. From preliminary analysis of our own findings it appears that "others" e.g. parents, spouses, siblings, doctors, etc. serve either directly (through persuasion) or indirectly (by example or modelling, e.g. :"my sister did it") to help or motivate the respondent to initiate change-directed action or learning. Yet, even in some of those cases, respondents will say that the real motivation came from themselves: "I had to want to do it." Do not these kinds of findings serve to strengthen the argument that SDL is more function of a situation than a lifelong trait which some possess in abundance but others do not?

Knowledge Integration into Action: The Practical Dimension.

The categories emerging under the heading of "Receiving Knowledge" are significant for two reasons. First, they back solidly the view that for most of the respondents, even when it is being 'learned', knowledge is something to be put to use. Quite literally, 'you haven't learned something until you've demonstrated it'. In the third category, there is near synonymity between learning and action: "I have to do it myself" (Connie); "you don't know until you screw up" (Lynn). Even, in the first category, where respondents discuss learning by instruction and guidance, it appears that the emphasis is not so much on becoming more informed and having more knowledge about the issue of WL. Instead, respondents stress the 'structured' nature of the environment and the fact that they are being **shown** what to do. Classes, it almost seems, are good if they get you to do something, not good if they get you merely to think.

Finally, with respect to acting on the knowledge received, two observations need emphasizing with respect to the concept of SDL. First, there are more examples among the respondents of attempts to modify the WLP guidelines than cases where the guidelines were followed faithfully. Is the unwillingness to do so a sign of self-knowledge, i.e. knowing what works for oneself and what doesn't (after all most of these women have tried to lose weight before, and for some the issue goes back to childhood)? In other words, even though the decision to participate in a WLP, an 'other-initiated learning episode', seems to suggest that these individuals are not behaving in a self-directed way, as was the case with Ross's sample, might it not be the case that the decision to enter such a program is a more mature (self-directed?) decision than the 'inability' to make any decision?

On the contrasting side, it can be argued that lack of compliance with program guidelines suggests both an unwillingness or inability to 'stay the course': you pay the money but are afraid to undergo the regimen. Hence, modifying the course might be 'self-directed' but it would not count as self-directed learning. Similarly, joining a program as opposed to doing it alone might represent a more independent, mature and responsible approach to the problem because it means owning up to it, hearing and digesting facts which are not to one's liking, making a decision that whatever the program directors request one is willing to do, etc.

All that can be said at this juncture is that the people who mentioned why they chose a particular program over another often cited such factors as 'structure' ('I'm not real structured but when I'm going to do something like that I can't do it, it has to be structured. I have to follow the directions' [Sarah] or lack of it as a major consideration (besides that of cost).

Emphasis on structure suggests to us that respondents are at the very least grappling with the issue of self-directedness, whether they are capable of it or even desire it.

This study is an attempt to draw the attention of researchers to areas normally considered outside the domain of adult education. It does this by extending the logic of the SDL concept to the whole notion of embedded learning in the day-to- day life of the individual.

REFERENCES

Aslanian, C. and Brickell, H. (1980). Americans in Transition: Life changes as reasons for adult learning. New York: College Entrance Examination Board.

Bandura, A. (1964). Social learning theory. Englewood Cliffs, NJ: Prentice-Hall.

Bonham, A. (1991). Guglielmino's Self-directed Learning Readiness Scale: What does it measure? Adult Education Quarterly, 41, 92-99.

Brookfield, S. (1984). Self-directed adult learning: A critical paradigm. Adult Education Quarterly, 35, 59-71.

Courtney, S. (1992). Why Adults Learn: Towards a theory of participation in adult education. London: Routledge.

Field, L. (1989). An investigation into the structure, validity and reliability of Guglielmino's self-directed learning scale. Adult Education Quarterly, 39, 125-139.

Houle, C. O. (1980). Continuing Learning in the Professions. San Francisco: Jossey-Bass.

Jarret, J. (1960). Adult education and freedom. Adult Education, 10, 67-73.

Jarvis, P. (1987). Adult Learning in the Social Context. London: Croom-Helm. Lincoln, & Guba, E. (1985).

Lincoln, Y. and Guba, E. (1985). Naturalistic Inquiry. Beverly Hills, CA: Sage.

Long, H. (1990). Psychological control in self-directed learning. International Journal of Lifelong Education, 9, 331- 338.

Long, H. and Associates (1989). Self-directed Learning: Emerging theory and practice. Norman, OK: Oklahoma Research Center for Continuing Professional and Higher Education.

Marsick, (1990) and Watkins, K. (1991). Informal and Incidental Learning: A challenge to human resource developers. London: Routledge.

Merriam, S. (1988). Case Study Research in Education. San Francisco: Jossey-Bass.

Oddi, L. (1986). The development and validation of an instrument to identify self-directed continuing learners. Adult Education Quarterly, 36, 97-107.

Patton, M. Q. (1980). Qualitative Methods. Beverly Hills, CA: Sage Publications.

Ross, S. T. (1985). The Process of Personal Change: A case study of adults who have maintained weight loss. (Unpublished doctoral dissertation, Northern Illinois University).

Strauss, A. (1987). Qualitative Analysis in the Social Sciences. New York: Cambridge University Press.

Strychar, I.M., Griffith, W.S., Conry, R.F. and Sork, T.J. (1990). How pregnant women learn about selected health issues: Learning transaction types. Adult Education Quarterly, 41, 17- 28.

Tough, A. (1982). Intentional Changes. Chicago: Follett.

APPENDIX A -- PROFILE OF RESPONDENTS   (N=13)

AGE	NUMBER
25-34	5
35-44	3
45-56	5

EDUCATION LEVEL	NUMBER
High School Graduate	3
College Degree	3
Some College	3
Postgraduate	4

Dimensions of SDL in Personal Change

MARITAL STATUS   NUMBER OF CHILDREN AT HOME

Divorced	1	0	7
Single	3	1	1
Married	9	2+	5

SOCIO-ECONOMIC STATUS (ESTIMATED)

Upper Middle   5;   Middle 6;   Lower Middle   2

APPENDIX B -- Interview Protocol

I.   Throughout your life time you have probably experienced various changes in yourself and your activities. Some of these changes probably happened accidentally, but today we'll focus on the intentional changes, the changes you have decided to achieve. I know that in the past you have been involved in a weight loss program. Therefore, I want to ask you some questions about that.

1.   Tell me the story about your decision to lose weight.

A.   How did you get there in the first place? (what was the trigger?)

B.   Who and what encouraged you?

C.   What did you expect to get from the change?

D.   How do you measure success?

E.   Did you think you could do it? Why?

   2.   Give me an example of how it affected your life.

      How did it feel to change old habits?

   3.   What was the hardest part?

4.   Easiest part?

II.   People learn or undertake learning projects throughout adulthood for a variety of reasons. Learning and change sometimes overlap in a person's life.

1.   What comes to mind when you think about learning something or a learning experience?

A.   What feelings or emotions do you associate with learning?

B.   How do you learn?

C.   Why do you learn?

2.   Think of an experience where you really thought you learned something, what happened?

3.   How did learning affect the change that you made?

A.Has learning been a real effort in your life? Why or why not?

III. Motivation

1.   Losing weight sometimes involves changes in lifestyle, etc. Please tell me about another major change in your life.

A.   Were you successful in making the change? (How did you know?)

B.   What helped or hindered your success?

C.   What would have helped you be more successful?

2.   Was the effort you put forth worth it?

A.   Did you get what you expected out of your effort?

3.   Describe how it felt to make a change when other people were making the same change.

A. How is that different than when no one else is making a change?

4. People can be influenced by many different things, e.g., books, religion, other people, etc. Tell me about things in your life that influence important decisions that you make.

CHAPTER TWENTY-TWO

ADULT SELF-DIRECTED LEARNING IN A PROFESSIONAL PROGRAM

Maribeth Moran & Francene Weatherby

Traditionally, education for the health professions has been lock-step in approach, designed for young students committing their lives to study their chosen profession. Prior to the 1960s, students of nursing were expected to be young, single, selfless females dedicated with almost religious fervor to becoming servants of the sick. They lived in special isolated dormitories and their training revolved around the services they provided. Instruction followed the apprenticeship training model with learning occurring through imitating the actions of others rather than through conceptualization and reasoning. Educational experiences were not formalized or structured but occurred serendipitously as the situation arose. There was no opportunity for students to control or even have input into their course of study.

As the nursing profession matured and nursing education moved out of the hospital training model and into the university model, learning the rationale for therapeutic measures rather than simply imitating procedures became the primary focus of professional education. Technology expanded rapidly with therapeutic measures and protocols for handling various illnesses constantly being updated with newer treatments and machinery. In order to function in increasingly complex health care situations, nurses had to be able to think and act independently.

In spite of the move into the academic setting, nursing education in the 1960s and early 1970s continued to be designed for young students with few extracurricular responsibilities who were entering college directly after high school.   Curricula were developed with rigidly sequenced courses containing highly specific behavioral objectives with vast amounts of technical information.   These programs of study were based on the belief that beginning nursing students with few life experiences knew only what they were formally taught in the classroom.   In addition, each school of nursing often felt that their particular curriculum was unique and special.   Thus, transfer of nursing credits from one institution to another was virtually impossible.   Students changing schools of nursing generally had to begin at the beginning.

While the educational process was changing from hospital-based apprenticeships to college-based programs, the characteristics of the student pool initially remained relatively unchanged.   Applicants were generally white, middle-class, single women with little health care experience.   During the late 1980s, however, applicant pools for schools of nursing began to show radical shifts (Holtzclaw, 1983; Fotos, 1987; Linares, 1989).   Several societal factors contributed to the changes.   Some of the more significant factors included:

1. declining numbers of students entering college as the baby boomer generation matured;
2. rising costs of education which affected the manner in which students financed their higher education;
3. the women's rights movement which enabled women to seek careers not traditionally considered female-dominated;
4. large numbers of college graduates seeking second careers because of unemployment or job burnout; and
5. increasing numbers of students with family responsibilities.

In addition to these factors, a unique aspect of nursing education itself further contributed to the changing nursing student population.   This unique aspect is the multiple educational entry levels into beginning nursing practice. Since the 1950s there have been several avenues a student could choose to become a nurse.   The various tracks, described in Table 1, vary in length of study and scope of practice for the graduate. With the exception of the practical nursing program, all prepare a student to practice as a registered nurse.

Once considered terminal courses of study, practical nursing programs, associate degree nursing programs and diploma nursing programs are now considering a rung on the career ladder of nursing by many. Additionally, as the nursing profession has evolved, not only is the bachelor's degree a prerequisite for graduate study in nursing, it is also now considered necessary for professional advancement and increased career opportunities. Consequently, large numbers of currently practicing nurses, from a variety of educational and experimental backgrounds, began seeking the Bachelor of Science Degree in Nursing (B.S.N.)

Influenced by these changes and with an eye on the need to increase enrollment in order to combat a growing nursing shortage, nursing faculty at the University of Oklahoma began to design an educational program to meet the needs of these adult self-directed learners. The faculty recognized that the changing student applicant pool demographics would reflect different learning needs in the student body as well as different time frame requirements for learning. These requirements offered a challenge to faculty to be creative and innovative in designed a course of study to meet individual learner's needs while at the same time, maintaining the rigor of the traditional program.

This chapter reviews the development of a program of study for career ladder adult learners in a baccalaureate nursing program. Application of the principles of self-directed learning to the career mobility nursing curriculum are described in detail.

ASSESSMENT OF BARRIERS TO LEARNING

During the initial development phase of new options for career ladder students, the faculty collected information from a variety of sources -- past and current students, potential applicants and the literature. As faculty analyzed information from needs surveys, barriers to continuing formal education began to be identified. The barriers to learning for adults described by Cross (1981) were used as a framework to organize data. The three categories of blocks to continuing education included attitudinal barriers, institutional barriers and situational barriers.

Attitudinal Barriers

A number of personal attitudes that interfered with potential students' pursuit of additional formal education were identified. Anger, frustration, feelings of inadequacy and fear were among themes.

The first major attitudinal barrier centered around the students' basic program of nursing study. As can be seen from Table 1, the three options for becoming a registered nurse, regardless of program length or educational setting, all lead to the same licensure exam and title of registered nurse. Graduates from the different programs often felt competitive and defensive about their own basic preparation programs. Some were angry that a lack of time or money in the past had "forced" them to choose a shorter, seemingly more expedient educational route. Now with the rapid advances in the health care system, they found their preparation inadequate for career advancement.

Other nurses seems to lack self-confidence in their abilities to succeed. A personal fear of failure made them reluctant to face the challenge of senior college level course work.

Negative attitudes toward higher education were accentuated by the impersonal rigid procedures students encountered in university settings. Students were frustrated when they realized that academic institutions often failed to recognize knowledge gained outside the classroom, usually requiring these nurses to repeat basic beginning nursing courses alongside traditional students.

Table 22.1

Characteristics of Basic Nursing Education Programs

Type	Learning Length	Institution	Course of Study	License
Licensed Practical Nursing Program (L.P.N.)	1 year	Vocational/Technical Schools, High Schools, Hospitals	Technical Nursing Care	L.P.N. (practices under the supervision of an R.N.)
Associate Degree Nursing Program (A.D.N.)	2 years	College or Junior College	Prereq. Courses Bedside Nursing Care is major focus	R.N.
Diploma Nursing Program (Diploma)	3 years	Hospital	Prereq. Courses Bedside Nursing Care is major focus	R.N.
Baccalaureate Degree Nursing Program (B.S.N.)	4-5 years	College or University	Wider Variety Prerequisite Courses; Bedside Care is emphasized with additional focus on Wellness Care, Community Health, Leadership/Management	R.N.

Institutional Barriers

Institutional barriers revolved around the regulations and requirements of academic institutions. These formal operating procedures often stifled students' motivation to pursue a baccalaureate degree. Major barriers in this category included prerequisite requirements, transfer credit and time limitations on course work.

Prerequisite requirements for nursing at the University of Oklahoma include 67 semester hours of course work in the biological and behavioral sciences, physical sciences, mathematics, English, political sciences and the humanities. The number of subjects and the breadth of the material often discouraged potential career ladder students from returning to the academic setting after a long absence.

A second major institutional barrier was presented by the lack of a mechanism to transfer hospital-based units of study into academic credits. Diploma programs often were not affiliated with institutions of high education. Thus, study completed in these programs was impossible to transfer into academic credit for the diploma career ladder student.

A final barrier was the time limitation placed on acceptable transfer course work. College of Nursing policy required that all prerequisite course work in the sciences needed to be taken within the ten years preceding admission to the college. This policy assumed that knowledge in a particular subject was gained only in formal classes and could not be expanded or updated by any means other than additional classroom studies. For practicing nurses, however, continual updating in the sciences is necessarily accomplished routinely in the clinical setting and through personal study.

Situational Barriers

Complex work and family situations often present situational barriers for the adult learner, barriers which are the most difficult to overcome. According to Valentine (1990) time constraints are reportedly the most important of these barriers and more universal than any other deterrent to adult education. Survey respondents reported that inflexible class scheduling designed for full-time study was extremely problematic for those trying to juggle work and family responsibilities along with course work.

A second limiting situational factor was money. Many bright, capable nurses reported that lack of finances kept them from seeking a four-year college degree. Single parents who were the sole source of family income found funding college work particularly difficult.

DEVELOPMENT OF THE CAREER MOBILITY PROGRAM

Faculty recognized that the barriers identified by adult career ladder learners had to be reduced or removed in order to provide viable ways for nurses to continue their formal education. The final plan would require creativity, flexibility, and risk taking on the part of students and faculty alike. Faculty particularly were concerned that "flexible" would translate into "substandard" and that the integrity of a strong nursing curriculum would be lost. The arrival of a new dean at the College of Nursing served as a catalyst for change. With extensive experience in working with career mobility students, the dean stimulated and encouraged innovation and experimentation; faculty responded by developing an educationally-sound new program especially designed for self-directed adult learners.

Major features of the program included:

* flexibility in awarding credit for prerequisite course work through the removal of artificial time limitations;
* options for completion and easy transfer of prerequisite course credits from any accredited college in the state;
* credit earned by passing nationally standardized examinations for the entire junior year nursing courses including clinical courses;
* flexible classroom and clinical course scheduling including evening hours and compressed time frames;
* innovative teaching methods such as audiotaped lectures and computer assisted instruction for self-paced learning;
* opportunities for completing certain clinical requirements in familiar work settings;

* financial assistance from scholarships, tuition reimbursement plans and paid leave programs through area hospitals.

These strategies aimed at leveling barriers related to prerequisite course work, nursing courses and scheduling, attitudes, and financing were incorporated into the new program.

Prerequisite Course Work

Obtaining the 67 hours of prerequisite courses was identified as a stumbling block by many returning adult students. Faculty decided to decrease this impediment by removing artificial and often indefensible time limits on previous course work and take into consideration each nurse's continued informal learning. This step provided a more individual sensitive method of awarding credit.

Methods for obtaining prerequisite credits were expanded to include challenge examinations such as the College Level Examination Program (CLEP) tests, correspondence courses and transfer credit. Equivalency tables from all the accredited colleges and universities in the state were used to facilitate transfer of courses from other institutions.

Nursing Courses and Scheduling

In considering returning to school, many practicing nurses had reported being discouraged or even angry at the thought of having to repeat basic elementary courses in nursing with beginning traditional students. The new program eliminated this concern by providing RNs and LPNs with the opportunity to take nationally standardized examinations in order to receive credit for up to 30 hours of nursing courses -- the entire junior year of study. these examinations, developed by the National League of Nursing (NLN) are offered four time a year and can be taken any number of times until successfully passed. The pass rate for practicing nurses, particularly those who had been in the clinical setting over 5 years was well over 90%. Students who passed the NLN challenge exams can then complete the remaining nursing course work in two semesters of full-time study. A part-time program schedule was developed for those students who were unable to attend classes on a full-time basis.

Generally, career ladder students face extremely demanding schedules, often working full time while raising families. Daytime, evening part-time and compressed scheduling helped to decrease the added stress of returning to school. Audiotaped lectures and computer assisted instruction provided students with the opportunity to schedule their own learning time around extracurricular responsibilities. These multiple teaching strategies also place increased accountability for learning with the student who was then responsible for seeking out faculty for clarification, discussion and debate over issues presented by the various media.

Attitudes

Students' attitudes that affected the learning process were addressed by several different means. Setting the appropriate climate for the learners was especially important since it was noted that career mobility students in the past were often defensive, critical, and sometimes even hostile. Faculty recognized that the "warm climate for learning" suggested by Malcolm Knowles (1975) needed to be an integral part of the new program and would help students overcome fears and insecurities that could hinder their learning.

Several strategies were designed to overcome these attitudinal barriers. A great deal of preplanning helped insure that classes and activities operated efficiently. A workshop designed to help welcome students to the College of Nursing and to ease their transition back into the student role was offered prior to the beginning of classed.

In recognizing career mobility students as competent self-directed learners with varying areas of expertise, faculty realized that clinical experiences would need to be tailored to meet individual learning goals. In order to facilitate this individualization, students were given the opportunity to develop personal learning objectives to meet the broad overall course objectives as well as the opportunity to complete certain clinical assignments in their own work settings. These options not only validated the students' abilities to be self-directed, but also helped students feel comfortable and self-confident in familiar surroundings.

Effective communication and support were encourages. An active peer support group provided an excellent opportunity for creative problem-solving in managing school work and family responsibilities as well as a safe arena for the expression of negative feelings. Personal and academic counseling was made available free of charge. A career mobility newsletter and a 24-hour hotline service were designed and implemented to provide immediate answers to questions and to communicate vital information to students and potential applicants. All of these endeavors worked together to create a climate that nurtured self-respect and promoted learning as self-directed behavior.

Financial Arrangements

Because finances were almost always a problem for returning students, financial assistance was made an important part of the specially designed career mobility program. In addition to the usual monies available to students through academic channels, many health care facilities in need of well-prepared, experienced nurses were willing to provide financial aid and educational leave plans to career ladder students. The new baccalaureate prepared nurses were then required to work for the aid-granting institution for a specified period of time after graduation. Several area hospitals agreed to provide matching funds to students who had received money from other sources. This added income helped ease the students' stress and freed time for studying.

Evaluation

In the first semester of program implementation, 32 returning nurses were admitted into the nursing curriculum. Twenty-six of these were full-time students and six were part-time.

Of the twenty-six full-time students, twenty-three successfully completed all course work and graduated after the spring semester. Three students failed one nursing course and repeated that course in the summer session.

Preliminary data suggested that students progressed well in the course of study and were pleased overall with their educational experience. Faculty likewise expressed their satisfaction with the students and with the program.

An extensive evaluation plan is being implemented using evaluations collected from students, faculty, administrators and employers. Since the majority of the new graduates are already licensed nurses, successful completion of the state licensing exam, a typical measure of success for nursing programs, cannot be used as an outcome criterion. Instead, added emphasis will be placed on post-graduation follow-up and employer evaluations of the graduates.

In keeping with the philosophy of the College of Nursing, faculty affirmed their belief that practicing nurses were capable of being self-directed learners in completing their baccalaureate nursing degrees. Students clearly demonstrated that they were highly motivated and willing to take responsibility for their own learning. Faculty responded with a commitment to provide an individualized approach to formal education. The development of the unique career mobility program at the University of Oklahoma helped facilitate this philosophy of the teaching-learning process. The apparent success of the program demonstrates how sensitivity to specific student learning needs can lead to a rewarding and satisfying experience for both teacher and learner.

REFERENCES

Ash, C. R. (1985). Applying principles of self-directed learning in the health professions. In S. Brookfield (Ed.), Self-Directed Learning: From Theory to Practice. San Francisco: Jossey-Bass Publishers, 63-74.

Cross, K. P. (1981). Adults as Learners. San Francisco: Jossey-Bass Publishers.

Fotos, J. (1987). Characteristics of RN students continuing their education in a BS program. Journal of Continuing Education in Nursing, 18(4), 118-122.

Holtzclaw, B. (1983). Crisis: Changing student applicant pools. Nursing and Health Care, October, 450-454.

Knowles, M. (1975). Self-Directed Learning. Chicago: Follett Publishing Co.

Linares, A. (1989). A comparative study of learning characteristics of RN and generic students. Journal of Nursing Education, 28(8), 354-359.

Valentine, T. (1990). Deterrents to participation in adult education: Profiles of potential learners. Adult Education Quarterly, 41(1), 29-42.

CHAPTER TWENTY-THREE

THE CONTINUUM OF SELF-DIRECTED LEARNING WITHIN A GRADUATE PROFESSIONAL COURSE

Constance M. Baker & Herbert A. Nishikawa

Microteaching a is course within the graduate program in nursing at the University of Oklahoma, College of Nursing on the Oklahoma City Campus' Health Sciences Center. This two-hour semester long course is required of all students as basic preparation to implement the teaching function of the nurse in clinical practice and as a foundation for those graduate students selecting a career as educator in institutions of higher learning. This course is based on the successful adaption of the Stanford University teacher-education course (Allen, 1969) at the University Of California, San Francisco Campus, School Of Nursing (deTornyay,1983).

The Microteaching course is based on the following propositions:

1. Microteaching is REAL teaching. The teacher and the learners are all engaged in using knowledge that is unique to nursing.

2. Microteaching controls the complexities of normal classroom teaching. Class size, content selection and time are all controlled.

3. The focus of the course is achievement of specific tasks. The practice of identified teaching strategies.

4. The practice sessions allow for control of time, learners, feedback, and teacher responsibilities.

5. Feedback on performance is immediate and enhanced by the use of videotaping procedures. Feed back is from the teacher (self), the learners and the course faculty. This is a safe environment to try new strategies.

COURSE STRUCTURE

Before presenting the application of this course to self-directed learning, a basic overview of the structure of the course is necessary. The course consists of a one hour classroom review and discussion of the teaching strategy to be demonstrated followed by a three (3) hour practice lab session. The number of students in the one hour class ranges from 12 to 14 students. Each class is then divided into two lab sections of 6 to 7 students. Both labs are conducted simultaneously requiring a faculty in each lab. In the practice lab sessions, each student conducts a five (5) minute presentation performing the teaching strategy while the remaining students function as learners. Within the five minute presentation, the student-teacher demonstrates the behaviors of the teaching strategy discussed and modeled in the earlier one hour class. The student-teacher chooses the topic\content to be taught and utilizes the teaching strategy or behaviors to enhance the presentation. In other words, the topic that is taught is not as important as the actual performing of the teaching strategy demonstrated within the five minute presentation. The entire five minute presentation is videotaped for the purpose of replay and critique. Immediately after each five minute presentation, verbal comments and feedback is solicited from the student-teacher and learners. The videotaped performance is then reviewed and written evaluations by the student-learners are completed and handed directly to the student-teacher. This pattern continues for each student in the lab until each student has demonstrated the teaching strategy as the teacher and all have responded as learners. After each student has demonstrated the teaching strategy in a five minute presentation and reviewed the videotape replays, a general discussion is conducted by the faculty member to re-examine the strategy.

TEACHING STRATEGIES APPLICABLE TO NURSING

The identified teaching strategies are: positive reinforcement, writing behavioral objectives, varying the stimuli, use of examples and models, questioning, team teaching, use of silence, set induction and closure, seminaring and higher order questioning, use of teaching aids, and lecturing. The student is responsible for selecting content for each teach and the evaluation of the teach is on the process, i.e. demonstration of the skill, without any comments on the chosen content. The teaching strategies selected for this course are based on applicability to nursing, student identification of meaningfulness and faculty experience of effective teaching behaviors.

The general characteristics of the graduate students in this course are: RN's with a minimum of two years clinical practice, hold a B.S. in nursing, admitted to Graduate College and College of Nursing and available for the course. Most students elect this course early in their program because of the "grape vine" assessment of "enjoyable even though videotaping in involved".

In summary, the purpose of the course is to identify and practice the selected teaching strategies deemed important in facilitating the teaching-learning interaction between nurse and patient and the teacher and student. Self-directed learning is the key ingredient in the students' benefiting from the opportunities offered throughout the semester.

SELF-DIRECTED LEARNING

Self-directed learning is viewed on a continuum with teacher-directed learning (Knowles, 1985). The degree of self-directed learning is determined by the extent, deliberate choice, to which the learner is willing to assume control and responsibility over the several learning variables built into the course. Within the general course guidelines, clearly spelled out in the syllabus, the student is invited to determine the outcomes from the course for him/her self and to be responsible for the learning variables identified in the general course objectives. Each student is allowed to individualize his/her own learning experiences within the scheduled practice (lab) sessions. The extent of control initiated by the student depends upon his/hers needs and/or goals.

The course learning variables available for student control are:

1. identification of learning needs
2. focus of learning activities
3. expected outcomes
4. learning resources
5. environment
6. timing
7. pace
8. evaluation of own performance (Knowles,1985).

Variables Defined

1. Identification of learning needs is defined as the ability to freely state what the student desire to gain in cognitive and/or psychomotor activity. For example, students have stated that they would like to be able to utilize more A/V materials into their presentations or be able to be more creative in their presentations. Students have also been appreciative of the creativity of their peers in using the same teaching strategy.

2. Focus of learning activities is defined as the identification and choice of activities which will enhance the desired outcome. Students have made statements such as "I need to continue to write cognitive type objectives" or "I need to move to writing affective type objectives".

3. Expected outcome is defined as the specific product within the general course objectives as interpreted by the students. For example, the student may decide that based on their prior experience they already are comfortable with speaking before a group of people; but need to consciously think of providing positive reinforcement in their interaction with the group.

4. Learning resources is defined as the methods available to the student in creating and/or achieving desired outcomes. Students have utilized the group of peers for feedback on specific attributes or techniques the student is trying to change or enhance. For example, students will ask each other these questions: Do I talk too fast? Do I use my hands too much? Is my voice too much of a monotone?

5. Environment is defined as the physical and/or psychological set created that is perceived as safe to try new behaviors. For example, after the initial set creation by the teacher of a safe and caring atmosphere, the students maintain the set with each other to enable themselves to test out different teaching strategies and innovative ways of presenting "old content".

6. Timing is defined as to when to perform and/or practice new behaviors. For example, depending on how comfortable the student is with the teaching strategy of the week, the student may choose to only perform that behavior/technique only once during their five minute teach or the student may choose to be the first or the last performer during that lab session.

7. Pace is defined as the amount of repetition needed to achieve the desired outcome and identification of learning needs. For example, students decide when they are ready to deal with constructive feedback from their peers. They also decide if and when they need to continue to perform variations of a particular teaching strategy.

8. Evaluation of own performance is defined as the identification of positive attributes within the performance of new behaviors. For example, at the beginning of the semester, students are asked to identify "one good thing that they liked about their teach/performance". Closer to the end of the semester, students are identifying positive attributes of their performance and possible changes they would make without any prompting.

Based on their prior classroom experiences, the students enter the course expecting teacher-directed learning. They anticipate a passive learner role and teacher criticism of their performances. By mid-semester, the students accept that they can control each of the learning variables.

They can decide the focus of discussions and they can determine the structure of the practice labs. By the end of the course, they could possibly function without the teacher!

EVALUATION

The final worth of any teaching endeavor is its effect upon the student. The comments concerning the course, Microteaching, are offered as the ultimate "evaluation" of allowing self-directed learning to occur according to the students needs.

MICROTEACHING: Course evaluation comments from students.

This course has really helped me polish my skills at lecturing, seminaring and writing objectives.

In this course I learned to write objectives, stand up when I had a teach and developed courage to speak in front of a group.

The immediate weekly application of the content was very helpful.

This was a fun, positive learning experience.

It was great to see everyone grow so much in their ability to teach and/or speak to groups.

Learned a lot about teaching techniques and as a new instructor, I could take this back to my college and try it out again.

This is probably the highest rated class by all students, the faculty are great. They are supportive, non-threatening, non-interfering and practice what they preach.

In this course I learned the basics and essentials that I can use everyday in my job as a nurse instructor

Gained confidence in my teaching ability. The videotaping was wonderful in providing data for self evaluation and critique.

Learned to experiment with different teaching techniques, had the opportunity and encouragement to be creative and learned to work as a team.

Super enjoyed this course and videotaping. Found out how much one can accomplish in a short period of time and am more aware of what I am doing and what the objectives are.

I loved it! I had such a good time and my students could tell what the technique of the week was because I used it on them.

I have applied the knowledge gained here in other courses and at work. I now can critique the effectiveness of other teachers.

I will never forget the teaching techniques taught

One of the most fun courses but yet a real eye opener for an "old" teacher to learn new and better teaching techniques. I gained a great deal of insight into my own teaching.

One of my favorite courses. Who would ever think that so much could be learned from just watching yourself on tape and having the group encourage you.

Delightful! one of the most fun courses anywhere. The structured atmosphere seemed to be unstructured.

Microteaching manual is now my bible in teaching and writing objectives. What a good and helpful course.

The degree of self-directedness increases as the student becomes more explicit in defining each course variable in relationship to his/her needs. The self-directed role of the student is a direct consequence of the faculty commitment to implementation of adult learning principles in a graduate professional course and in the continuous use of the skill of positive reinforcement.

REFERENCES

Allen, D. & Ryan, K. (1969)   <u>Microteaching</u>.   Calif: Addison-Wesley Publishing.

deTornyay, R (1983) <u>Strategies for teaching nursing</u>, (2nd ed.).   New York: Wiley.

Knowles, M. & Associates (1985)   <u>Androgogy in action</u>. San Francisco: Jossey-Bass.

DATE DUE

DEMCO 38-296

Please remember that this is a library book,
and that it belongs only temporarily to each
person who uses it. Be considerate. Do
not write in this, or any, library book.